PRESENTATIONS OF GENDER

PRESENTATIONS OF GENDER

ROBERT J. STOLLER, M.D.

Yale University Press
New Haven and London

Designed by Nancy Ovedovitz and set in Times Roman type by The Composing Room of Michigan, Inc. Printed in the United States of America by Vail-Ballou Press, Binghamton, N.Y.

Library of Congress Cataloging in Publication Data
Stoller, Robert J.
   Presentations of gender.
   Bibliography: p.
   Includes index.
   1. Gender identity disorders. 2. Masculinity (Psychology)
3. Femininity (Psychology) I. Title.
RC560.G45S76   1985   155.3'3   85-2376
ISBN 0-300-03507-1 (cloth)
       0-300-05474-2 (pbk.)

The paper in this book meets the guidelines for permanance and durability of the Committee on Production Guidelines for Book Longevity of the Council on Library Resources.

10   9   8   7   6   5   4   3   2

CONTENTS

Preface   vii

Acknowledgments   xi

1. Naturalistic Observation in Psychoanalysis: Search Is Not
   Research   1
2. A Primer for Gender Identity   10
3. Marked Femininity in Boys: An Emphasis on Mothers   25
4. Marked Femininity in Boys: An Emphasis on Fathers   43
5. How Biology Can Contribute to Gender Identity   65
6. Dialogues on a Somewhat Feminine Boy   77
7. A Child Fetishist   93
8. Origins of Male Transvestism   137
9. Near Miss: ''Sex Change'' Treatment and Its Evaluation   152
10. Two Feminized Male American Indians   171
11. The Development of Masculinity: A Cross-Cultural Contribution   181
12. A Preliminary Program for Naturalistic Observation of a
    Psychodynamic Issue   200

References   207

Index   215

PREFACE

Though of book length, the present work is simply another chapter in my ongoing search to understand the origins, development, dynamics, and pathology of gender identity—masculinity and femininity. As always, I work from the psychoanalyst's viewpoint. I occasionally disagree with other analysts' findings, often with their theory, almost always when their jargon leads to the rhetoric of scientific surety, but I agree with them on at least three tenets: that psychoanalytic treatment is a unique way to enter and share another's interior life; that events of infancy and childhood contribute to later behavior; and that these events can be untangled by infant observation and, in adults, by treatment that shifts the events from being unconscious to conscious memories. I also believe that however much our short-range enthusiasms may unbalance our view, the overall contribution of psychoanalysts to understanding gender identity is significant, a necessary piece of a research structure that must also include the techniques and theories of other disciplines. If I say little about these other modes of study, I nonetheless know that they are vital.

For studying subjectivity, we still have no tool as powerful as psychoanalysis, that most delicate and uncertain technique in which one person's subjectivity is measured by another's. Practicing analysts are constantly aware that the measuring instrument we use—ourselves—is inexact and susceptible to gross errors from our neuroses (countertransference). Yet, the publications of analysts, especially when theory is being built, do not begin to account for the influence of the analyst's personality on his or her observations and the conclusions (theories) that result therefrom. The situation is not hopeless, but we had better reveal ourselves more so that others can more clearly judge our findings.

This book-as-chapter, then, has two main themes. First, I want to lay out present-day thinking in regard to gender identity, shaping the findings in the field to my own perspective. Second, the book is a preliminary sketch of how a psychoanalyst can set up hypotheses and check them. For I feel that, as primitive a research instrument as analysis is, its basic concept is sound: we need a microscope in order to understand the nature of behavior from the subjective, nonneural side. Psychoanalysis, practice and theory, is still too crude for reliable scientific work, but perhaps its workings, like those of other inventions, can be refined.

Complementary to trying to create a research tool out of psychoanalysis is my conviction that analysts' reports are not constructed when the investigation has finished but are part of its living tissue. Though that is not true of the scientific method with which we are familiar in the natural sciences, *all* the findings in a psychoanalysis are interpretations, and even worse, interpretations that can never be checked by an outside observer. So our audience is always at the mercy of what we choose to report, how we first experienced it, and what words we use for our descriptions. This puts a burden on the analyst as writer that may be heavier than we can bear. At any rate, our clinical reports so far can be read only as interesting stories. Confirmation will take much more time and care than psychoanalysts have yet offered.

For the present, I want to ease this problem in communicating honestly by trying for a style of writing that is to simulate, in print, the way I talk. For I find that the usual manner of psychoanalytic writing—for example, "to cathect the other sex with libido," "the manifestation of certain fleeting transitional stages in the movement of the narcissistic libido, in particular during times when the patient was on the way to re-establishing the basic mobilization of his grandiose self in the merger-twinship relationship"—is, at bottom, disreputable. Psychoanalytic theory, appearances in the literature to the contrary, starts in the belly, not the head. At this still primitive stage of our development, we analysts should not disguise those origins but—I plead—should enthusiastically reveal the unsureness of our ideas. When we do otherwise, we only irritate our critics, who rarely succumb to our pseudoscientific rhetoric.

A note on a great problem facing those who use analytic treatment to study origins of a disorder: one gambles. An analysis takes years, and yet we may not find all we want. One had better, therefore, love the practice of analysis for itself and be able to put aside research interests. Freud was wrong when he said that a research interest must be inimical to analytic treatment; it was, to say the least, complex for him to thus pronounce, considering that the research interest was rampant in him. Though you must take my word for it (as I keep saying you have to about everything any of us reports), if there were time I believe I could convince you that my curiosity interferes less with my therapeutic work than do some colleagues' concerns with, say, money, their chronically bad back, their untreated depression, their bad marriage, or the strain of working with ten patients a day. In fact, I think my interest in my studies helps the treatment more than it hinders. At any rate, you can see that a gamble like this makes it even less likely that we can study enough cases to satisfy the demands of scientific method. One has only one lifetime. Still, we need not be defensive, for, to repeat, our assignment—not a mean one—is to be the sharpest of naturalists, not natural scientists.

From these comments let me build a few guidelines for reading this book. It does not pretend to be a scientific treatise presenting findings created by acceptable scientific method. The arguments are not polished so as to appear airtight, and I tend not to hide my idiosyncrasies in polite objectivity. I think, therefore, that this material is better read if you drink rather than chew it, swallowing and digesting without worrying about the chemical constituents and molecular configurations of the recipe's ingredients. Let us converse together—argue together—knowing that as yet we do not know enough.

ACKNOWLEDGMENTS

I thank Gladys Topkis for being the editor I needed: firm and full of good judgment.

I am also indebted to my colleague, Prof. Gilbert H. Herdt, for introducing me to ethnography and for joining with me to write up our ideas on gender development among the Sambia, but even more for making it possible for me to glimpse directly what he had taught me.

And let me thank my secretary, Mrs. Flora Degen, whose constant dependability, good sense, and skill left me free to enjoy thinking and writing.

I also want to thank the following publishers and journals for granting permission to draw on materials previously published by them:

A Contribution to the Study of Gender Identity: Follow-up. *Int. J. Psycho-Anal.* 60 (1979):433–441.

Fathers of Transsexual Children. *JAPA* 27 (1979):837–866.

Near Miss. In *Eating, Sleeping, and Sexuality.* Edited by M. Zales. New York: Brunner/Mazel, 1982.

Two Feminized Male American Indians. *Arch. Sex. Behav.* 6 (1976):529–538.

The Development of Masculinity: A Cross-Cultural Contribution. *JAPA* 30 (1982):29–59.

Gender Identity. In *International Encyclopedia of Psychiatry, Psychology, Psychoanalysis and Neurology* vol. 5. Edited by B. B. Wolman. New York: Human Sciences Press Periodicals, 1977.

Gender Identity. In *Encyclopaedic Handbook of Medical Psychology.* Edited by S. Krauss. London: Butterworths, 1976.

Maternal Influences in the Precocious Emergence of Fetishism in a Two-Year-Old Boy. In *Parental Influences.* Edited by E. J. Anthony and G. H. Pollock. Boston: Little, Brown & Co., 1985.

Disorders of Masculinity and Femininity. In *Basic Handbook of Child Psychiatry* vol. 2. Edited by J. D. Noshpitz. New York: Basic Books, 1979.

1

NATURALISTIC OBSERVATION IN PSYCHOANALYSIS: SEARCH IS NOT RESEARCH

In the earliest stage of the development of a discipline that studies an aspect of the natural world, we usually simply look around or, if we already have preconceived ideas, begin digging for what we suspect. Using the available tools and inventing better ones as the task becomes clearer, we gradually collect data that delineate the shape and quality of our subject. This exciting, free-wheeling period, a fundament of science, should, however, shift to a next stage: the findings and their related theories must be confirmed in new circumstances, from different perspectives, and by others. Both processes—naturalistic observation and confirmation—are necessary; leaving either out endangers the adventure.

Because I enjoy it (not because of a belief that it is better), I emphasize naturalistic observation when studying gender identity. For this effort, I have collected data in three ways: by seeing briefly—in evaluation and/or short-term treatment—many people with gender disorders; by analyzing adults with these conditions; and by working for years with families, using psychoanalysis as a means of learning about psychic influences on earliest development. The gross and the microscopic styles of observation support each other and, by providing feedback, help correct earlier faulty impressions. All, of course, are preliminary to studies researchers might do that have predictive value and that conform better to experimental method.

From the start, my purpose was to find nonbiologic roots of gender behavior. I am not trained or suited by temperament to work in the laboratory or to approach the subject by means of experiments—proper selection of samples and analysis of variables—in animals or humans. Though I enjoy studying severely aberrant people, in the past ten years I have seen few such people. Instead I have moved in from the extremes of the continuum, having learned with the grosser cases what to look for in ordinary folks (I use circumlocutions to avoid the word *normal*). After twenty-five years of studying gender identity, *anyone* will serve me as a subject.

Residing in a university and surrounded by colleagues who are scientists, I know not to inflate my work with allegations that it constitutes experiment (for example, ''every psychoanalysis is an experiment'') or science (''our science''). *Research* is not a synonym for *search* and should not appear in a psychoanalyst's sentence if it is there for propaganda. At our best, we analysts are naturalistic observers of behavior with techniques—unstable but powerful—that no one else has. That's a good start. I shall settle for words such as *work* and *studies*.

How did I come to study gender identity? To answer is not to grant myself autobiographic indulgence but to make a point that should be among the most central for those who would aspire to psychoanalytic research: when one's primary technique is analysis, the instrument used, quite literally, is one's self. This delicate mechanism cannot be calibrated, and so the data (*data* shall be used as synonymous with *observations*) produced are hard to evaluate. Beyond that, since the data are arbitrarily plucked from the analytic hour—that tangled mass of syntax, memories, movements, affects, and fantasies—and further modified when edited into written form, the final report is dangerously removed from the original events in the analysis, not to say the experiences from the past that the patient has been reporting. And so, whatever the risk—even that we may show our data to be biased and our conclusions unsure—I think analysts' case reports must be written differently or should be ignored.

Medawar (1963) says:

The scientific paper may be a fraud because it misrepresents the processes of thought that accompanied or gave rise to the work that is described in the paper. . . . The starting point of induction, naive observation, innocent observation, is a mere philosophic fiction. There is no such thing as unprejudiced observation. Every act of observation we make is biased. What we see or otherwise sense is a function of what we have seen or sensed in the past. . . . The scientific paper is a fraud in the sense that it does give a totally misleading narrative of the processes of thought that go into the making of scientific discoveries.

If we know nothing of the analyst—the instrument—doing the work, most of his other findings are beyond judgment. In the belief that this problem also exists when an analyst is creating a method for formally studying a problem, I shall write in an informal style and show the haphazard aspects of my method; without that, I could, at the least, disguise the realities, especially the weaknesses, of the data and ideas. (And hiding weaknesses would fool few respected readers and keep the rest from confronting the strengths.)

Perhaps it helped in this endeavor not to know, in the first years, that this was to be a long-term interest. Otherwise I might have done as researchers do: prepare a plan. This, shaped by the need to influence granting agencies, would require a research protocol, in which are presented a careful literature review; a statement of hypotheses; the steps to be taken to assault these hypotheses with proper samples, controls, and sophisticated defense of data with statistics; a technology for data collecting; evidence in advance that the data would test the hypotheses and generate useful conclusions; and reassurance that the findings would be important, would justify the spending of a lot of money, and—important in sex studies—would be defensible against politicians and other concerned citizens. From the overall subject of gender identity I could have selected a manageable question or two; or (more impressive even though unmanageable by me) the program could be grander, requiring a lot of time, money, subjects, and researchers.

But I was mostly interested in talking with patients, usually though not necessarily in a treatment situation, and I had no idea where the interest would lead and no consciously stated hypotheses to test. With no plan more complex than to enjoy each day's work and none of the burdens of organized research, I could roam about, guided not by an agency's regulations and traditions but by my curiosity.

Our motivations, then, are a crucial factor in the form our findings take. So let me say a bit more on that. The primary cognitive reason I did not get interested earlier in the study of sexuality—gender identity and erotic excitement—was that I could not discern significant unresolved problems when confronted by patients. Whatever my own contribution, conscious and unconscious, to that attitude, psychoanalytic training in the 1950s contributed its share. At that time, analysts were raising few questions about the origins or maintenance of gender behavior; analytic theory seemed sophisticated enough to account for any clinical event, any observation, any data collected by any method. Indeed, the final defense against new ideas was the plausible though glib argument that loose pieces could be accounted for by biology (the biology of philosophers—for example, death instinct, libidinal cathexis, psychic energy, inherited fantasies—not practicing day-to-day scientific biology).

Despite an ongoing research project by colleagues in our department at the University of California, Los Angeles, I still found the subject uninteresting, even after they invited me to interview patients for their study (the first careful one ever done) on transsexualism (Worden and Marsh 1955). The one patient I recall seeing for them did not interest me, either in his clinical condition, though it was bizarre enough, or in the unknowns he presented that I thought worth pondering. He was an anatomically normal man who needed to put on women's clothes and be enchained in order to become sexually excited: so I found him no more than a pervert, readily enough understood by considering the vicissitudes of instincts, libidinal fixations, and oedipal traumas. In those days—the mid-1950s—psychoanalysts and analytic candidates could handle such data without batting an eyelash.

What threw me off with such people was the grossness of their pathology; explaining it took no effort. This innocence died one day in 1958, literally in a single moment. My friends were done with their project but had made an appointment with a patient whom they had not seen but who was categorized as a "transsexual woman" (a biologic female who nonetheless considered herself a man). They asked me to see her to tell her the research was finished.

Shortly before the appointment hour, I was approaching stupor at a committee meeting in a conference room with a glass wall that allowed us to see people pass. A man walked by; I scarcely noticed him. A moment later, a secretary announced my eleven o'clock patient. And to my astonishment, the patient was not what I expected—a woman who acted masculine and in the process was a bit too much, grimly and pathetically discarding her femininity. Instead it was a man, unremarkable, natural appearing[1]—an ordinary man (and eight years' follow-up until his death never changed that impression). Analytic theory, though it can explain everything, did not, I felt, account for the naturalness of his masculinity, its presence since earliest childhood (confirmed in photographs from the family album), his nonhistrionic quality, and his unquestioned acceptance in society as male. Generalizations on oedipal conflict and metapsychologic descriptions relying on "ego," "superego," "id," "cathexis," "libido," "instincts," and the like had, I felt, to give way to data—the realities of this patient's presence. (And some years later I came to think that our metapsychology[2] worked no better to describe anyone, not just someone as aberrant as a transsexual.)

My version of contemporary psychoanalytic answers was now inadequate; though the theories were finely tooled to account for bizarreness, they could not clarify naturalness. I was now into issues of self, identity, identification, the relationship of culture and the historical past to the development of the individual, perhaps even the unexplored territory (notwithstanding Hartmann's ideas) of conflict-free development. For instance, how are acting, imitation, impersonation, imposture, multiple personality, habituation, incorporation, introjection, identification, and internalization related and different?

The next year, this patient referred a friend, a butch homosexual "female" who turned out to be a male pseudohermaphrodite. A paper published on this case (Stoller and Rosen 1959) brought the referral of an intersexed patient ("testicular feminization syndrome" it was called then) who years later was revealed as really a male transsexual (Schwabe et al. 1962; Stoller 1964, 1968b). By now I knew there was no shortage of questions; my patients were all confusing me—were releasing my latent confusion.

None of these uncertainties were manifest in me at that moment, but in the twenty-five years since, I have discovered that they had been present in some form. Time has brought them to consciousness, which then let me ask the

---

1. Years before, he had had a mastectomy and a panhysterectomy, and he had been taking male hormones.

2. I shall use *metapsychology* not as a synonym for psychoanalytic theory but, as Gill (1976) has recommended, for those aspects of theory based on a belief that psychic energy is a real energy, as that word is used in physics: more than a metaphor.

questions that have made up the greater part of my studies. Owing to the fortunate circumstances of being an analyst set free in a congenial university, I have roamed about the subjects of masculinity and femininity and of erotic desire haphazardly, in accord with what interested me.

I have seen hundreds of patients and their family members in consultation or treatment. Anyone who came, by whatever way of referral, was worked up, and all those with severe gender disorders who asked for help were treated, as were their families. As a selection process for an orderly research project, this is unacceptable; as a way of learning, it worked well for me. At first, with roots sunk in medicine but those in analysis still forming, I was especially occupied with biologic issues—the relationships between demonstrable physical defects and gender behavior—and with diagnosis—discovering syndromes and the physiology and/or psychodynamics that underlay them. So I studied those in whom the condition itself—a change from the expected brain function—energized cross-gender behavior (for example, congenital hypogonadism, such as some cases of XXY—Klinefelter's syndrome) and those in whom the aberrance was produced by the response of society (which includes parents) to abnormal anatomic appearance (hermaphrodism), not by a biologic force. These patients confirmed hypotheses described earlier by Money (1955) and Money and the Hampsons (1955a, 1955b, 1957), who found that the masculine and feminine behavior of one who was intersexed was usually and heavily determined by the sex assignment at birth and the subsequent rearing of the child in accord with that assignment.

But none of this was psychoanalytic; I was just an analyst arriving at the same conclusions reached by others who had no analytic training. The obvious difference was my seeing patients in more depth, for I was following my natural tendency to talk with people on whatever basis they wished in regard to duration or intensity of the relationship.

Along with those with biologic disorders came patients without physical aberrations. Uninterested in studying sexual aberrations in general, I worked with people with gross abnormalities of masculinity and femininity, the main visible manifestation of which was wearing clothes of the opposite sex. There were some who wished sex change and some who put on clothes of the opposite sex for other reasons.

This accumulation of patients over a dozen years led gradually to my discerning several categories of cross-gender behavior, a classification that not only fit my clinical experience but seemed compatible with syndromes others had observed though not described in detail. Naturalistic observation expanded into taxonomy. A workable differential diagnosis for cross-gender behavior condensed out of the fog (see chapter 2). Only at this point did I feel that my interest was taking on organized form. Though this classification might have practical use, pointing toward different treatments, it serves me mostly for studying the development and maintenance of ''gender identity'' (a label I coined for the differing degrees of masculinity and femininity that can be found in a person).

For clarity, a short vocabulary exercise: *sex* (maleness and femaleness) refers to a biologic realm with these dimensions—chromosomes, external genitals, gonads, internal sexual apparatuses (for example, uterus, prostate), hormonal state, secondary sex characteristics, and brain; *gender* (gender identity) is a psychologic state—masculinity and femininity.[3] Sex and gender are by no means necessarily related. In most instances in humans, postnatal experiences can modify and sometimes overpower already present biologic tendencies.

Though I was by now interested in the subject, I did not intend to study gender identity. The shift to commitment occurred with the entry into treatment of the family of the very feminine boy sketched in chapter 4. This introduced psychoanalysis into the observing process, where before one could have said only that it was an analyst who was making the observations.

A nice way to find something new is to go look (or to be there and notice it when it happens). This approach has two weaknesses; it can take a long time, and the data are only suggestive unless confirmed. So to save time and cross distances, one takes risks: the scientific method. That is, one sets up experiments that approximate the discovery for which one searches. But I cannot do that, so, to simulate the scientific method of checking naturalistic findings by means of controls, for years I have seen in analysis adult patients and parents of children with related but different gender disorders. I have also observed, without using analysis, other families and subjects.

I wanted to use analysis to study origins of gender behavior, not just manifestations and classification. For personal gratification, then, as much as for scientific reasons, I came to use analysis more and more. This shift began in the midst of the see-a-lot-of-patients phase but has increased so that now almost all my clinical work is done by analysis.

This effort is weak, however, for several reasons to be noted as I proceed; the bluntest is that I cannot find patients with massive gender disorders who want analysis. They wish only to change the outer world—their anatomy, the people they know, society. So for some years my analytic practice was restricted mostly to parents of children with gender disorders. While the child and one of the parents are seen by colleagues, I have analyzed the other parent—thus far, only mothers. Fathers of the gender-disordered boys I have studied (I am, so far, less experienced in working with gender-aberrant girls) will not enter treatment themselves, a reflection of the part they play in

---

3. One often finds the terms *sex role, gender role,* and *gender identity role* used. *Role* refers to a part one takes; there is no reference to one's intensity, intent, or commitment to the behavior. *Identity,* on the other hand, implies that one's very being is involved. One *plays* a role; one *is* one's identity.

creating their children's pathology. The nature of analysis obviously precludes one's seeing many patients, and so one has to be satisfied with the depth of the data; the breadth—numbers of people seen—is terribly inadequate (not that the depth is good enough either).

Along with others, I have come to believe that if one wishes to understand origins of character structure in childhood, one cannot settle for information gathered in the transference.[4] Though analysis of the transference is a fine source of data on how the patient experienced childhood, one should not confuse that with what actually happened. To get closer to the latter, we must also find what the parents did and felt. To me, a great advance that may move psychoanalysis toward being the science it claims to be is detailed and controlled observation of children. When one adds to this the analysis of the parents, who are in the midst of the child's development, one gets a better picture, though still not complete, than one can get by analyzing only adults. So I am strongly biased in favor of looking for answers by seeing the child and the parents in deep and extended treatment.

So, for over fifteen years, I was involved in a psychoanalytic "experiment," in which I slowly worked my way along a sequence of families, the focal case being a very feminine boy and his parents. (Until recently I called such children "transsexual boys," because they so powerfully wished to be girls, but it is safer not to give them the diagnostic label since we cannot say how often they grow up with that impulse unchanged. Chapters 4 and 5 deal with this problem further.) In this "baseline" case, the analytic situation revealed the dynamics that I think cause this condition (Stoller 1968a). With these dynamics in the open, I went on to see a total of fifteen families with such boys (some in treatment, though not analysis, some just for evaluation) to test the hypotheses that had developed in the first family's treatment.

On confirming these findings, I have come to feel that the degree to which such dynamics are present in any family will determine the degree of femininity in a boy. The next step, then, was to find other boys with comparable but not identical conditions to see to what extent the family dynamics varied. And so I have also worked in analysis with the mother of another very feminine boy, but one who also had masculine qualities, to determine what was different in *that* family to produce a different form of femininity (chapter 8); with the mother of a then two-and-a-half-year-old boy who became sexually excited when fondling her pantyhose (chapter 9); and with the mother of an adolescent transvestite (chapter 10). Suffice to say here that there were differences among these cases in the attitudes of the parents, the way they handled the child, and the relationship between mother and father that could account for the dif-

---

4. For readers not familiar with the term *transference*, let me define it as the process, during treatment, of reliving, not just remembering, the past in the present.

ferences in the gender disorders of the boys. Unfortunately, psychoanalyses take years, and so this "experiment" proceeds slowly. One who wishes to do analytic research that uses the practice—not just the theory—of analysis must not be overeager to finish his or her work.

Grossly feminine boys are very rare; yet their infancy gave glimpses of dynamics that, far less intense but qualitatively similar, illuminated for me the dynamics of masculinity and femininity in general, of perversion, and of sexual excitement. The original finding was this: if an infant male has too intimate a relationship with his mother (her body and psyche) and if she tries to maintain that intimacy indefinitely in an ambience of trauma-less, frustration-less pleasure, he will fail (not be well motivated) to separate from her body and psyche in the way boys usually do. As a result, from the start, he is feminine. The consequent hypothesis is that the less these factors are present, the less feminine he will be. In what is called normal masculinity, these factors should be minimal. And if there is *no* intimacy between mother and infant, there are risks of "excessive" masculinity—the phallic character—something like what is seen in the development of female transsexuals or some phallic warriors.

Generally, of course, there is a period of marked intimacy between mother and infant, necessary for healthy development. But I hypothesize that even this minimal period and milder degree of intimacy leave behind, in boys, a trace, a touch of uncertainty that their masculinity (identity) is intact. (In females this will be an anlage for femininity, but that should not be a problem.) This early, usually reparable flaw suggests that masculinity in males may not be quite as absolute and stable a state as Freud indicated and puts in doubt part of his theory of the development of masculinity and femininity (see chapter 2).

Against the series of very feminine boys I counterposed fourteen families with a very masculine daughter. If too much mother and too little father made for feminine boys, too little mother and too much father might yield masculine girls. It does (Stoller 1975a).

Though the subject in those days was always gender identity, and though the deeper aim was to understand more about ordinary people, I was bound to work at times with perverse people. Especially as I came to understand better the origins of extreme femininity in boys, I began thinking that not all aberrations were perversions in the usual sense in which that term is used in psychodynamic circles. We analysts tend to believe that aberrant behavior of any sort is, in the absence of a clear biologic force, the product of attempts to resolve traumas, frustrations, intrapsychic conflicts.[5] Thus were explained the perversions, and—without adequate evidence—all aberrations were considered per-

---

5. I am surprised that many people's observation that conflict is not the only cause of aberrant development is claimed by Kohut (and acclaimed by his followers) as one of his great contributions to analytic theory.

versions. But I was seeing people whose behavior, though most unusual, was not, so far as I have been able to determine, always the result of trauma, frustration, or intrapsychic conflict.

So—the third phase of this study—I have tried to define the perversions, to understand their dynamics, and to see how they differ from other aberrations. In doing so, I came on the curious fact that women are not represented in most of the diagnoses of perversion; whatever their fantasies, women practice perversions less than men do. Could this be related to men's fear that they are not masculine enough, a fear stemming in part from the blissful merging with mother and its encouraging of femininity (Stoller 1975b)?

In this third—current—phase, I see only adults with gender/erotic disorders, in analysis or in something as close to analysis as they will allow. Since I now feel that case descriptions of less than book length can be at best fables and even a full book no more than a biopsy—and since it takes me several years to write a book—few reports will emerge from this present phase.

This, then, for better or worse, is how an interest in a patient or two with marked gender disorder led to the study of gender identity. Whether my hypotheses are in time confirmed or not, I have tried, in doing this work, to establish a method of operation so that the analyst need not continue to be the victim of data-gathering techniques that preclude testing and prediction. For all the inherent weaknesses in such work, the task may not be hopeless.

Here are idosyncratic suggestions for putting into action a program of psychoanalytic investigation for these early days in the creation of analysis.

1. Do what you enjoy.

2. Be very curious (an essential feature of skepticism, which in turn is an essential feature of scientific behavior).

3. Do not have a clear-cut plan.

4. Do not know what your conclusions will be or even where you are heading; do not head.

5. Have patience; then always be impatient.

6. Think it over; let it soak; listen closely to the repetitions; let the discoveries find you.

7. Use whatever techniques for data collecting appeal to you, but never stop psychoanalyzing.

8. Find people more honorably committed to scientific method than yourself and stick them with the grubby work of properly confirming hypotheses.

9. Do not try for a grant if acceptance means you must accomplish what you promised.

10. Since no research anywhere comes to final conclusions, you need not rush. Act as if you will live forever; it will not make any difference to you if that estimate is wrong.

2

A PRIMER FOR GENDER IDENTITY

This chapter serves as an overview of my ideas about gender identity and its major disorders. For readers unfamiliar with the subject, the following is an introduction; for informed colleagues, it is a baseline description of my perspectives against which to play their own opinions and data. And for both audiences, the chapter presents the background needed for understanding how I use later chapters as checks on the present hypotheses.

DEVELOPMENT

Concerns about the origins and maintenance of masculinity and femininity have been essential to psychoanalytic thinking from the start. With such concepts as castration anxiety and penis envy, Freud placed problems in masculinity and femininity at the center of his theories regarding the origins of all psychopathology. Though he elaborated these concepts over the years, his conviction about the nature of such issues—to be reviewed below—was unchanged throughout his life, and for more than a generation thereafter analytic theory held to these positions. Recently, however, this aspect of sexuality, gender identity, has been intensely reexamined by analysts (for example, *JAPA* Supplement 1976). It has become the focus of work by non-analysts as well—animal psychologists, neurophysiologists, endocrinologists, geneticists, learning theorists—whose provocative findings have helped us rethink and change the established psychoanalytic beliefs.

The term *gender identity* reflects these new data and ideas (Stoller 1964). It refers to the mix of masculinity and femininity in an individual, implying that both masculinity and femininity are found in everyone, but in differing forms and to differing degrees. It is not the same as maleness and femaleness, which connote biology; gender identity implies psychologically motivated behavior. Though masculinity fits well with maleness and femininity goes with femaleness, sex and gender are not necessarily directly related. Many biologically intact men have to try to avoid having what they feel are feminine impulses and behavior; the converse is true for women. There can even be rather complete gender reversal, as in the case of biologically normal males or females who live as members of the opposite sex.

But these designations do not serve us well unless we are also clear what is meant by masculinity and femininity. Masculinity or femininity is defined here as any quality that is felt by its possessor to be masculine or feminine. In other words, masculinity or femininity is a belief—more precisely, a dense mass of beliefs, an algebraic sum of ifs, buts, and ands—not an incontrovertible fact. In addition to biologic anlagen, one gets such beliefs from parental attitudes, especially in childhood, these attitudes being more or less those held by society at large, filtered through the idosyncratic personalities of parents. Therefore, such convictions are not eternal truths; they shift when societies change. An American Indian warrior wore his hair long and felt masculine; a Prussian represented his claim to manliness with very short hair. Masculinity is not measured by hair length but by a person's conviction that long or short hair is masculine.

Core Gender Identity

The earliest stage in the development of masculinity and femininity can be conceptualized as the sense of one's sex—of maleness in males and of femaleness in females, and in rare cases of anatomic hermaphrodites, of being a hermaphrodite, or even a vague sense of being a member of the opposite sex. It is part of, but not identical to, gender identity, a concept that covers a much wider range of behaviors. Core gender identity is a conviction that the assignment of one's sex was anatomically, and ultimately psychologically, correct (Stoller 1968a). It is the first step in the progress toward one's ultimate gender identity and the nexus around which masculinity and femininity gradually accrete. Core gender identity has no implication of role or object relations. By age two or three, at which time one can observe clear-cut masculinity in boys and femininity in girls, it is so firm that it is almost unalterable. Efforts to shift it in later years will probably fail (Money et al. 1955a, 1955b).

Core gender identity results, I think, from the following:

1. A biologic "force": originating in fetal life and usually genetic in origin, this effect—so far as is known—springs from neurophysiologic (central nervous system) organizing of the fetal brain.

2. The sex assignment at birth: the message that the appearance of the infant's external genitals brings to those who can assign sex—the attending physician and the parents—and the subsequent unequivocal effect of this assignment in convincing them of the child's sex.

3. The unending impingement of parents' attitudes, especially those of

mothers, about *that* infant's sex and the infant's constructing these perceptions, via its developing capacity to fantasize, into events—that is, into meaningful, motivated experiences.

4. "Biopsychic" phenomena: early postnatal effects caused by certain habitual patterns of handling the infant—conditioning, imprinting, or other forms of learning that, we speculate, permanently modify the infant's brain and resultant behavior without the infant's mental processes protecting it from such sensory input. This category is related to item 3; it is listed separately for emphasis and to distinguish it from mental processes (also the result of parents' impingements) with which we are more familiar, such as castration anxiety (Freud 1909).

5. The developing body ego: the myriad qualities and quantities of sensations, especially from the genitals, that define the physical and help define the psychic dimensions of one's sex, thus confirming for the baby its parents' convictions about their infant's sex.

In the usual case—by far the most common—each of these factors contributes to the resultant core gender identity. Only in the case of aberrance, however, do we see any of these factors clearly. In other words, they have been discovered in the pathologic, not in the normative. Some examples follow:

1. *The biologic "force."* In all mammals, including humans, anatomic maleness cannot occur without the addition of fetal androgens. For mammals, the resting state of tissue is female, and male organs (except testes) are produced only if an androgen "pulse" is added (Jost 1972; Ohno 1978). This process of sex differentiation is set off by the Y chromosome, whose function is to induce production of histocompatibility—H-Y—antigen. This molecule, the testis-organizing plasma membrane protein, has been assigned the task throughout mammalian evolution of changing the at-first undifferentiated gonad into a testis (Ohno 1978). This is true whether the chromosomes are male (XY) or female (XX). Masculinization of the brain, however, is most likely due to a complex process in which, in males, testosterone is transformed into the *female* hormone, estrogen, the immediate agent of brain masculinization. In the female fetus, which produces little testosterone but a significant amount of estrogen, the effect of the estrogen is perhaps blocked by a plasma estrogen-binding system or by progesterone (MacLusky and Naftolin 1981).

If these fetal hormones are present at the right time, in the right amount, and of the right chemical structure, both anatomic maleness and postnatal masculinity will be possible regardless of chromosomal maleness or femaleness. This rule has so far been found invariant in all species tested. Since direct experimental manipulation is impossible in humans, "natural experiments" have been used, all of which confirm the general mammalian rule. Thus, for instance, all people studied with the complete form of androgen insensitivity syndrome have been feminine girls and women despite their having male (XY) chromosomes and their producing normal amounts of testosterone (from cryp-torchid testes). Because these people have a somatic inability to respond to testosterone, their anatomic appearance is female and their gender identity feminine. Comparably, all people with Turner's syndrome (XO) are feminine, there being no fetal androgens present.

We know, nonetheless, that the more advanced the evolutionary develop-ment, the less absolute is the effect of somatic factors and the more we are dealing with a psychology into which the concept of choice enters. And the factor of choice leads to meaning—fantasy, interpretation—and the need for a vocabulary of behavior useful only for describing humans: masculinity and femininity. (The best review of these issues is Money and Ehrhardt 1972.)

2. *Sex assignment.* When the appearance of the external genitals is unequivo-cal, the infant is assigned to the appropriate sex; whether the parents are pleased or not, they do not question the assignment. Though their pleasure or displeasure may contribute to the intricacies of the child's developing mas-culinity or femininity, the child, if not one of those under the influence of prenatal cross-sex hormones, does not question that its body is that of the assigned sex.

3. *Parental attitudes.* Let us use as our example here a female who was born with genitals that appeared neither male nor female but rather bisexual. On delivery, the doctor told the mother that she had just had a hermaphrodite, that this was not quite a boy or a girl; his attention caught, however, by a female-appearing part of the genital anatomy, he added, ''You might as well raise it as if it were a girl.'' The mother did so and in the process communicated her belief to the child, who was given no reason to doubt in early childhood that it was neither a male nor a female but a member of another sex. Such a child feels that it is the only such case in existence. As an adult, the patient believes herself to be neither male nor female but an ''it'' who imitates women.

4. *''Biopsychic'' phenomena.* Environmental stimuli that, at the beginning of life have no mental effect on the infant, permanently ''condition,'' ''im-print,'' or ''fix''—we do not yet understand these processes and so do not yet have an accurate language for them—certain modes of behavior. In the rare case, despite biologically normal genitals and proper sex assignment, core gender identity can still be influenced by such subliminal or unconscious communications from mother to infant. This occurs, for instance, in primary transsexuals, feminine boys who believe that they are somehow female, while still acknowledging their anatomy or sex assignment. Though suffering no demonstrable congenital defect, with external genitals normal and sex assign-ment correct and accepted by their parents, these boys within the first year or two of life, as we shall see, show the effects of their mothers' too-gratifying ministrations. I do not find evidence that these infants are traumatized in the

symbiosis or subjected to frustrations that could cause intrapsychic conflict, as is seen in effeminate homosexuals.

5. *Body ego.* To the large literature on this subject of one's sense of the dimensions, uses, and significance of the body, I can provide a footnote (Stoller 1968a). Even when anatomy is defective, so that the appearance of the genitals and their sensations are different from those of intact males or females, the individual develops an unequivocal sense of maleness or femaleness if the sex assignment and rearing are unequivocal.

Classical Analytic Theory and Gender Identity

The following is a review of Freud's theory of masculinity and femininity in terms of core gender identity.

First, the classical description of the development of masculinity in males: in brief, Freud believed that maleness and masculinity are the primary and more natural states and that both males and females consider femaleness and femininity less valuable (Freud 1933). Both maleness and femaleness, however, are invaded by attributes of the other sex, and this innate bisexuality has consequences for both normal and abnormal development (Freud 1905). The boy, Freud said (1905, 1909), enters life better off than the girl. His genitals are visible, available, and capable of easily produced and reliable erotic feelings. And though what he already possesses can be threatened, potential danger is not as fundamental a problem as having been deprived from the start, the condition of females. Then—another powerful edge—the boy begins life as a heterosexual. Because his first love object, his mother, is of the opposite sex, his sexual development is off to a proper start. As was true with his genitals, it is only threat, not primary absence, against which he must struggle, for he is endowed with a biologically guaranteed, postnatally conflictless core gender identity.

However, despite this wholesome lead, in time he will be more or less threatened, and to just the extent that he is masculine and heterosexual. It is his predicament to be endangered by his natural desire for his mother: he discovers that his father is a too-powerful rival. The more he shows he wants his mother, the more will his father forbid this, threatening the very part of him—his genitals—that most clearly announces this wish. Castration anxiety intervenes, for instance, when the boy observes females—penisless creatures. Such trauma blocks what would otherwise be an uneventful progress to masculinity and heterosexuality.

Thus the boy is forced to maneuver through his oedipal conflict with techniques that avoid (imagined, expected) castration. If he is to succeed, his parents must help him. They do so in two ways. First, they teach him to displace desire for his mother onto other females, to wait until later years and maturity bring him loving and erotic relationships with women. Second, his father will act so as to serve not only as a rival but also as a model for masculine identification. If the threats to maleness and masculinity are too severe, perversion or neurosis intervenes; in the happier situation, however, the outcome is ''genital primacy,'' of which masculinity and heterosexuality are essential parts.

The girl, on the other hand, is in trouble from the first, says Freud. Her genitals are inferior and her original love object is homosexual. There will never be a direct route to femininity; instead, from birth on, she must struggle to achieve femininity. As a result of being deprived of a penis, she is filled with envy. How she manages this pain determines her future sexuality. If the envy is too great, she will attempt to get a penis in fantasy; or by developing masculine qualities that will substitute for a penis; or, aware of her biologic inferiority, she may simply accept defeat and be fixed in a passive, masochistic, lifelong hopelessness; or, believing her clitoris to be a phallus, though an inadequate one, she may focus her genital erotism on that inadequate organ, deny the inner, feminine reproductiveness of her vagina and uterus, and then be left with a strongly masculine tinge—the complex of fantasies focused on her clitoris—without the compensating, enriching acceptance of her female, reproductive interior.

However, if she can vanquish her penis envy and fixation on her clitoris as a penis substitute, she will have turned toward femininity. When that occurs, she can then bear to give up her mother and turn to her father as a new love object. Now she has the impulse to heterosexuality and to having a baby. Only then—when she has already become feminine—can she enter into the risks and promises of the oedipal conflict. But, felt Freud, it is the unusual girl who lets go of her mother (homosexuality) and turns to her father (heterosexuality), abandons hope for a penis (homosexuality), and accepts the potentials of vagina and uterus (heterosexuality). This means that few girls are even competent enough to engage fully in oedipal conflict, in contrast to boys, who almost always do. Even then, such a girl must go on to resolve this conflict: forsake her father by postponing her genital maturity and at the same time draw femininity from identifying with her mother. Femininity for Freud, then, is a secondary, defensive state, acquired rather late in development, and more the product of renunciation of hope than of pleasurable experiences or expectations.

The anatomic differences between the sexes add to boys' and girls' conflicts. For boys, the discovery of penisless creatures brings home the reality of the threat of castration, while for girls, seeing a penis in the real world underlines their lack and therefore increases envy.

It was Freud's conviction that men are more likely than women to negotiate these obstacles successfully; so he concluded that men are a more admirable class than women (Freud 1933).

Core Gender Theory

Almost no one questioned Freud's belief that maleness and masculinity were acknowledged by mankind (perhaps at even what he considered the profoundest level: racial unconscious) as superior to femaleness and femininity. Though males recognized this superiority, their maleness and masculinity were constantly endangered from infancy; and females, admitting male superiority, from infancy on suffered envy of males' better equipment and status, forever trying to end their despair at not having a penis, or perhaps at having had their penis taken from them, by finding a substitute for this absent penis. These two central features of personality development—castration anxiety in males and penis envy in females—set the form of all normal and aberrant personality formation, not just masculinity and femininity; in almost all psychopathology—neurotic or psychotic—these primordial conflicts were found.

The concept of the core gender identity, however, modifies Freud's theory as follows. Though it is true that the boy's first love is heterosexual, and though fathers are too-powerful rivals, there is an earlier stage in gender identity development wherein the boy is *merged with mother*. Only after months does she gradually become a clearly separate object. Sensing oneself a part of mother—a primeval and thus profound part of character structure (core gender identity)—lays the groundwork for an infant's sense of femininity. This sets the girl firmly on the path to femininity in adulthood but puts the boy in danger of building into his core gender identity a sense of oneness with mother (a sense of femaleness). Depending on how and at what pace a mother allows her son to separate, this phase of merging with her will leave residual effects that may be expressed as disturbances in masculinity.

This theory is tested by the boys I have called primary transsexuals—boys who, without anatomic abnormality, have been feminine from the first year or so of life. I shall here use these boys as the control locus for pinning down my understanding of the development of masculinity in less odd circumstances. Let me summarize the findings I shall expand on in chapters 3 and 4.

As an infant, such a boy usually has an excessively intimate, blissful, skin-to-skin closeness with his mother. This, unfortunately, is not interrupted by his father, a passive, distant man who plays no significant part in bringing up this son. He is not present in the household enough to serve as a model for masculine identification or to shield his son from mother's embrace. He does nothing to encourage the two to separate. For masculinity requires a boy in time to separate from his mother's intimacy. Femininity requires also that a girl separate from her mother, but not particularly from her mother's femininity.

A second test that points to a first stage of protofemininity in both sexes is found in the forms that masculinity typically takes in cultures everywhere—the macho belligerence that degrades women, makes many men fear tenderness and intimacy, and contributes, I think, to the finding that the perversions are more common in men than women. I attribute these sex differences not only to brain and hormones but to males' need for constant vigilance against their unacceptable yearning to return to the merging in the symbiosis.

Female transsexuals and other very masculine females suggest a third test regarding the postulated protofemininity. I have found (Stoller 1973a, 1975a) that these females have suffered a premature and massive disruption of the mother-infant symbiosis, the opposite situation from the one that occurs in the too-feminine males.

But given this earliest stage of protofemininity, I find Freud's theory of gender development accurate: boys' choice of their first love object—mother—is a heterosexual act and girls' is homosexual, bringing on the conflicts and consequences first discerned by Freud (1905, 1933).

If my theory is correct, femininity is not, as Freud thought, an inherently pathologic state, for the girl is now seen to have an advantage. From the start she is identifying with a person of the same sex. Though the potential homosexual nucleus is there, her first love object being female, the development of her femininity no longer seems so risk laden. Those conflict-free aspects of gender identity (for example, those that result from identifying with the gratifying aspects of being a woman) are present from earliest life. On the other hand, though the boy moves to heterosexuality early on, he must have already separated himself sufficiently from his mother so that he is an individual and knows his mother is a separate, different-sexed person. Then he will prefer to have, not to be, a woman.

With these fundamentals in place, as the years pass refinements in styles of masculinity and femininity are willingly drawn into him or her from the outside world or are beaten in by culture's demands. Later conflicts or gratifying reinforcements, physiologic shifts, or life's exigencies will have their effects on gender identity into old age, but the early patterns are the framework through which these later modifications will develop.

Given prenatal conditions normal for the individual's anatomic sex, the two main factors in creating gender identity—whether it is the gender congruent with anatomy and with what one's culture defines as the proper behavior for one's sex or a distorted gender identity—are the silent effects of learning and the more sharply experienced modifications resulting from frustration, trauma, and conflict, and the attempts to resolve conflict. Thus, parents, siblings, and in time others outside the family may shape masculine and feminine behavior in boys and girls by complex systems of reward and punishment, subtle and gross. Additionally, prohibitions, threats, and mixed communications that combine both reward and punishment are taken up by the developing child and, at different stages of maturity and experience, are interpreted to have different meanings. Preoedipal and oedipal conflicts and their resolutions are filled with such development.

In brief, this newer view of gender identity holds that femininity in females is not just penis envy or denial or resigned acceptance of castration; a woman is not just a failed man. Masculinity in males is not simply a natural state that needs only to be defended if it is to grow healthily; rather, it is an achievement.

GENDER DISORDERS

In the descriptions that follow, one can see the distortions in masculinity and femininity; these conditions clearly belong in a classification of gender disorders. There are, however, other behaviors—the erotic perversions—in which gender disorder is at work but not obvious. Though I take these up in depth elsewhere (Stoller 1975b, 1985), they are worth briefly considering here.

I suspect that the problem boys have with creating their masculinity from the protofemininity leaves behind a "structure," a vigilance, a fear of the pull of the symbiosis—that is, a conflict between the urge to return to the peace of the symbiosis and the opposing urge to separate out as an individual, as a male, as masculine. In that conflict, a barrier must be raised against the impulse to merge. Much of what we see as masculinity is, I think, the effect of that struggle. For much of masculinity, as is well known, consists of struggling not to be seen by oneself or others as having feminine attributes, physical or psychologic. One must maintain one's distance from women or be irreparably infected with femininity.[1]

When we look closely at the behavior that makes up a man's perversion—when we get an in-depth subjective description of the erotic behavior—we find, regardless of the overt form of the behavior, that he is under pressure from envy and anger toward women (Stoller 1975b). The evidence is found in the fantasies these men have that they are degrading women. Examples are rape, coprolalia (dirty language as an erotic stimulant), voyeurism, fetishism, exhibitionism, pedophilia, necrophilia. In all these you will find evidence of uncertain manliness. And so, though there may be no desire to put on clothes of the opposite sex or otherwise to behave (or fantasize behaving) as a member of the opposite sex, in the perversions is nonetheless buried unsureness of gender identity. (Classical psychoanalysis discusses these issues in terms of "castration anxiety," a concept I find too anatomic, too stripped of identity connotations.)

---

1. This explanation ignores biologic factors. I believe, nonetheless, that such factors also participate in differentiating the erotic behavior of men and women and contribute, in ways not yet measurable, to the greater incidence of perversion in men than in women. I am thinking, for instance, of the power of androgens in driving men's erotism.

Transsexualism

By now most physicians are familiar with the fact that "transsexualism," used as a diagnosis, is a problem. There are—though not everyone knows this—multiple meanings for *transsexualism* and no generally accepted definition. Though *ism* implies a state, a condition, a dynamically organized complex of behaviors and thoughts, the label is most frequently used, by both laymen and physicians, to refer to anyone who wants or has had a reassignment of sex. As a result, a term with a scientific, diagnostic ring to it—transsexualism—in fact bears no such weight. At best, one might consider this usage to refer to a syndrome, but even that is not accurate, since within the request for "sex change"[2] or the accomplishing of it are myriad behaviors and attitudes. Certainly, when one is familiar with a number of such people, one recognizes that transsexualism, as the term is commonly used, does not refer even to a syndrome but rather to a mix of different syndromes, symptoms, signs, desires, proclamations. And if a diagnosis is a label for a set of interdependent signs and symptoms (syndrome), underlying dynamics (physiologic and/or psychologic) with common etiology, then "transsexualism" falls as far short as would descriptions such as "cough," "abdominal pain," "greed," "stamp collecting," or "desire to be a psychiatrist." The individuals who experience any one of these states share in less than they differ.

A CLASSIFICATION

I divide those who wish for or have already received "sex change" into the following categories (which, like most psychiatric diagnoses, are more clearly defined in print than in the clinic). In the following, because only males fit several of the categories, I shall mostly present a differential for males.

Male Primary Transsexuals

These are anatomically and physiologically normal males who are, at the time you examine them, the most natural-appearing feminine males you have ever seen. In their ordinary daily behavior, they are indistinguishable from girls and

---

2. I shall use "sex change" rather than "sex transformation," "sex reassignment," "sex conversion," "sex surgery," or "gender transmutation" because "sex change" is the shortest, most direct, and least euphemistic expression of what the patients desire and therefore most clearly measures the failure of the effort to change sex. When quote marks are used, I am referring to the effort; without quotes, I indicate the wish. At present it is not possible to change sex; the punctuation is used to indicate the falsity of the claim that such an option exists. In males, "sex change" consists of amputating penis and testes, creating an artificial vagina, electrolysis to remove facial and body hair, and estrogens and mammoplasty to create breasts and other feminine rounding; in females, mastectomy, panhysterectomy, testosterone (to lower voice and to grow facial and body hair), and creating—never successfully—a penis.

women considered feminine by their society. This description is true at whatever age you see them: early childhood, later childhood, adolescence, young adulthood, middle age, or senescence. They give a history, confirmed by family and others, that they have been this feminine all their lives, from the beginning of any behavior that can be called masculine or feminine (which may be as early as a year), and with no episodes of masculinity or of even transient commitments to typically masculine roles (such as marriage, masculine professions, service in the military, heterosexual erotic behavior). Hence ''primary.''[3] They know they are biologically male, but since early in life they have openly said that they want their bodies changed to female. From early childhood, they have wished to dress and live exclusively as do females. They get no erotic pleasure from putting on females' clothes. They do not consider themselves homosexual, except in the anatomic sense that they are turned on exclusively to males—men they consider masculine and heterosexual—and they reject sexual advances made by overtly homosexual men; a prime indicator to them that a man is homosexual is that he is interested in the transsexual's male genitals.[4]

Male Secondary Transsexuals

This is a wastebasket category made up of men requesting ''sex change'' whose life history is different from that of the primary transsexual's in that the cross-gender behavior does not begin in earliest childhood, is punctuated with episodes of unremarkably masculine behavior, and (with rare exceptions) is laced with experiences of pleasure from the male genitals.

I can make out four life patterns that precede the announcement by these people that they are transsexuals and therefore have a right to ''sex change.'' The most common, I think (there are no adequate statistics, so one cannot be sure), is via a progression over years during which the patient feels himself to be a homosexual, with a slant toward the feminine or effeminate side and with,

---

3. By definition, all primary transsexuals have been uninterruptedly feminine since earliest childhood, but we do not know how many boys who are extremely feminine in earliest childhood grow up to be transsexual. It still must be proven, however, by following such boys, without treatment, into adult life, that they remain transsexual. So far my evidence is only that, when evaluated in childhood *or* adolescence *or* adulthood, the most feminine males have come out of the below-described family constellation. Green (forthcoming) has followed a series of feminine boys—few, however, as feminine as these primary transsexuals—and finds that the majority are homoerotic by their late teens or early twenties; only one wants a ''sex change.''

4. For years, this was the group I called transsexuals (or true transsexuals), relegating the rest of those requesting ''sex changes'' to some vaguer category, such as ''pseudotranssexual'' or ''nontranssexual seeking sex reassignment'' (Stoller 1968a, 1975a). However, this terminology confused colleagues, since for them ''transsexual'' had always had the broader meanings of a person who wants sex change or who claims to be trapped in the wrong body. I feel that it is better, therefore, to accept the common usage. We can then add clinical strength to our labeling if the subcategories of primary and secondary are used.

in time, a sense that he would do better if female. The second group proceeds via transvestism (fetishistic cross-dressing): after a longer or shorter period of putting on women's garments to get excited, these men notice that they enjoy dressing less for the erotic pleasure it brings than because it makes them feel like (their version of) a woman. The third group arrives at the desire for sex change via a more or less exclusively overtly heterosexual commitment, including marriage, fatherhood, and a work history in typically masculine pursuits. In the fourth, there has been no strong commitment to any erotic style— heterosexual, homosexual, or perverse—but instead only a weak or absent erotic need in a man who had not been manifestly aberrant in gender behavior. (I have not studied such a patient. Though I worked for years with one who made such a claim, he finally admitted it was not so.)

Female Transsexuals

The female transsexual is a biologically normal female, recognized as such at birth and properly assigned to her sex. Nonetheless, since the beginning of any behavior that can be called masculine or feminine, she acts and fantasizes as if she were a masculine boy. This masculinity is not interrupted at any time in life by episodes of feminine behavior or interests. Comparable to male primary transsexuals, the child impresses observers as being masculine, often passing undetected as a boy; plays only with boys; takes a boy's name; and wants to become male. By adolescence, the transsexual is living permanently as a male, working in a typically masculine field, erotically drawn only to women she judges very feminine and heterosexual, and trying to transform her body to male.

I do not believe female transsexuals should be divided into primary and secondary groups but rather that these very masculine females are the far end of a continuum of butch homosexuality.

Fetishistic Cross-Dressers (Transvestites)

The term *transvestism* has been used for any cross-dressing. (In fact, such a vague clinical concept can seem precise only if one transforms it with the scientific-sounding Latin.) I restrict it, however, to those, again biologically normal, who put on clothes of the opposite sex because the clothes are sexually exciting to them. Though this fetishism can occur in childhood, usually it is first manifested at puberty or later in adolescence. It is almost always found in men who are overtly heterosexual, of masculine demeanor, in occupations dominated by males; and it occurs only intermittently, most of the subject's life being spent in unremarkably masculine behavior and appearance. Such men usually marry and have children.

As the years pass, for many the fetishism cools down but does not disappear, and there is an increased nonerotic need to dress and consider oneself temporarily a woman. A few such men in time have strong transsexual wishes (secondary transsexualism), but for most transvestites the impulse for sex change is contained by the much more dominant masculinity. In no cases has the primary transsexual family constellation been reported; rather, one frequently finds that in early childhood the boy was cross-dressed by a girl or woman for the purpose of humiliating him. In time, the humiliation is converted, via the perversion, to a triumph, especially as manifested by the ability to achieve an erection and orgasm despite being in women's clothes.

Fetishistic cross-dressing is found almost exclusively in males.

Cross-Gender Homosexuals

These are boys and men, again biologically normal, who, knowing and accepting themselves as males, prefer males as their sexual objects, and conversely with girls and women. A few—no one knows the percentage—cross-dress. They do not do it because they believe they somehow belong to the opposite sex (as do primary transsexuals) or because cross-dressing excites them sexually (as is true for transvestites). The men do it to feel feminine without also wanting to be female, and conversely for the women. Though some of these people have occasional thoughts of "sex change," the males prefer their maleness and the females their femaleness. Butch homosexuality in women differs from effeminate homosexuality in males in that these masculine women do not have the element of caricature that defines effeminacy.

Intersexuals

These are people with biologic disorders of sex that influence their gender behavior. They suffer defects of the sex chromosomes (for example, XXY—Klinefelter's syndrome); or of the genes, without gross chromosomal disorder (for example, androgen insensitivity syndrome); or iatrogenic prenatal conditions (for example, progesterone-induced androgenizing effects in girls whose mothers were given progesterones to prevent abortion). These states somehow influence brain function (causing either abnormal masculinization of the brain, as in adrenogenital syndrome in otherwise normal females, or failure to androgenize the brain, as in XO—Turner's syndrome).

For a fine review of this and the following states, see Money and Ehrhardt (1972).

Feminization

Chromosomal abnormality: XO (Turner's Syndrome). Missing a second chromosome and having no gonads to produce sex hormones, these people nonetheless develop anatomically in the female direction, in accordance with the general rule for mammalian development. In addition, such persons grow up feminine in behavior and heterosexual in object choice.[5]

---

5. These "experiments" of nature are not yet highly suggestive. We need more information before we can decide if the adult femininity in these patients is related to their unandrogenized brains or simply to their having been raised from birth unequivocally as girls.

Complete androgen insensitivity. With male (XY) chromosomes, the subject nonetheless develops to adulthood as a normal-appearing female but with cryptorchid testes that produce normal testosterone and minimal or absent internal reproductive organs, including the vagina. Probably the hormonal defect is in the target organs (the extragonadal tissues), which, unlike the norm, fail to respond to circulating androgens. Subjects are feminine and heterosexual.[6]

Constitutional male hypogonadism. In the case of these males, who appeared physically normal at birth, some are discovered in adolescence or later to have had testes markedly deficient in androgen production since fetal life. In the case of Klinefelter's syndrome, they may develop gynecomastia (female-appearing breasts) and weakened erotic desire. An unusually large number cross-dress from early childhood on and feel more or less feminine; some state in words and behavior that they believe they really should be girls.

Temporal lobe disorder. A number of reports (reviewed in Blumer, 1969) implicate paroxysmal temporal lobe disorder with cross-gender behavior— oddly enough, only in males. The behavior (usually dressing in clothes of the opposite sex) comes on with the paroxysmal electrical burst; remission of the brain disorder with treatment leads to immediate loss of the aberrant behavior.

Masculinization

Progesterone effect. Otherwise normal human females have been masculinized in utero by large doses of the female hormone progesterone (which is biologically closely related to androgens) given to their mothers to prevent spontaneous abortion. In addition to having masculinized genitals (hermaphrodism) more of these little girls (compared to a control series) have developed into tomboys (masculine in behavior but heterosexual in object choice).

Adrenogenital syndrome. Fetal hyperadrenalism causes masculinization of the external genitals in females because the fetus's adrenals produce excess androgens. Though these girls are otherwise normally female anatomically and hormonally, they, like those influenced by prenatal progesterone, are often tomboyish, though heterosexual.

Those with Hermaphroditic Identity

Like the previous category, these patients have a biologic defect—genitals not unequivocally male or female—but in this instance the condition (hermaphrodism) does not act directly on the brain to produce cross-gender behavior. Instead, the behavior is the result of aberrant sex assignment; when

---

6. The same footnote again: these are not yet highly suggestive. We need more information before we can decide if the adult femininity in these patients is related to their unandrogenized brains or simply to their having been raised from birth unequivocally as girls.

parents are unsure if their child is male or female, that uncertainty will be reflected in the child's gender identity. Such people feel freakish, as if they are neither male nor female, or as if they were both at the same time.

Psychotics

Cross-gender impulses in psychotics have long been described. I break this category into two classes. The first, the familiar one, is made up of those psychotics (more frequently men than women) who suffer hallucinations and delusions in which, against their will, they feel their bodies are being transformed into the opposite sex or they suffer hallucinations (for example, of being homosexual) with voices accusing them of being flawed in their sex. The second group are psychotics who wish sex change, the transsexual wish being independent of the psychosis; when not psychotic, they still want to change sex.

Casual Cross-Gender Behavior

Without strong intent, children often experiment by putting on clothes of the opposite sex. In addition, adults, especially in carnival situations, will also "for the fun of it" put on a display of cross-gender behavior.

Now I shall expand the ideas sketched in this review chapter and, especially, load the argument with cases that test the hypotheses regarding family dynamics and very feminine boys. Let us start in the next two chapters by looking at family dynamics that shape very feminine boys.

3

MARKED FEMININITY IN BOYS: AN
EMPHASIS ON MOTHERS

In this chapter, I again take up the hypotheses, proposed since 1964 and still not well tested, that (1) extreme femininity in some boys comes out of a specific set of family dynamics, and (2) the femininity in these boys, though not in all feminine boys, is not primarily a defense against primitive, overwhelming anxiety but rather is due to too much gratification.

Considering that, if it exists, I am talking about a very rare condition and that most everyone who has discussed femininity in males disagrees with me, you should wonder why I persist. I do so, first, because, despite their rarity, these boys represent the far end of a continuum that reaches all boys; therefore, they tell me something about gender development in all boys (and perhaps girls too). Second, I persist because the arguments against the hypotheses are presented, almost without exception, without the observations one needs to refute the conclusions I draw from my observations. Though I must attend to others' theories and sensible reasoning, refutation should come from clinical cases. For instance, if I claim and quote their words that the boys' mothers find their sons beautiful, I can relax if someone shows me to be wrong by presenting a series of families of comparably feminine boys whose mothers did not tell of their sons' beauty. To counter my claim by reporting on laboratory mice or narcissistic cathexes of the self-object satisfies me no more than a plastic hamburger.

So I go at it again. Let us start with the simplest form of the hypothesis: in boys, in the absence of special biologic circumstances (for example, certain chromosomal disorders), the more mother and the less father, the more femininity. The hypothesis lies within the category of developmental arrest, for it is tested in circumstances in which an excessively close and gratifying mother-infant symbiosis, undisturbed by father's presence, prevents a boy from adequately separating himself psychically from his mother's female body and feminine behavior. The hypothesis predicts that the more intense these family dynamics, the more feminine the boy will be. I do not believe, however, that this factor is the only one contributing to the gender identity of most gender-aberrant boys. As infancy progresses, conflict situations—preoedipal, such as the discovery of the anatomic differences between the sexes, and oedipal, such as the struggle to create a safe and loving erotic bond with parents—increasingly make their contribution to gender development, as analysts have demonstrated for decades. And the more conflict rather than pleasure plays a part, the less extreme is the femininity.

Beyond this hypothesis—beyond proof—I want also to suggest something quite controversial, at least for psychoanalysts: in some boys this gross aberrance—femininity so marked that they are dreaming of changing into females—is not at the start the product of conflict. It is, then, not an active arrest, a frozen defensive state, but, rather, at its core a comfortable, primitive character structure that only after a time picks up its anxiety and conflict components.

As a consequence, the prognosis for treatment to remove marked femininity in these boys, especially that which developed in the first year or two of life, is guarded. (See chapter 2 and also Green, 1985).

Whatever the risks, I shall present these ideas by means of clinical descriptions rather than by mobilizing the literature, metapsychology, or clinical theory on developmental arrest.

BACKGROUND

Among the ideas likely to upset analysts these days is the suggestion that nonconflictual gratification can lead to developmental arrest. Yet we know that that idea is at the center of our theory. Freud always used it as a building block in constructing a model of development, for he knew that the processes we now call separation/individuation were threatened by gratification: if the blissful conditions of intrauterine life and the early symbiotic fusion were not invaded, maturing ego functions would not emerge. These functions need, in addition to a biologic epigenesis, the goad of dissatisfaction—trauma, frustration, and other pain. The oedipal conflicts exemplify how painful reality forces the psychic apparatus (that is, the child) to modify itself in opposition to its own self-centered, pleasure-driven, pain-avoiding bent to float dreamily in the tensionless maternal soup. Humans, prodded by biology and reality, are doomed/privileged to invent themselves out of the struggle between the opposing demands of bliss—that is, stasis—and growth.

Yet, though this ground plan of development is almost universally accepted by analysts, I do not recall any report, not even an anecdote, in which Freud described one of his own patients in whom a nonconflictual, gratifying, primary (that is, starting at birth) experience thwarted development. And it is my judgment from several readings of his works on the origins of sexual behavior that he would not have considered extremely feminine males or extremely masculine females to be anything but perverse, which pretty much meant: the product of conflict and attempts at conflict resolutions. (He would footnote, however, that as time has shown, marked gender aberration can be biologically driven.)

In other words, in theory he believed that excessive or extended gratification could lead to perversion; perversion was fixation of a component instinct allowed somehow to persist in conscious life.[1] But when he presented cases, the clinical picture was explained by such concepts as oral aggression, anal aggression, castration anxiety, penis envy, and other defensive maneuvers that indicated underlying conflict.

Conflict is the cornerstone of any explanation to be considered analytic, for many analysts even a sine qua non. If no conflict, then not analytic. Though I agree that the study of intrapsychic conflict has been perhaps the greatest contribution psychoanalysis has made to understanding human behavior, I think this criterion can—in pursuit of purity—be applied too severely. If we want a comprehensive theory of development, we ought to leave room for recognizing the power of nonconflictual forces in shaping fundaments of behavior.

This preamble serves as a defense for my argument that a massive non-conflict can support a massive aberrance: marked femininity in boys. But I must underline at the start that I cannot imagine how, in the tumultuous world of clinical reality, we can avoid two factors that will defeat any efforts to test this last hunch. First, we cannot get into an infant's mind. (We can scarcely do it with cooperating adults.) Second, having decided that infancy is a time permeated—some say ravaged—by conflict and anxiety, one leaves no space in the resultant theory for the quiet moments of infancy that do not have conflict/anxiety in their structure. If anxiety and conflict—at the least, present unconsciously—are from early infancy on universally present, then how could I ever demonstrate a non-conflict-laden infantile experience? In this state of weakness of argument, I try to keep the heavy doors of theory from slamming shut by saying that no one knows: we are all guessing. Even when we have observations, they can be challenged (one reason, for instance, why some colleagues deny that infant observation is psychoanalysis).

I am unhappy about publishing once again my old story of the family dynamics I think lead to primary transsexualism. I must do so, however, or the reader unfamiliar with this description has no clinical baseline for judging the cases that follow.

Were you to judge by the length of the following description, you would

---

1. You recognize, of course, that the above impressionistic glance at Freud's beliefs proves nothing. Citing authorities never does (especially authorities as textured as Freud, with his parentheses, footnotes, and emendations, augmented by his immense correspondence, the insatiable snooping of biographers, and the picking over his entrails to read portents, the ''If-he-had-lived-I-am-sure-Freud-would-agree-that . . .'' and the ''It-is-my-judgment-from-several-readings-of-his-works-that . . .'').

think primary transsexualism is as important as, say, schizophrenia. So, to orient the reader, I must note again that it is a rare condition. Its importance for me lies in what I have learned from it regarding the development in every-one—male and female—of gender identity. Studying these people, I saw how the early mother-infant relationship contributes to some of the original mas-culinity and femininity in us all. Only after finding these factors in the extreme case was I alerted to look for their effects when they are less intense.

In the case material that follows, the hypothesis that too much mother and too little father yields femininity in boys is confirmed. But my belief that the boy participates in the symbiosis with little conflict is neither confirmed nor disproved.

SUMMARY OF THE CASES

Each of the boys, anatomically normal, was graceful, charming, and feminine in appearance and carriage. Each liked to dress all day in girls' clothes and to play exclusively with girls in girls' games; each wanted his body changed to female. His parents said he had been this way since the beginning of any behavior one could judge as masculine or feminine, starting around a year of age. Having by then seen a number of adult males requesting sex change, and being unsure how much of their histories could be believed, I thought it would be interesting to study a child with his family to see if we could find clues to this behavior. Mother, father, and boy entered treatment, each with an analyst. The father never got started; he was not interested. The boy was treated by my analyst colleague Dr. R. R. Greenson, the mother by me. The two effects of treatment pertinent here were that the boy became more masculine and that his mother gave us an explanation for his femininity.

Because they are described elsewhere (Stoller 1968a), the findings are merely summarized here, but I ask you to remember that the constellation of effects first emerged from a psychoanalysis in a long and laborious process of uncovering. I like to think it was the analytic treatment situation and an analytic perspective toward the data that made this possible. I suppose it was; yet now I am sure anyone can find these factors without using analysis. Further, though the full array of influences surfaced in this treatment, I did not know that for a few years. Some factors struck me immediately as pertinent, but it was only after seeing three more families[2] that I decided others were true findings, not coincidental or artifact.

Here is what analysis uncovered in the first family studied. (The findings were confirmed and clarified in the later families, though, of course, not every detail was the same in each family nor to the same degree in each case.)

---

2. Now fifteen, some children and some adolescent when first seen. The last family (below) was evaluated in 1978; after twenty or more years, my interest in studying transsexualism died away. (The reasons are imbedded in chapter 9.)

One must study three generations in order to understand the process. The mother's mother—the transsexual boy's grandmother—is a cold, harsh woman who has no love for the daughter who is to be the transsexual's mother. The girl, who is unquestionably female, is made to feel from birth on that being female is worthless. She is treated with no affection or respect by her mother but serves simply as slavery to do the household tasks. On the other hand, her father loves her; they are close for a few years. Unfortunately for her femininity, however, the attachment is one in which father has his daughter join him in his masculine interests, encouraging her to be like him. Then somewhere between age six and puberty he abandons her, by death, separation, divorce, going into the service, and so on. In the first case studied, when the girl was six, a sister was born, and the father instantly turned his love and attention exclusively to the newborn. (This factor—father's rejection—was less constant than the others listed here.)

With father's desertion, sometimes within days, the girl begins acting like a boy. She refuses to wear her girls' clothes, insisting on dressing only in boys' clothes, from underwear out. She cuts her hair short in the manner of boys. She refuses to play with girls but will play only with boys, in exclusively boys' games and becomes a fine athlete, better than most of the boys. Even more, she wants to become male, talks of changing sex, and prays to God for a penis. Up to this point, the story sounds much like that found in females who grow up to be transsexuals (Stoller 1975a). But, with the changes of puberty and their proof of oncoming adult femaleness, the girl stops waiting for maleness, becomes manifestly depressed, and puts on a feminine facade, giving up her boyish ways. In time, without romance, heterosexual fantasies, or premarital erotic enthusiasms for men, she marries. Having decided that she must act as if feminine, she has pushed herself toward marriage, but her wish to be male, though consciously renounced, and her hatred and envy because she is not persist.

The man she marries is chosen by her to fulfill her unhappy needs. He is not effeminate, but he is distant and passive. (It is unlikely that a more manly man would marry such a woman.) He is not involved with his family, not respected by his wife, and not physically present most of the time. When this boy is young, his father—hard working—leaves home before the boy is awake and does not return until the child is already in bed. On weekends, having worked so hard, he wishes to relax; his wife encourages him in this so long as relaxation continues to keep him removed from the family. In each case, the father was therefore not present even on the weekends. One, for instance, spent every weekend in a photographic darkroom; another drank beer and watched football on television all weekend, with the children instructed not to disturb father; another was a painter, isolated in his studio.

It is likely, of course, that not every man and woman who fit these descriptions marry and have children; I never see those who do not. But those who do follow this scenario do not have a houseful of transsexuals. In fact, for years I was puzzled by the fact that all the families I observed had only one transsexual son, and there were no reports of families in whom more than one such boy occurred. The reason only one transsexual was appearing, even though often more than one son was born, was revealed in each mother's story, as we shall see shortly.

Contrary to what one might expect before analysis revealed differently, the mother was happy to give birth to this son. Like others before me, I at first thought that those very feminine boys who were not the result of an inherent biologic force were produced by a mother who was disappointed not to have had a girl. Yet these mothers were overjoyed. In addition—a mystery clarified by analysis[3]—each boy was given a strongly masculine, phallic name at birth, which hardly seemed to predict a continuing impulse in the mother to have her boy be feminine. And when one recalls that these are women who hate men and who learn to despise the penis they envy, one is surprised to learn that the proximate cause of the femininity is an excessively intimate symbiosis, present from birth indefinitely onward until external forces end it, in which the mother is trying to produce a frustrationless, traumaless, blissful state. Nothing is to split mother and son apart.

It is this passionate motherhood that produces the femininity or—to flip the coin over—that arrests the development of masculinity. Should another set of family factors arise that also leads to too much merging, it too, I predict, will lead to boyhood femininity *as long as mother and son are merged too well too long*.

This intimacy, more complete than any I have seen under other circumstances or have ever found reported, is set off by the infant's perceived beauty and gracefulness. If this mother finds the baby to be ideal—beautiful, cuddly, responsive to mother—he becomes the beautiful phallus for which she has yearned since her sad, hopeless girlhood. Finally, from her own body has been produced—just as she had hoped and then despaired of ever getting—the perfect penis. Though all others—her husband's, her other sons', all other men's—are ugly, this one is not. Because her other sons are not considered beautiful and graceful, they are spared this intense symbiosis and are not feminized.

With this cure for her lifelong depression in her arms, she is not about to let go of it. There is nothing complex about this motivation: when she holds the baby she feels marvelous; when he is out of reach she feels less so; and if he were out of sight, she would be anxious. Therefore, she simply acts on her desire and keeps him unendingly in contact with her, skin to skin, day and night, with as little interruption as she can manage. Father may be driven from

---

3. This needs amplifying in order to manifest a problem in using psychoanalysis to look for origins of behavior. This question, like others, was answered during the analysis, but I ignored the answer—did not assign to the data the status of "answer"—until hearing the same conditions described by other mothers in the next few years.

the marriage bed, the infant taking his place for extended periods. In time, and at appropriate ages, though, mother allows ego functions to develop—sitting, crawling, standing, walking, talking—none is aborted or delayed in the symbiosis. Rather, in her love and pride, she encourages her son to develop his intelligence and creativity (especially artistic sensitivity). However, she does so only with him constantly within sight and reach.

When one hears of a mother and infant in a blissful relationship in the first months of life, one thinks that this is normal, even ideal. One does not expect it to go on day and night with the mother trying to keep it from being interrupted, and certainly one does not expect it to persist for years. But in these families, we observe it still active when the children come to us, usually around age four or five. Every impetus to referral for treatment indicates the process. By this age the boys act and look like beautiful girls, but their mothers refuse to recognize this; they consciously cannot understand why everyone mistakes their child for a girl. (We, too, on first seeing the children, find them beautiful, graceful, and feminine.) So the mothers usually do not bring their sons for evaluation spontaneously, but are driven to do so only after months of questions about whether the boys are girls. Between four and five, in our society, children begin moving out into the world, for instance, to school, and it is especially then that pressure builds up for the mother to consider her child abnormal and to get help.

Dr. Paulina Kernberg, in a personal communication, enlarges on my ideas about the boy's meaning to his mother:

My suggestion is that the mother of these boys does *not* consider the child as a narcissistic object, but as an idealized version of themselves or of the child they believe the maternal grandmother would have liked. Hence, the support for the various interests and sublimatory activities and the mother's apparent unawareness of any problem in the children. The mother in turn would reenact an O-R [object relations] in which she herself plays the role of her own mother, this time enchanted with her daughter-boy; namely, her feminine son. The boy submits to mother's need while enjoying his own importance in fulfilling mother's needs.

A character structure with secondary gains or illness develops, explaining the apparent lack of conflict. The mother sees the child as a daughter, an improved self-image, whereas normally the mothers of sons see them as ideal objects (Chasseguet-Smirgel). This would not be, from this point of view, pre-objectal, but a reenacting for the mother of a dyad of ideal-mother (herself) and ideal-self (her son).

This mother, thus, is doing all she can to maintain the close relationship with this ideal product of her body. At this point, one would expect the father to interrupt the process. But he was chosen as a person who would not be there— and he is not. (Recall that with every family seen we could not involve this father in treatment; father does not participate beyond the initial evaluation.)[4]

---

4. If he did participate, we probably would not see the families, for he would already have been strong enough to end the symbiosis that creates the femininity.

Mother is therefore free to continue the symbiosis uninterrupted; no one moves in as a shield between mother and son. Father's second main function—to serve as a model for his son's masculinity, as most fathers do—is also not possible. He simply is not present, and, additionally, masculinity is so disparaged in the family by mother's remarks about this weak and absent father that the boy is never encouraged to look on masculinity as a state he would admire and wish to identify with.

Once the femininity begins to appear, somewhere around one to two years, mother is thrilled to see it, all the while denying that it is strange behavior for her phallicly named, unquestionably male son. She defines it as lovely, fine, adorable, creative, graceful, gentle, and appealing, not as feminine, and so encourages him to continue.

As soon as the child can manage, he spontaneously begins putting on girls' clothes (it is not first done by his mother) and takes girls' parts in all his play. He has no interest in masculine activities, and in his choice of stories to be read to him or of television programs, he shows that his fascination is with the females. When he is old enough to play with other children, he joins the girls, in girls' games. The girls diagnose his femininity accurately: a masculine boy would be excluded from games played only by girls, but the very feminine boy insinuates himself effortlessly into their group, and the girls sense that he is one of them. By age three, four, or five, he has given himself a girl's name and is talking of becoming both a girl (an identity and a role) and a female (a biologic state) when he grows up. He may even announce that he wishes to have his penis removed.

School becomes increasingly painful, since his femininity marks him for teasing by the other boys but, interestingly, not often by girls. Sooner or later, under the pressure of his peers, teachers, or neighbors—but not his parents— he may try to hide his femininity, but this does not succeed; so he finds himself almost friendless. The ensuing state of sadness and loneliness leads to poor school performance, further isolation from other people, and a picture of a generalized neurosis. This, however, is only an appearance, for the depressive neurosis is not generated from inner conflict. It is, rather, a collection of symptoms, the result of a painful external reality; for when the primary transsexual is given permission by some authority in society, such as a physician, to embark on the task of passing into membership in the female sex, the anxiety, depression, and withdrawn behavior arising from social disapproval disappear. But lasting relationships with others seem beyond his/her grasp.

The story so far comes from the mothers, fathers, grandparents, and neighbors and is confirmed by our observations of the families when the boys are four or five or older. But at this point in the explanation, crucial data are missing: never observed by an outsider and not articulated by the mothers or their transsexual sons is the process by which, within the first year or so of life, the little boy draws forth his femininity. One can presume that the pleasures of the symbiosis are transmitted in measurable ways: mother's soft and cradling arms, warm skin, pillowy muscles and bosom, cooing voice, and the innumerable other movements, behaviors, and attitudes that, though minute, pass clearly onto the infant's body so that he is in an ambience molded for constant bliss. But how does that lead to feminine behavior? I do not know. Shaping by positive and negative reinforcement?

Here may be a clue. All the mothers mention that these sons' eyes are large and beautiful, which draws the mothers to look constantly into the babies' eyes. I doubt if there is a more intense way available to humans for merging with each other than to look deeply into each other's eyes; lovers have always known this, as have mothers. When we look openly and fully into another's eyes, at the same instant we are equally penetrating and penetrated. There probably is no other interpersonal experience in which activity and passivity are simultaneous in time and equally powerful. It is a process so intense that few persist for more than moments. Yet these mothers keep it up as long as possible; in no other way do they so profoundly sense their unbroken connection with this beloved infant. Perhaps in this way, especially, the boys drink in, merge with, sense they are part of their mothers' femaleness.

A most odd oedipal situation develops in these families: there is no oedipal conflict. Other boys emerge from the mother-infant symbiosis to become separate persons. They then desire their mothers as sexual objects and fear their fathers' retaliation for such wishes. The conflict between desire and fear complicates—deepens—their developing masculinity, especially when resolved by identifying with father. In that way fathers can help their sons delay consummating this first heterosexuality, displacing it out of the family and to a later time. Father is converted from overpowering rival to ally when he encourages his son to identify with him, while mother serves the process of renunciation by being a model for future love objects. Heterosexual masculinity is the consequence.

None of this occurs with the very feminine boy. His mother, not his father, is the model for his gender identification, and she is not the object of his erotism. He wants *to be* like her rather than *to have* her (Greenson 1968). His father, all too absent, is neither rival nor model. The boy is deprived of the needed conflict.

THE "TRANSSEXUAL EXPERIMENT"

Those are the family dynamics, found first in the uncontrolled setting of an analysis. How is one to test the validity of this explanation of the boys' femininity? First state it in testable form, as hypothesis. Then test. (Hypotheses are testable propositions; there are very few in psychoanalysis.)

Predictions from the hypothesis: if a woman like this marries a man like this and has a beautiful, graceful son, she will create the above-described symbiosis, making her son feminine by a year or so of age. She will then encourage his femininity, and father will fail to intervene, so that the boy (in the absence of treatment or other circumstances that disrupt these family dynamics) will continue to develop in a feminine way. He will be feminine throughout his life, never having episodes of natural-appearing masculinity; he will not dress, walk, or talk like a man, want sexual relations with women, desire to be a father, seek out a masculine profession, or otherwise live in roles his society defines as masculine. No exigencies of life will get him to turn from his femininity. In time he will try to change his sex.

If this hypothesis is to be testable, we must be able to turn it around as follows: I also predict[5] that if we have an adult, biologically normal male who is at present the most feminine of all males and has been so without interruption since earliest life, then he will have a mother as described and a father as described, will have been perceived in infancy by his mother as being beautiful and graceful, and will have been excessively close to her.

Corollary: to the extent that any element in this constellation is less strong or absent, the femininity will be lessened.

Corollary: the less these family dynamics are at work, the more likely masculinity will occur.

Note again that the hypotheses do not state that the boy's femininity is the product of an atraumatic, conflictless symbiosis. Though I believe that is so, I cannot prove it, for the reasons given earlier.

Interview with a Feminine Boy's Mother

s: He has been dressing up in girls' clothes since he was how old?

M: Three and three quarters. [He is now eight.] Around that time, somewhere around three and a half and four. In the beginning I thought maybe this was just theater; I didn't discourage it at all. I thought it was just pageantry, fantasy. Then it started again; it was a compulsive act; there were very few male things around for him to identify with. For a long time I wanted to think that he was just being lyrical. Then he went to nursery school. They had a lot of clothes and wigs. I would go and pick him up, and maybe two times a week he was dressed up as a woman.

s: How did he look?

M: He looked beautiful. He looked beautiful. It's terribly disturbing to me now [but not then, unfortunately] when he dresses up as a woman: softer female, ultra gestures. I don't know where he learned all this. Then two years ago, I went away for ten days, and I left him at home with two of his young teachers. They told me when I came back that he at one point had shoved his penis between his legs and put a bandaid on it; he was totally compulsive at that time when I was away about wanting to be a woman. He

5. I do not expect, however, that it always ends up this way.

had a trunkful of clothes he called his dress-up. At that time, there were two little girls about his age living in the back of my house. The three of them used to dress up and hang things on the clotheslines; they had a theatrical thing too.

The other day I took him to a friend of mine. I went shopping. When I came back, there was David dressed up in drag to high heaven again, in an orange suit with grapefruits in his breasts—tottering around all over [in high heels]. He had stopped it for a while. And then three weeks ago, he had a little girlfriend over. I came into the room; he was dressing in one of my dresses. I got angry and said, ''I thought that didn't interest you any more.'' And he said, ''Well, you were wrong because sometimes it really does interest me.'' The little girl said to him, ''Do you want to be a girl?'' and he said, ''I'd make a pretty good girl.'' She said, ''Why do you want to be a girl?'' and he said, ''I've got a good build for it.''

s: Tell me about his father.

m: My husband was [they are divorced] extremely intense, always living on the edge of a very high drama. Fantastic voltage in the air all the time; slightly ambivalent about his own sexuality, a very strained and anxious man, extremely intelligent on an utterly neurotic level, and totally obsessed with me. When David was born, he left the next day for Europe. He just disappeared. He couldn't handle it at all. He was very odd about the whole thing even though he claimed he wanted a child. He was so obsessive toward me that he really did not acknowledge David for the first year and a half. He would come in and out of rooms and never change his diaper. He is full of tension, rigid, totally untactile with David. I overcompensated a lot because I have no relative here, no grandparents. So David has no other safe place. He has not a safe place with his father, who is either highly emotional about him or very dark. He filled me with a dread, and an apprehension, the same old thing my father must have done to me. Also he desperately wanted me, and he wrote wonderful letters. And also I had a lot of guilt about not loving him completely. I felt the only way I was going to get out of it was to go into it [marry him]. I thought I had to go right through and come out the other side.

I wanted to have a baby; I really wanted to have the baby; I really wanted to have a boy. I've always wanted to have a boy. I used to have nightmares about having girls. It was a moment of—I couldn't believe I had this sort of blessing. Someone had kissed me on the forehead, and there was a boy. I couldn't believe you want anything as much as that and then there it was. I got a boy. I always thought if you wanted something desperately, it was bound not to happen. I just felt incredible. Plus I had had three abortions before. I just felt incredible. I had thought I was going to be punished, have a mongoloid girl or something. I just felt full of ecstasy. He looked—he looked—he looked like he had been here many times before. He looked so old and so wise; he looked like such an old soul: I had the feeling of totally—I felt like I had seen him ten thousand—had encountered him many times before. He had this—I guess all mothers feel like this—this great sort of huge stare. He looked tremendously intelligent. The nurse thought I was totally nuts. I had this huge conversation with her: didn't she think he looked very intelligent? I had this instant kind of rapport with him. Maybe I filled in too much; maybe I made too heavy an emotional strain in the atmosphere when he was around. I was incredibly intimate with him from the beginning. I used to talk to him for hours; I had this totally lyrical sort of vision of having a child, very like a French impressionist; I had images of walking through long grass, trailing kites; I didn't have an image of him and another child [sibling]. This totally lyrical image of me in Provence with this child, on donkeys, and stuff like that. Then I got pregnant again, when he was nine months old.

S: That was not on purpose?

M: No. He was nine months old. I went through ten days of trying to make a decision whether to have this second child. My husband wasn't with me; I didn't want to stay with my husband, but on the other hand, I didn't want David to be an only child; I didn't want to stay with my husband. So I had an abortion. Then I unconsciously was through [having children].

I had dinner with this girlfriend of mine last night, and she said, "When David was very young, you were so concerned about him being creative that you reinforced this side of him." I didn't buy him trucks; I didn't buy him those male-image numbers; I didn't. I would sit down and make collages with him and all kinds of things I thought would be better for him to do.

S: Was he artistic?

M: He's extremely artistic; he just loves to make things. He does nothing but fine sculptures; all you need give him is a box of nails, glue, and scissors, and he's in heaven. All he wants to do is create. He's fabulous at music. He remembers the lyrics and sounds—terribly receptive. The other day I put on some Bach. It was very solemn, and he just loved it and wanted me to play it all over again. He's very beautiful. He was always beautiful; he was a gorgeous baby. He's a beautiful child. Physically. I was filling out an application for him: "What's the best thing about yourself and what's the worst." He wrote the worst thing about himself is that "I hate ball games."

S: So who are you?

M: I am an actress [in style, not profession]. As a child, I was very lonely. I have this feeling of it being always wet, cold, and solitary. I felt safe with my mother and in a state of total apprehension with my father. My father was extremely stiff, conservative, and my mother was an alcoholic. He was a drunk but not an alcoholic; she was an alcoholic; she was emotional, warm, a victim. They have a relationship which is so sarcastic—just dreadful. I was very close with my mother, but I grew incredibly enraged at her being so victimized by my father. He was totally pissed off I wasn't a boy. And then when I grew up and became attractive he became extremely attracted to me and bought me gifts—ribbons and underwear. I felt this odd sexual thing. [Her husband is old enough to be her father.] I just thought that men were first-rate citizens and women were second-rate citizens. He thought that. I thought so too.

s: Were you tomboyish?

M: No.

s: Were you good in sports?

M: No, terrible. [This is different from the other mothers.] That frustrated him a lot.

s: How much time did you spend with David when he was little?

M: A lot. Most of my time. The marriage ended when he was three or three and a half.

s: Does your husband play much of a part now in David's life?

M: He sees him on Sundays for a few hours, three Sundays a month. He's erratic about it. David strangely enough recently has more desire to see his father. His father picks him up but not consistently. His father will say, "I will take you to X next weekend"; the following weekend is Labor Day weekend, and I know there is no way they are going to go to X. And then David is in tears, and his father is always saying, "I'll pick you up."

One must, of course, treat with care the remarks spoken in an evaluation. But I must say that, having heard similar comments time after time (and not coming on these factors in boys and men without gross femininity), they jump right out at me.

Here again is the mother desperate to grow a boy out of her body and, on doing so, trying to keep the two merged into each other. And the absent father. And the beautiful infant, artistic and sensitive, with a masculine name. Once more the mother who, as a girl, was "always wet, cold, and solitary," not adequately attached to her unattending and, in this case, reportedly alcoholic mother, and who had a father who wanted her to be a boy.

There are differences too (as in each of the families studied). This mother, unlike the rest, is beautiful, in the sense of "histrionic."[6] And *her* mother,

---

6. Here is a hunch: The beautiful son of a histrionically beautiful woman is at risk for becoming homosexual. The key word here is *beautiful*. In the boy, it means the stunning good looks associated with females. (Otherwise, the word would be *handsome*.) In the woman, *beautiful* as used here refers to a dazzling, dramatic, compelling appearance coming from the woman's surface and without clues to what—if anything—is inside. Perhaps the gender disorder has more of a homosexual than transsexual cast if the boy's father is not absent but, rather, present—brutal or forbidding.

Perhaps these women's having homosexual rather than transsexual sons is related to the mothers not having powerful, overt transsexual desires the way mothers of primary transsexuals do. In this family, the factors making up the transsexual constellation are less extreme than in the paradigm cases. My guess with this boy is, then, that without treatment, he will grow up to be a very feminine homosexual, maybe even of the sort who in time ask for sex change.

anchored in the role of victim, may have given the girl some closeness (or so I judge the remark, ''I felt safe with my mother'').

One cannot give heavy weight to this report in the absence of far more corroboration, but still, here is that constant repetition from family to family.

DISCUSSION

Were you to review the data—the tapes of the interviews or the published excerpts—you might agree that one route to marked femininity in boys without demonstrable biologic abnormality is too much mother and too little father.[7] I presume you could also agree that this situation is an example of developmental arrest, since a process that would otherwise have unfolded in a predictable manner was blocked. (Recall that the mothers powerfully encourage precocity in many areas, such as locomotion, speech, and intellectual function, for they try to undo their own traumatic childhood by means of their sons' successes. We see this, for instance, in the artistic sensibility typically reported in these boys.) A second aspect of developmental arrest—too complex to be considered at length here—is the failure of these boys to develop a capacity for rich and intimate relationships with other people from childhood on throughout life (Stoller 1975a). Sensing themselves to be little more than appendages of their mothers—never having an adequate experience of separation and individuation—they grow up with some clinical features of that diffusely defined state called borderline.

But, different from the developmental arrests the clinician usually confronts, here is one that is not the result of either overwhelming trauma or disruption of neurologic development. (In fact, neurologic disruption does not lead to gender disorders, according to what my colleagues Doctors Dennis Cantwell [attention deficit disorder], Edward Ritvo [autism], and George Tarjan [mental retardation] tell me.)

In brief, I am suggesting that marked femininity in anatomically and genetically normal boys can begin in an ambience of excessive gratification and too little conflict, trauma, and frustration. It need not be due, I theorize, simply to regression induced by anxiety (for example, castration anxiety) as is the case in most gender disorders and as would fit present-day psychoanalytic theory.[8] If there were regression, there would have to be evidence of past masculinity

7. You might also believe (as I do, though without strong data) that even when the family constellation is present, it may not always produce a feminine boy. My hunch is that some boys are so biologically male—whatever that means, especially in the newborn brain—that they have more inherent power to resist the effects of the excessive maternal intimacy. I must be careful, though, and not claim, without evidence, that when a boy is in such a symbiosis and not feminized, he is more biologically male. That sort of arguing wipes out the possibility of a disconfirming case.

8. Though even in most gender disorders in males, if femininity (or effeminacy: feminine impulses contaminated by caricature) appears as a fixation point to which one has regressed, we still need to explain whence came that original femininity. I think it came from the mother-infant symbiosis: blissful merging.

from which the boy had regressed. But there was no masculinity when the femininity began to appear—at a year or two of age—in these most feminine of boys.

The problem with proving this idea is that it is impossible, except in the abstract, to find an infant who has been subjected to no conflict, no trauma, no frustration, no anxiety. If my theory is to be disconfirmed by one's demonstrating, let us say, anxiety, then I am lost before I start. For by the time a child can communicate, anxiety from many sources is endemic.

I shall take the position—not everyone does—that intrauterine life is pretty much (but not completely) amental and pretty much tensionless. I also say—again without proof—that, from birth on, there are periods, lasting from moments to hours, of blissful, rather objectless merging[9] with mother and that some babies have more of this glorious intimacy than others. If you grant that, then perhaps you will allow that some infants get too much. You might even think, as I suggest, that those who get much too much are given it by mothers who had much too little and who need to keep their infant sons as if still part of their own bodies in order to cure the terrible feeling of being worthless because of being female.

Then, of course, in the reality that complicates the idealized state of theory, we can wonder to what extent an infant, though constantly surrounded by mother's effort to nullify pain and frustration, will nonetheless try to wriggle out of her unending embrace. I presume all infants have such impulses to separate (in part genetically preordained), but I also believe that some have this capacity more and some less, and that those infants who complain least, who are the most embraceable, are at great risk when born to a mother desperate to do the embracing.

I also presume that mother's efforts to prevent her son's escape will bring on primitive (diffuse, unverbalizable) anxieties, but once again I think that in

---

9. A word like *merging* is vague. The work of Stern and others (reviewed by D. Stern, "Some Implications of Infancy Research for Clinical Theory and Practice," *Dialogue* 6 [1983]:9–17) shows us how early and in how many sectors of mental life the infant is distinguishing between itself and the outside world, especially mother. "Given these capacities, which are functioning well shortly after birth, it is difficult to imagine the infant lingering in a long phase of undifferentiation. . . . The infant need not individuate from an initial symbiotic position. The infant can form, in parallel, various schemas of self, and of self-fused-with-other from non-differentiated experiences" (p. 13). I am not sure about using the concept "self" for mental states of the first months of life; self is an organized condition of separateness more than is a fragment of motivated behavior such as pointing to an object. But I can imagine periods of feeling fused with mother, at first global and with the passing weeks episodic, that would persist in us all throughout life. My idea is that the preprogrammed development of separation and individuation can be retarded by inherent (for example, central nervous system) and/or external (for example, too much mother) factors and that certain "atomic" functions, sectors, or syntheses of function can be selectively slowed down or arrested while others proceed on schedule. Stern talks of primitive states of "communion rather than communication" between parents and the infant (p. 17). In noting these moments, he uses a vocabulary that implies merging-at-the-same-time-as-separating: "to align the adult with the infant," "to 'be with' the baby," "to share," "attuning process," "moments of communion," " 'fueling' " (p. 17)—con- and transsubstantiation.

these feminine boys the anxieties are less biting, less traumatizing, less able to motivate the boy to get away from mother than is the case with boys who will move toward masculinity.

The latter boys, I believe, gradually create a psychic structure that functions to keep them forever separating from their mother-on-the-outside and from their inner impulses to stay merged with her. This is a vigilance—a "symbiosis anxiety," or "barrier to symbiosis," or "fusion anxiety"—erected to serve as a more or less successful, more or less permanent avoiding of merging that allows the boy to sense himself as having a separate body and separate identity from his mother. (I suspect that such barriers are also created from the first months of life on, in both boys and girls, in order to ward off the temptation to stay at one with mother in regard to other qualities relating to dependence/independence besides masculinity and femininity.) This willingness to resist the pull toward merging is a piece of neurosis—that is, a product of conflict, trauma, and frustration—but, like the oedipal conflict (of which it is an early part), it is necessary for development. Without it, arrest results. In other words, as we know, neurosis is part of normal development (though you may prefer, as I do, to drop *normal* and settle for less loaded words, such as *normative, expected,* or *adaptive*).

To the extent that a boy can mobilize defenses against his desire to merge with mother, the less feminine he will be or the more the femininity will be mixed with masculine behavior, and the more the boy will want to be male. He may be neurotic or perverse, but these are more advanced states than this empty femininity.

Limentani (1979) states clearly the issue that also troubles everyone else. "It is difficult to regard as nontraumatic the behaviour of a mother who actively distorts the process of separation and individuation." I agree that it is difficult, but I ask my colleagues to stifle their analytic reflexes for a moment to see if they can conjure up an image of an infant/child who would enjoy lengthy periods of closeness with a warm, embracing, adoring mother. And suppose, as the child's neuromuscular, speech, and other systems developed, his mother was thrilled at his progress, encouraging him to artistic and intellectual precocity—as long as he was in constant contact (voice, eyes, and touch) with her. Is that really trauma? In time even these boys fuss about their mother's attention, but by then they are four or five or six. If the rules of the game are that fussing—in the absence of other clinical evidence of pain—is accepted as a sign of response to trauma great enough to reverse gender identity, then I am lost.

To repeat: the pure form of this condition exists only in the theory. In the real world, we deal with continua, degrees, complex interweaving of factors, algebraic sums, clinical impressions. If, for instance, I talk about a blissful symbiosis, that can be only a generalization. Though these mothers are almost superhumanly motivated to create mutual bliss, they of course cannot succeed. But they do a pretty good job, much too good. And of course, try as they will, they cannot protect their sons completely from anxiety. (We all presume, anyway, that anxiety has infantile origins so inevitable, even so organic, that no maternal style can prevent its generating.)

You will also wonder, considering how intensely these mothers have envied males, if they can keep that hostility out of their love for their sons. (We know how the mothers of some homosexual males barrage their sons with soul-threatening hostility.) Yet I believe the mothers of feminine boys. They are not hostile toward these sons. (They certainly can be with their other children.) In fact, were the mothers nastier, I think the boys would begin to modify the femininity with defenses against their mothers' hostility, defenses that, though leading to neuroses, character disorders, and perversions, allow at least a bit of masculinity to appear.

Keep in mind that in describing this excess of love, this swamping of the boy's development in a rather frustrationless ambience, I am not pointing only to a disorder of excess but also to a deficiency disorder. The boys do not have enough frustration, enough pain, enough trauma, enough conflict. And they do not have enough father. He is not there as a person with whom to identify and with whom to fall in love, and he is not there to protect his son from mother's unending engulfing behavior. The resulting "borderline"[10] disorder is more the result of inner emptiness—being mother's thing rather than her child—than of a frozen defense against unbearable anxiety.

For the clinician experienced in gender disorders, let me add two notes. First, remember that I am not talking here about the majority of the boys who grow up to ask for "sex change." Most of them do not fit the clinical description of *these* very feminine boys nor do they come out of families with the constellation of forces described above. If you try to fit most of the males called transsexuals into the picture I have presented, you cannot succeed. In that failure is a bit of success, not disproof, for these theories.

Second, a caution to myself. Though I have studied children, adolescents, and adults who fit the clinical picture and the dynamics I have sketched, I have never followed one of these little boys untreated[11] into adulthood to see if the predictions hold up. Of those we studied who are now adolescents, none looks now like a primary transsexual, though each is gender aberrant and/or has homoerotic desires.[12]

10. The quotation marks indicate that I am unclear about what the clinical dimensions of this "borderline" are.

11. Mere evaluation, even without treatment, can change the family's dynamics to some degree.

12. So far our follow-up studies are too flimsy for more than the wispiest of impressions. I have, however, been a close observer of the unprecedented follow-up study of Dr. Richard Green, who has observed a series of forty-four gender-disordered boys for fifteen years (Green 1985). He has found none who appears to be a primary transsexual, though over half his cases are either gender-aberrant or homosexual. Two of his cases are from my fifteen; they are homosexual, not transsexual. The rest cannot, however, quite be compared with mine, since probably none of his cases when seen in childhood was as feminine as the most feminine of those I studied. Nonetheless, in some of his cases he finds dynamics similar to those described above.

I have now described how mothers contribute to their very feminine boys' gender identity. In the next chapter, let me expand on earlier descriptions of these boys' fathers. In doing so, I can also adjust the perspective that in some circles sees the fundaments of behavior only in earliest infancy and in the mother-infant relationship.

As is the case for the mothers, I feel that studying the aberrant fathers of these aberrant boys helps us understand better the contribution of parents of any sort to their children.

4

MARKED FEMININITY IN BOYS: AN EMPHASIS ON FATHERS

Perhaps in the beginning, there were in humans as in lower animals no such mental states as masculinity or femininity, sex-differentiated behavior following precisely from the exigencies of protecting oneself and the species. But man, being man, introduced stylized behavior whenever a few moments' leisure could be found: drama, theology, law, games, art, tradition. A man nowadays need not club down the brutes of the night either to save his own life or to protect his family; instead, his maleness and masculinity almost functionless, he can sit, stoned on beer, watching war, football, rape, and murder on television, letting advertisements for fast cars and fancy clothes *be*—not just signify—his masculinity. In the nondesperate societies, his masculinity is increasingly ceremonial, with one exception that concerns us: fathers promote the formation of their children's identity.

Struck by the great discoveries on childhood that emerged from the analyses of adults and by the intuitions of artists and mythmakers, analysts for years were not drawn—despite the occasional anecdote—to observations of infants and children, ordinary or odd. But the view from the dramas produced in the theater or the transference can be, in terms of psychology at large, distorted. Especially in the case of more ordinary infants and children, our knowledge of the frights and ecstasies must be balanced with observations regarding the mundane, quiet moments, hours, and years of development.

Though obvious, the idea of learning about development by watching children with their parents took a long time to flower in psychoanalytic thinking. With data derived almost entirely from the analyses of adults, from analysts' imaginations, and from productions of artists, our received texts have been—to me—a bit histrionic, filled by descriptions with too much Grand Guignol and not always true to the vaudeville that makes up wide sweeps of the early years of life. Nightmares have their truth, but so, too, has the commonplace order of daytime.

We would be nowhere without the drama—Oedipus, earth goddesses and

Lady Macbeth, child-gnawing Chronos and the devoured Christ—and yet this must be supplemented by extratreatment observation of ordinary parents going about their ordinary business with their children (for instance, Abelin [1971, 1975], Kleeman [1971], Mahler [1968]). In addition—the direction in which my data take me—we can study aberrant children to see more easily which types of abnormal parent behavior are involved in what childhood disorders. From the origins of analysis on, cross-gender behavior has served for this purpose. We need only think of such fundamental concepts as bisexuality, castration anxiety, penis envy, and oedipal conflict to recall the importance of cross-gender impulses in Freud's theories (though we know that his view of preoedipal matters was more obscured than ours).

Freud did not have time to follow through on his awareness, late in his life, that a huge domain—the preoedipal relationship with mother—lay behind what he had discovered in the oedipal period. In opening up this dimly perceived world, analysts, with increasingly sophisticated research designs, have observed infants and children, via the children's fantasy lives (as revealed, for instance, in play) and in action with their families. Because of her primary role, preoedipal mother—correctly—has been the more studied parent.

Not that we are totally ignorant about the preoedipal father. He has been seen to have four great functions early in his children's lives: first, he serves as mother's main support, his effect on the child less often direct than mother's; second, he later directly modifies behavior by reward and punishment; third, especially but not exclusively, he is a model, in boys, for identification; and fourth, especially but not exclusively, for girls he becomes a love object. There is another function, crucial for boys, that my data emphasize: a father serves as a shield to protect the child against impulses mother might have to prolong the mother-infant symbiosis. As Abelin (1975) remarks, ''During the practising subphase of the separation-individuation process the father is now thought to play an important part in the development of the child's exploratory and early phallic attitudes; and in the subsequent rapprochement subphase his role may be crucial in the disentanglement of the ego from the regressive pull back to symbiosis. Mahler (1966) placed special emphasis on the nonsymbiotic origin and quality of the father-child relationship—which was what enabled the father to remain 'uncontaminated' during that stage'' (p. 293).

To what extent father serves the same function with his daughter is unclear. Blum (1976) notes that father complements and helps orient and guide his daughter's feminine individuation.

It might be a good idea to turn again and think on the role of the father in preoedipal years, not only because we wish to balance the recent concentration on mothers' effects, but because we still have so much to learn. Perhaps my data on the fathers of children who are markedly feminine males and markedly masculine females can suggest how more ordinary fathers contribute to their more ordinary children.

A SERIES OF CASES

In the hope that you will see precisely the nature of these fathers' absence, I shall present typical quotations culled at random from nine of the fifteen families referred to in the last chapter. You will see how the same themes repeat. (Space limitations make it wise not to demonstrate the fact that the dynamics were at work in all fifteen families.) These are direct quotes, taken either during evaluative interviews with me or during conferences with our research group. I have edited the spoken material only by cleaning up stammering and repetitive speech, deleting sentences impossible to follow without hearing inflections, or adding a few words in a present sentence that may have come from a few sentences back, in order to condense or make clear the sense of the speaker.[1]

Case 1

Like all the mothers in this series, this woman had been depressed all her life. She was, however, one of only two who had been treated for depression. In the rest, this condition did not present as frank depression but rather as a sense of hopelessness. All these women despaired at being female, which they believed a worthless state, and were undone when puberty did not change them into males. The wish to be male was consciously abandoned in each case with the appearance of female secondary sex characteristics.[2]

Let this following hopeless wish to be male stand for the other mothers. (Their words are presented in earlier publications [Stoller 1968a, 1975a].) Assimilating it, perhaps you will sense why they could bear to marry only passive and distant men.

M: I was interested in boys' clothes. All my playtime, I spent in boys' attire. I never played with girls. I was quite a fighter; not many people would hit

1. The reader, unfortunately, must suffer an inconvenience that may change his perception of data: transcripts of conversations are a different language from that spoken by the people who were conversing. Hearing people speak spontaneously and reading the words spoken are not the same. Those of us who report such raw quotes must either risk losing our audience's interest or, in paraphrasing or otherwise transforming the material into readable English, change the data to something genuinely different from the original situation. I find the integrity of the data to be less threatened if one reports verbatim; but this can anaesthetize a reader.

2. "I was the only girl in the neighborhood in my day that would wear a pair of pants. My mother was furious at me all the time. She had a bad time with me. I gave her a very bad time because I was a quite healthy, husky girl. And I loved sports so much, always in the ball field with boys, always playing with boys. I could always hold my own with the boys until I got to be about fifteen, and then I started working and I changed right along, growing up [puberty]. I didn't start to develop really until I was fourteen or fifteen. Getting a woman's body was a little disappointing to me, because I rode bicycles and everything, but the feeling I had came mostly from the boys, because I no longer wanted to play ball or anything. I can still remember when I was around fifteen, a boy wrapped a rope all the way around me, getting it around my breasts. It was real tight, and he said, 'Now I'm going to squeeze the milk out of you,' and that embarrassed me so much I never played with boys after that."

me, not even boys my own age. I ran everything. I had my own football team, my own baseball team; this was a team of boys, not girls. If they did not like it, they did not get to play. And I would attempt anything that boys can do. I wanted to be a boy as far back as I can remember. I felt very put out that God didn't give me a penis. This started when I was about four or five. I can remember at night, I'd say my prayers that I would wake up a boy the next morning.

So she married this man:

M: My husband is an alcoholic. As you know, when a person is drinking there is no communication between husband and wife at all. And his drinking was done away from the home most of the time. At the beginning, it wasn't too bad; he didn't drink a lot, and he was at home most of the time the first couple of years that we were married. [A son born in this period is masculine.] It just progressively got later to a point where he was going right from work to a bar and drinking and drinking until most of the time when the bar would close; he was rarely home. He was out. And, of course, this was when my little one was fairly small, and I don't think he even knew he had a father, because he never saw him, maybe on Sundays, but my husband was getting home at two, three, four, five, sometimes even at seven-thirty [A.M.], and he would shower and leave for work, and this was an every night thing. I mean this was—and, of course, I kidded myself along. If I had any sense at all, I would have thought that he's not going to be home for dinner—"I won't fix dinner for him"—and go ahead and eat. But I always waited; every night we'd wait. And I'd wait and I'd wait until seven, seven-thirty, and we'd be eating so late. Because he never came home for dinner. Some nights he might get home at eight-thirty. I don't know why—I guess he must have fallen out of the bar by mistake—but he sometimes would get home at maybe eight-thirty or nine; but this was very rare. Most of the time it was two or two-thirty, and he would usually stay home on Sunday, but of course he would drink all day.

Now he has given up drinking; my husband now has taken up photography, and we have no companionship at all. He comes home, and he eats, and he goes out to the garage. He has cabinets built out there, a darkroom and the whole bit. So almost every night he's out there, and on Sunday— last Sunday—he played golf in the morning, and in the afternoon he had a schedule set up to take pictures for someone. So all Sunday we were alone, and I was pretty upset about it. In fact, we had an argument about it before breakfast. About him going out. I insist that Sunday is the day for him to spend with the family. It's the only day he has off, and I feel that the boys need this, and I do too."

The fathers usually failed to come in for evaluation interviews. When, this work completed, a conference was set up and its importance emphasized for the boy's future, some fathers still did not appear; that was so with this family.

Then, when we recommended that the fathers participate in the treatment, not a single one was able to cooperate; the two who tried it discontinued, one after a few visits, the other after a few months.

M: My husband is at work today; he did not ask for time off. He said he could not get time off, but I think he could have, had he asked. He works with his mother, and I am sure that had he told her what it is for, she would have been willing to allow him to have time off. I found out last night that you had called him. Just before we went to bed, he said, "Oh, by the way, I cannot get off tomorrow." And I said, "I didn't know you'd planned to." He said, "Dr. Stoller called up." And I said, "What did you tell him? Did you tell him you were coming in or not?" He said, "I told him I would try." And I said, "Did you?" And he said, "No, I was afraid to say anything to my mother. I was taking too much time off." Now, what he has been taking time off for I don't know: he hasn't been spending it with the family.

My husband is very, very quiet. He usually reads or he's out in the garage with his camera equipment and developing pictures. I know tomorrow he's going to spend all day on some wedding pictures that he took at a wedding. He has to get those done tomorrow. For a while, he was working on this every night, the type of thing where he got up from the dinner table and went right out and started working in the garage on his pictures. When we first moved into our home, we bought a pool table, and for nights and nights he read [up] on the best shots, and he played pool almost every night. He would invite someone up, or he'd go out and play by himself. He spends very little time with the family.

S: What is your husband's reaction to your son's dressing in girls' clothes?

M: He didn't like it at all, even the first few times that the boy would wear this dress. But he didn't do anything about it. He would blame me for it that I shouldn't allow him to wear the dress, and what was I trying to do, make a sissy out of him and that kind of thing. When my husband saw him dressing up, he made fun of him and told him that little boys didn't dress this way *but did not make him stop* [my italics].

In most of these families, there were other sons, who were masculine. For each, there was precise information that the family dynamics were different from those with the feminine boys: the fathers were present during the masculine boys' infancy and early childhood, and there was no excessively close mother-infant symbiosis. In this family, for instance, father's alcoholism did not start until the feminine boy was born. Father was home and not drinking when his older son was little.

Case 2

M: I'm much more domineering than my husband. He, through the years, has let me be taking over everything; he said it just seemed easier to him to let me do it. Like in disciplining; it seemed that I was always the one doing the disciplining and . . . I have a habit of making the decisions and of saying . . . "I" instead of "we." And I pay the bills, handle the money. So it has really been where I have definitely been the strong one in the family, wearing the pants, I guess, so to speak, and I haven't enjoyed it that much at all. I never pretended to the kids as if my husband was the dominant one; I did not create that image, not at all. He hasn't been filling in enough as a father, and he doesn't feel he has either. Like at home, he'd many times rather watch TV than go out and play with the kids or to talk more with them, share their problems. And he said he's not the athletic type; he's more of a watcher than a doer. And if there's a good game on TV, he would rather watch that.

My husband is well-bred; he comes from a very nice family. One thing I always said was the man I would marry would have to be ambitious and hard-working. Of course, I didn't know about him, and he isn't, and that has been a disappointment to me. And I feel that this has shaded my opinion and changed my view of him through the years, which I try to convince myself is not right because he has too many other fine qualities; but I feel that this has made me less respectful of him. . . . He was brought up mostly by his mother; his father was on the road most of the time.

F: My part [in the family] is more in a lackadaisical type of nature where my wife, shall we say, ran the whole show or was more or less wearing the pants as far as the children are concerned. And I'd come home and she'd tell me what transpired, what she [did] and what she didn't do about it, and I took the easy way out: it was done; why make an issue out of it. She had handled it. So, in bringing it up in front of the kids, rather than making another scene or discuss it or argue about it, I just passed it on. Whether that was right, wrong, or indifferent, I do not know. At the time, I figured it was right; so, as I say, also taking the easy way out. So we tried to make, maybe even a year or two ago, one day out of the week or weekend, whatever the case may be, father-and-son day, just the two of us, regardless of everybody else: "This is our day." And unfortunately enough, I didn't get too headstrong into it; so, if he was misbehaving or what have you during the week, I'd tell him, "Well, we have to forget about our day." But I didn't do it enough times to let him believe that it was a punishment. A good part of it was my not spending the time with him when I should have: throwing a ball around or whatever it may be, where I haven't been in the past.

The place where I work would be open every night; I'd go in late. The store would open like 10–11 o'clock [A.M.] and we'd work until 9–9:30 [P.M.]. So I wasn't there at dinner when the kids went to bed. But we'd have breakfast in the morning together, and when he wasn't going to nursery school or school, we'd play a little bit or I'd be sleeping—I don't know—so I hardly was with him. We'd have a day off during the week, and then I'd try to spend it with all of us or do some other errands which had to be done that I didn't get a chance to do other times. Even when I was there, I was not with him as I should have been. He was more or less with my wife, and I was in the background, so to speak. And on Saturdays and Sundays, I'd be working; I'd have a day off during the week. . . . I did not like it, but what the hell are you going to do?

When I was home, I didn't play with P., not too much, because he was going to nursery school then. There never was any ball games or wrestling or going out together. It was either the family outing or . . . and then we started talking about this father-and-son day together, but he was about three or four, and a few times we'd do it and then more or less taper off, and that was the end of it. . . .

About my wife; to me, it's [his wife] mine, and beauty is a matter of opinion. And to me, she's beautiful, and to someone else she could be the most gruesome thing that walks. Who can say? Nobody is perfect. I would not be human if I did not argue. I could have $10 in my pocket and spend $50, if you know what I mean. It just burns a hole in my pocket; so that's why I left all the finances in her lap from the beginning, more or less, right, wrong, I don't know. Maybe this is where she felt the control of wearing the pants, being that she's controlling the purse strings. I took the easy way; so to me it was a relief. I did not have to worry about it with her. Her other responsibilities were basically raising the children, maintaining the house, a housewife, which is probably more work than a guy does going to business. I always used to kid to her and everybody that if I get reincarnated, I am going to come back as a Jewish housewife, because the Jewish girls, they have it made. But then about a year or so ago, a flu epidemic went through the house, where she was in bed with it for a couple of days and I was just recuperating. I was home too, but being able to maneuver and move about and get out of bed; I was doing a lot of the chores. So I said, "I am wrong; I don't want to be a Jewish housewife. You can have it; let me out of here."

Case 3

This was a fifteen-year-old boy, so hopeless at being a male forced into masculine roles that he was hospitalized as a dementia praecox. He was virtually unmanageable though locked in a seclusion room until he was told he would be evaluated by a research team familiar with gender disorders. He instantly lost the "psychotic" behavior and thinking; it never recurred. Once again the typical family constellation appeared, except for one feature different from the other cases: father participated in the treatment plans. However, he had been absent during his son's infancy and childhood, mother filling her loneliness with this baby, creating a great intimacy. An older brother, not subjected to the pathogenic symbiosis and not suffering an absent father, was masculine.

F: Having been in the service, I was overseas in '53 and '54, and that was the last time I was out of the family picture. My [transsexual] son was born in 1952. And on returning, the only difficulty is that I haven't been at home possibly as much as some parents due to the fact that I always seem to be landing in a situation where I had to commute quite a bit. [In order not to be transferred] when I returned from overseas in '54, rather than give up that beneficial living situation, I commuted the distance, so I didn't spend as much time with the family as I would possibly if I had been located in the immediate geographical area.

Case 4

The patient in this case was nineteen when first seen, a beautiful "woman" originally diagnosed as having a congenital endocrine disorder (Schwabe et al. 1962; Stoller 1964). It was only eight years later that "she" confessed to stealing estrogens from her mother since just before puberty, with the result that she had developed spectacular secondary female sex characteristics set off by normal male genitals. She had had "sex change" surgery, had married, and had been living for years as a woman when she finally permitted me to interview her mother. Before that time, she kept me from getting information about her infancy or childhood that could have tested my hypotheses.

Again, in this family there was an older brother, who was unremarkably masculine, having been subjected neither to the blissful symbiosis nor to an absent father.

M: My husband became ill with narcolepsy when C. [transsexual] was about two years old, and he had to take a lot of benzedrine to keep him awake because his narcolepsy was in the form of sleeping attacks. He would fall asleep in a plate of food or anywhere these attacks would come up, but he was very stubborn and cranky. He wouldn't take his pills at the proper time; he took them so he could stay up all night and work—which was very difficult for us at home to get along with him during the day, because he had no rest. The doctor said that maybe he felt he wanted them more at night than during the day because he could accomplish more at night. He worked nights. [This was in a shipyard during the war.] Then he went from one job to another, and he couldn't get along with anybody. So finally he gave up and did odd jobs; and finally he decided he wanted out. He didn't want any responsibilities—I had four children. He did not want us to go with him. . . .

My husband's narcolepsy began when C. was about six months old. He never was much a part of the family. He done things by himself. My husband tried but it did not work out. C. and him were never close. When C. was six months—a year old, he [the father] was drinking very heavily, and when he'd come home he'd just tear everything down in the house, just violent, and would beat me so severely that sometimes I couldn't get out of bed for two or three days. . . . There never was nothing between C. and him. In fact, I doubt whether he even wanted any more children. [C. was the last.] On the day the baby was born, he goes out and gets drunk. He saw the baby the next day; he was just bloated about having another baby, and that was all. I don't believe he even came to the hospital after that. Then he went to union meetings; he never was home very much. He didn't like to play with her [son]; he never paid much attention to her.

Case 5

This boy, when first seen at age fifteen, was extremely feminine, graceful, and pretty. Shortly thereafter, he left home to begin living as a woman and has done so ever since. Now, over twenty years later, she is a beautiful woman, with a feminine body and surgically produced "female" genitals.

M: As far as having any playing games with M. or doing anything along this order, my husband never did. He never said, "Come on, son, let's do this or let's do that." He always felt that M. hated him or was against him for some reason, even at a young age. After M. got out of the age of babyhood, which I would say was around two years old, even at that point my husband never found anything to do with M. at all. In fact, I remember we used to have big discussions on that when M. was young. I used to say, "Why don't you go and play baseball with him," and then he rejected the fact of all the psychiatrists saying this togetherness is so important; he felt that wasn't what really made a family, all this togetherness.

When he comes home, invariably he goes to work on something. That's his hobby. He does this until dinnertime. Then he'll talk to the kids, or a lot of times, he used to say, "Come on out and help me," which they never did. See, he wanted to become friendly with them on his terms. He had no contact with M. at dinner, none except "You're not eating; why aren't you eating; mother made the dinner."

After dinner, he goes and reads the paper or something of that sort. I never saw him actually sit down and play a game with any of his children, never. He would not read to them. Periodically he would discuss what's happening in the world, but reading, playing, anything like that—it just didn't exist. At bedtime, he'll say, "Why don't you kiss me goodnight?" He liked it when the kids kissed him goodnight. In the morning he's a very early riser, and then he would definitely get up and leave [before the children were up]. There was very little contact between them on the weekend.

Case 6

This mother also was treated for depression. Like others, she has no respect for herself as a female and no joy in femininity. In addition, she had a set of identical twin boys, both of whom were feminine. One, however, was even more so than the other, and this was the one on whom she had lavished the greatest attention. She also had an older son who was masculine, and, as in all other comparable cases, the family dynamics were different with that son.

M: My husband is far more passive than I am. He's a marvelous person. He is extremely unselfish—in giving and loving and doing—and I am selfish. I don't give much to him at all. I can't say the marriage is empty. I personally have not been capable of loving a man like it would be nice to be able to love a man. But the relationship is good as far as . . . aside from being passive . . . and aside . . . I can't recall exactly what it said [referring to something she had read] but this is true, the passiveness. . . . This I know is bad for the child's balance; this is wrong for the mother to be the aggressor and for the mother to be the dominant one and the father to be the giving and the unselfish and the passive.

My husband has always been around; it wasn't the case that he was not. He's a fantastic husband. He's a good father too, but because he hasn't been able to relate to his two boys I can't honestly say he knocked himself out with them to the extent he should. So, it's been serious, and periodically, he'll try to do something with them. He will be quite demonstrative with them sporadically, and they like it. But he doesn't do it frequently enough; he does it sporadically. There really isn't a source of relationship with them; I mean, I can't see it myself what he can do with them other than be demonstrative. He's a very fine man, he is very unselfish, he tries to make us happy in every way he can. I can't say he's passive; he's not aggressive particularly. His brothers are completely different, as far as daringness or aggressiveness in business and things like that; he is the opposite extreme. He's so fearful. I've had to push him constantly. I feel guilty about that, maybe I should be more satisfied with what I have and not push him so much. This is something I'm considering: not pushing any more. I'm dominating; I'm selfish, self-centered. Yet I'm glad he's not more so; if he was more aggressive he'd say, "Look; I have had enough of that," but he's not that way; so it's good in a sense for me, and yet maybe it isn't.

Case 7

This boy, first seen at age five, wants to be Alice in Wonderland. He asked to have his genitals removed. As with the other cases, there was an excessively close symbiosis with his mother from infancy on, and his father, a diagnosable obsessive-compulsive intellectual, never spent time with the boy. This hard-driving father left home in the morning before the children were awake and usually returned after they were in bed. On weekends, he worked at his hobby, the children instructed never to interrupt him because, considering the dangerous tools he used, they might be hurt. He attempted treatment, and though strongly advised to spend more time with his son, he was unable to force himself to do so. The best he did was to arrange what he called "dates" with his son, writing the appointments into his schedule; but the few attempts failed, and so the project was abandoned. The father's struggle to be cooperative against his natural tendencies was so great that the "treatment" was stopped after a few months when he developed an apparent heart condition. Though no clear organic evidence was found, he thought it best that he be relieved of his assignment as father.

M: I asked him, please, spend some time with T. that day. And he didn't get around to it. He was busy with his hobby; he was working on something in which he was very interested. And at about ten o'clock that night he finally came in. The children had gone to bed. He had seen them—he had stopped for dinner—and I said that I really felt that so much of what was wrong with T. was the fact that he had really a lack of father. My husband played it back, which he seldom does because he's very controlled and extremely patient and very mild-spoken: "It's a thing of genes and there's not a thing you're going to do about it."

And that just drove me crazy because I was just furious at that point because I don't believe it. And he almost at that point seemed to accept the fact, or he wanted to avoid the responsibility of T. disappointing him in what he grows up to be and accepting the fact that he will be a homosexual. When I decided to come here for help, his response was, "Don't get too involved." That's what he said. He thinks that T. is working the problem out nicely now, or will be. He is antipsychiatry. He thinks that it isn't a necessary thing and that some of it is make-believe on the part of the patient, that people are bored within themselves and find another way to get attention for themselves; and he does not think it is really necessary unless one is psychotic. And yet he has a sister who is quite ill, seriously mentally ill, and his brother is—my husband says, "Oh, I'm from a nice, normal, ordinary family." His brother is a big, high-powered-type fellow, outgoing, extroverted, happy-go-lucky type—except he drinks too much; he went into a kind of a depressed cycle two years ago and did not leave the house for six months. And his older sister is also extremely neurotic. So, it's a nice, normal, ordinary family.

My husband and I get along very well. No problems. A happy marriage. I wish he had more time to be at home, but no major problems. The only things that we genuinely argue about are the children. I feel he should spend more time, not be so compulsive about neatness with them, not yell at them, not expect so much; and he thinks I'm much too soft on them, I'm much too permissive, which is probably very well-founded, good criticism. We're very compatible; we like one another. We were not little kids when we were married. This wasn't any two little kids in high school finding a sexual attraction. Now that we have brought the problem up with my husband, he and T. have "man-to-man dates." In fact, as I was going out today, T. said, "When will Daddy be home? I want to have a date with him," which he never would want before. He's made much effort. Like Wednesday, they went out to have hot dogs together and go shopping in a toy store. This is the most time he has ever spent with his father in a few months.

Case 8

This was an adult, operated transsexual when first seen with mother. They came in only a few times, their manifest purpose being simply to help me with the research.

M: I used to feel that this child is not rugged and is never going to be—never, but I couldn't get his father to talk about it. He just wouldn't come down to facts. . . . When my son was little my husband was quite busy. When you start in the X business, you have to go out at night too. It was a good time; I had a wonderful early marriage, I thought. It was fine. But I know the baby was always handed over to me to do everything. If I said I thought "you ought to do more for him. I think you should put him to bed. Why don't you bathe him tonight?" my husband would say, "Oh, you do it better than I do. I'll run up the dishes or I'll do something else." And so when I stopped asking, and I thought: Well, if this man is not going to start doing anything for a little baby, then the little baby and the man are not going to be friends later on. . . .

The child was in bed at six o'clock; so maybe he didn't see him before he went to bed, but he would always go in and peek at him. But he wasn't there to handle him a lot of the time. There might have been warmth between him and his father, but he just didn't know how to show it. I know my husband was disappointed because it wasn't a girl; and I thought, "Well, that will pass after a while," like sometimes the mother turns away for a few days, no matter what kind of a baby it is.

Case 9

This, again, is a latency-age feminine boy. An older brother, not subjected to the intense symbiosis the younger one was, is masculine.

This mother did not marry until her mid-thirties, when she suddenly decided it was time. She found her husband, who was several years younger than she, and got him to marry her, though he says he was not in love with her, did not like her, and was put off by her appearance. He now feels he cannot stand up to her.

M: My husband is very quiet. He's had his problems. He tries to be active. A lot of it is awkward for him. When the babies were tiny, he couldn't pick one up and kiss him. The thing was that he just couldn't kiss a boy baby.

F: [I had a problem] I guess I never got over; I was always self-conscious about going to the bathroom, excusing myself. I tended to hold it more than I should and get myself into situations where I had to go through physical contortions to hold it, and I just didn't know how to solve it. It was socially embarrassing. Maybe, this was even before I sort of—I don't know how I got that—but I got . . . and I guess . . . I'd try to hold it longer and I suppose . . . I—you know—would go—shifting in my chair and this kind of stuff. [He was worked up by a urologist; no physical pathology was found.] I remember things like I'd be taking an exam in college and I wouldn't get up and excuse myself—you know—oh—just various times I—you know—social things, I'd just end up holding it. I wet my pants in class, I guess. That was my predicament, anyways; once in college I was coming home, driving home from, a long ways home from a date, I guess, when it happened. In a car, and I don't know if she ever knew I did it or not. I think I walked her up to the door or something at night and . . . things like that I guess. I remember trying to forget it, you know. And I'd think back on it. I look back on the whole mess, I sort of wonder why didn't I ever . . . how could I, sort of, just let it go without confiding in somebody or without getting any help, you know, I . . .

To recapitulate: it takes both parents to create extreme femininity in biologically intact boys. First there is the mother who, because she has been treated as a worthless female by her own frozen mother,[3] suffers a lifelong sense of hopelessness[4] and a powerful desire to become male.[5] She does not, however, go the full route the female transsexual does,[6] attempting to change literally into a male, but rather—we are speaking of a generation ago, when the nonmarriage options now available were less so (at least for these girls)—she marries. And with her envy of males she does not marry a masculine man.

---

3. Dream: "I was in a room trying to reach some wooden milk bottles—like children's toys—on a shelf."

4. "My childhood was kind of crummy. My mother had five nervous breakdowns. My mother and father were divorced when I was nine. I was very dependent on my mother. She's very critical, extremely critical."

5. "I wanted to be a boy. I used to actually wear boys' clothes. [This was over thirty years ago.] My mother said she used to buy me frilly little dresses and hats and purses, and the only time I'd wear them was when I went to Sunday school. I felt I could do anything a boy could, as well if not better. I almost always assumed the role of a boy. I felt very put out that God did not give me a penis."

6. "But I broke away from being the tomboyish person and began to be a young lady at the age of sixteen. I was maturing into womanhood physically."

Instead, each woman, without love, courtship, or erotic intensity,[7] finds—chooses—a man who will minimize her penis envy. To her he is weak, as good as castrated. She chooses with skill; he complies, not entering into the family as an active, adequate father.

So, when this baby is born and is chosen by the mother as the ideal phallus[8] (emphasizing physical beauty and grace)—grown from her own body—she holds onto this baby, who is to be the cure for her lifelong hopelessness. And she does not let him go. Having chosen a husband who will not interfere and who, as time passes, will not be present to serve as a model for masculinity, she is left free to help create the femininity we then see.

I suppose that had she married a more competent man (probably by mistake) the marriage would soon end. If the mother attempted to create the symbiosis, there would be battles as the father fought to prevent her from doing this to his son. A masculine man does not let this happen; he is, instead, a constant presence for his son's masculinity.

Though phallicness is not all there is to masculinity in our society, it certainly is an aspect of it. The following—to pluck from the psychiatric literature a type probably not seen in analysis—exemplifies the rule that masculinity is strengthened by a masculine father with whom his son identifies (Reinhardt 1970):[9]

Commanding officers of representative Navy jet squadrons were asked to select the most outstanding from among the upper tenth of their aviators. . . . Two-thirds of the fathers [of the outstanding pilots] had a background of some military service, but it was surprising that 85 percent of them had served specifically in the Navy. Nine percent of the [outstanding] pilots reported father deprivation . . . as compared with 20 percent of the failure group. Seventy-three percent [of the outstanding pilots] reported that the father was the more significant parent. Further, typical father-son relationships were distinguished by their intensity and the quantity of shared activities during the pre-college years. The time reported as being spent in shared sport, work, and play activities was so great that the interviewers were at first skeptical; but similar statements were repeated by most of the group. . . . Eighty-four percent of the study group [outstanding pilots] had never had a personal injury or accident (fracture or injury requiring hospitalization). . . .

Synthesizing the examination data, these pilots were practical logicians, men of the mind but very much of the world. They are less grounded in subjective processes or experiences than most and are more closely tied to external events. . . . They are explorers; they have a curiosity, a restlessness of mind and body that leads to the pursuit of new knowledge, even

7. "I couldn't adjust right away to boys [as sexual objects] because I felt like I was one and wished I had been one for so many years that I had a hard time adjusting myself to my husband."

8. "I wanted a boy. I wanted a boy so desperately. Maybe I caused him to be a boy. I prayed for a boy, but I figured nothing could go my way. So I was thrilled and happy when they told me it was a boy."

9. Though this is not a report on preoedipal fathers, it can—I trust—signify the process of identifying with father that starts in those earliest months. (Besides, there is a value in drawing from nonanalytic data and nonanalyst authors for cross-checking analytic ideas.)

for the sake of the search. They are polar opposites to the people commonly termed "dropouts." . . . Lacking in either altruism or dependency, they make friends easily but intense friendships rarely. This tendency toward interpersonal and emotional distance causes them not to be touched too deeply by life. (pp. 732–733, 734)

One need not argue whether this description is synonymous with masculinity—some would say yes and some no; perhaps you would agree, at least, that there is a clearly phallic quality to these men. But there is probably no argument, as one reviews these data, that if a father wants his son to be like him, that is more likely to occur the more the two are together.

VERY MASCULINE FEMALES

For brevity, the next data will be only sketched in; they are given in more detail elsewhere (Stoller 1973a, 1975a).

In my experience, the most masculine biologically intact females fall into three groups: female transsexuals, mothers of male transsexuals, and women who believe that literally they have a penis in their bodies.

Sight unseen, one might hypothesize that if an excessively close mother-child symbiosis and a distant and passive father produce extreme femininity in males, too little symbiosis with mother and too much father could produce very masculine females. That is so.

Female Transsexuals

In regard to female transsexuals, the mother-infant symbiosis was ruptured in each of the fourteen families studied (Stoller 1975a). In most cases this was due to mother's being depressed, but there were also other conditions, such as severe paranoidness or a physical illness, that required mother and infant to be separated for many months with no adequate mother substitute provided. During the first year or so of the girl's life, her father made two crucial decisions. First, rather than himself moving in to assuage his wife's suffering, he stimulated his daughter to precocious ego development so that she would serve in place of father to comfort this unreachable mother; this set up a poignant situation, for the little girl was already starved for closeness with mother and yet was not allowed to defend herself by rejecting mother as she grew older. Second, father, who was not distant or manifestly unmasculine, established a close relationship with this daughter.

Unfortunately, the basis for this was not masculine-father-with-feminine-daughter, an oedipal situation in which controlled erotism stimulates the girl's femininity and heterosexual impulses. Rather, father took this daughter as a buddy, encouraging her to behave as he did, to share his masculine interests, and to spend as much time as possible with him as he went about these masculine activities. Not surprisingly, at an early age the girl was already acting in a very masculine way; and there was no one present either to discourage that behavior or to encourage femininity.

Mothers of Very Feminine Boys

I have already told how, from birth on, the girls who became the mothers of very feminine boys themselves had frozen, empty mothers (the boys' grandmothers), women who, by letting their daughters know that they are purely female, make it clear that being female is worthless. That mother-infant symbiosis is cold and bitter. Where I have information on the fathers of these mothers of transsexual boys (the boys' grandfathers), some encouraged masculine behavior in their daughters and others were simply distant and passive men who, when their daughters expressed the desire to be a boy, did not discourage such a wish.

Females with "Penises"

A somewhat similar background was present in the family constellations of the three females I have studied who believed they had penises within:[10] a frozen mother and a father who encouraged his daughter to be masculine. (The data are reported in Stoller 1973a and so need not be discussed further here.)

DISCUSSION

If one knew nothing of how masculinity develops in boys or femininity in girls, I think hypotheses could be set up from the markedly aberrant conditions just described. One might say that if one wished a boy to be masculine, an excessively close symbiosis between mother and son must be prevented, not allowed to persist uninterrupted for years; and one would recommend that a strong and masculine father be present who would help encourage, at the appropriate time, the boy's separation from his mother's body and psyche and who would then encourage him by example to develop masculine attributes. In this way, the boy would be allowed to come to sense himself as a person quite separate from mother and of a different sex and, in this way, to desire her. With this forceful father around, the boy would then learn the limitations on that desire, falling back before this overpowering rival. In other words, an oedipal conflict would develop, as is not the case with the transsexual boys.

Comparably, if one wanted femininity in a girl, one would recommend that there not be a disrupted and frozen mother-daughter symbiosis but rather that the two have plenty of time to be as if one with each other—for that promotes

10. These are not patients who hallucinated a penis during a psychotic episode; rather, from childhood on, regardless of psychologic status, these three had an unending sense of a full-sized, anatomically normal, erotically active, abdominal or intravaginal penis.

femininity. (If we had no other evidence, we would still know that from the very feminine boys.) We would then want a father who is not too close too soon if that closeness is used to encourage identification rather than a desire to have father.

In brief, without these parental influences that produce in a child first identification and later rivalry with the same-sexed parent plus desire for the opposite-sexed parent, ordinary masculinity in boys and femininity in girls do not occur.

This sounds terribly simple; it may just be.

What a density of experience is compacted in a phrase like ''passive withdrawn father.'' Abelin (1971) remarks on how much more than just a rival a father can be for his children and how early in life that takes place: ''During the course of the separation-individuation process, the father becomes aligned with reality, not yet as a source of constraint and frustration, but rather as a buttress for playful and adaptive mastery. This early identification with the positive father figure precedes and prepares the way for the oedipus complex. Indeed, rivalry presupposes an empathic identification with the wishes of the 'other one' (i.e., the rival).''

We need no intuition to differentiate the experience of the boy deprived of a father but with a mother who respects and keeps the memory of father present from that of boys in families in which father, though physically scarcely there, is hated and scorned by mother. Constantly disparaged, he is not even there to defend himself or to give the boy opposite evidence. On the other hand, in the developing personality of a more ordinary boy, identifications occur with each parent; even more, the essential and complex gestalt that contains the *relationship* parents have with each other is reconstructed within.

My description of the origins of extreme femininity in boys stresses that hostility is not an essential dynamic in the mother-infant relationship (though these mothers are bursting with anger toward others than the favored son). But what about the boy's feelings toward his father: does he not experience his father's withdrawal, lack of interest, and withholding as hostility, as passive aggression toward both himself and his mother? To answer, I need—and do not have, for I have never been able to get one of them into analysis—adequate data from adult transsexuals.

The work with children, in their play and drawings, however, suggests two factors. First in time and importance, because of the father's physical and emotional absence, the boy has a lacuna in place of an adequate representation of a father. Second, coming months later as the boy learns words and concepts, a representation of father as a person who angers and frustrates mother is built up from the forms in which father is displayed to the boy by his mother. These versions of father and fathering result, by the time the child is about four, in a fantasy system in which father is present within as a number of separate father-entities grouped around the two themes of father as an absence and father as an unmovably inadequate presence.[11] Beyond all that, there are the boy's reactions to the frustrating circumstances of there being just beyond reach a father who is unwilling and unable to function properly as a father.

As a result of this mixture, the boy does not see his father as worthy, as someone to admire and envy, and therefore as someone to hate. Because of what his mother has said about his father and what the child himself has noted, the boy does not use his father as a model on which to build masculinity; masculinity has little value.

These impressions must be tempered by the following observation: I have never, in talking with a very feminine boy or an adult transsexual who developed from these family dynamics, heard one of them complain about his father or express anything I could even indirectly sense as anger. Nor is anger a part of their way of relating to me, except in momentary flashes of irritation or frustration when I will not do what they want. This contrasts markedly with the rage easily found in boys and men with other gender disorders, such as effeminate homosexuality or fetishistic cross-dressing.

Unfortunately, the very feminine boy I study does not early in life experience a father he can identify with, hate, or love. Deprived of these three requirements for masculinity, he has few resources with which to defend against his mother's overpowering need to merge her beautiful son into herself.

Missing is what Loewald (1951) has called "the powerful paternal force." Fathers, he reminds us, are a significant presence for their children long before they become a threat to the boy or a heterosexual erotic object for the girl. He says:

With this force, an early identification is attempted, an identification which precedes and prepares the Oedipus complex. It would seem that Freud has in mind this positive, non-hostile aspect of the father figure (preceding the later passive identification due to the castration threat) when he speaks of an identification which "plays a role in the early history of the Oedipus complex. The little boy manifests a special interest for his father, he wants to become and be like him. . . . *This behaviour has nothing to do with a passive or feminine attitude towards the father (or towards the male in general), it is, on the contrary, exquisitely masculine.* It is not in opposition to the Oedipus complex, but helps to prepare it." And further: the boy then "shows two psychologically different attachments, towards the mother a clearly sexual object cathexis, towards the father one of identification with an ideal." These two currents meet and, in mutual modification, help to form the Oedipus complex.

The father figure, then—and we are supported in this view by the above-quoted passage from Freud—is not *primarily* hostile, representing the threat of castration with which the

11. This is oversimplified, of course; there are fantasies within fantasies. For instance, each of the mother's insults about her husband implies that she yearns for a different sort of man; in this way a concept of a desired man—paper-thin, unfortunately—is also suggested to the boy.

boy copes by passive submission and/or rebellion. Earlier, and in my opinion more essential for the development of the ego (and reality), is his positive stature with whom an active, non-passive, identification is made; an identification which lies before and beyond submission as well as rebellion. (pp. 15–16)

We are used to finding oedipal conflict as a source of pathology. So we can forget that in that conflict—with its threats, envies, fears, and rages—are forces needed to produce the character structures, such as masculinity and femininity, that maintain the society. The transsexual boys, however, remind us again how necessary is painful development and suggest that too little conflict may also have its pathology.

RECAPITULATION AND PROBLEMS

The hypotheses cannot yet be adequately tested. To rule out the biologic etiologies to which most researchers subscribe, we need to understand, far more than we do, the biochemistry of prenatal androgens and estrogens and how and when they organize the fetal brain. We have to demonstrate that one or another of these steroids or their metabolites was present in the right chemical form and amount, at the right time, and affecting the right cells or connections in the brain. The techniques for such work in animals are still being discovered; the human fetal brain is beyond our reach. (Prenatal hormones may not be all there is to organizing the fetal brain in a male or female direction; every year brings new answers and questions.) When we make these discoveries, we shall have to find Freud's complemental series—that is, in which cases these somatic factors are powerfully and in which more weakly etiologic and when their effect is tripped off by or synergized by postnatal experiences. Even if these somatic factors are present, we need to know if they are the normal "background" physiology that we bring into the world to be modified by postnatal events.

And with all the experimental work done, we still need to explain the family constellation—if others confirm its presence. Ideally, to test my hypotheses, we should study an immense group of genetically and anatomically normal people from birth to adult life, to separate out those few who develop marked cross-gender behavior and see if the constellations I predict for severe male and for female aberrance show up.

The weaknesses in my work so far are clear. First, I begin the observations only when the children are well along in gender development—four or five or more, by which time so much has happened beyond an investigator's view. And that view, when experienced by talking with—treating—family members, is blurred. How can one get into infants' minds? To what extent does even a psychoanalysis allow an observer to move into a mother's or father's mind? Then there is the imbalance in that so far the mothers have been in treatment but not the fathers; the samples are too small; the controls are too thin in numbers and categories; there are too few statistical defenses against coincidence; the follow-ups are not systematically done.

These are major cautions. Yet I feel a beginning is there. Those who disagree should not simply ignore the findings of the constellations. If I claim, for instance, that some feminine boys have mothers who tried to create a blissful symbiosis, whose fathers were not sufficiently present, and who were beautiful and gratifying to hold, those with different hypotheses must show that these factors do not exist or are coincidental. No one has. And though my efforts at controls are crude and far short of good experimental design, the constellation does show dimly through the murk. A preliminary testing should not be difficult. Let someone, not an associate, draw on a population of children (in an outpatient clinic, for instance). Take only the most feminine boys, as evidenced by observing them and hearing their families describe them. Pick those who have been feminine since the start, not those who were masculine at times. Exclude those with genetic and anatomic defects. Then see if the mothers were too close and the fathers too distant. Do the same with extremely masculine girls and see how many have too little mother and too much father in infancy and early childhood. You will not need psychoanalytic technique for your measuring. The findings will not be subtle.

But do not, as is always done, with the exception of Green's (1985) and Zuger's (1984) studies, take adults coming to a clinic for ''sex change'' and ask them about their infancy. First, it is absurd to think you get a reliable view of infancy and early childhood from questionnaires or short and superficial interviews of adolescent and adult patients or their parents. Second, do not try to disprove the hypotheses by testing them on everyone requesting ''sex change.'' ''The primary transsexual Stoller describes—which he says is a rare condition—is unlike the transsexual patient others have reported'' (Eber 1982, p. 177). That is correct. So I suffer when the writer, talking about most transsexual patients described in the literature, still refers to ''Stoller's history of the nonconflictual origin of *this* disorder'' (my italics), for I have never believed in ''the nonconflictual origin of this disorder,'' when ''this'' refers to what others are calling ''transsexualism.''

Some of the fault is mine. When first writing on these issues in the 1960s, I divided the pool of people seeking ''sex change'' into such categories as ''true transsexuals'' and ''pseudotranssexuals,'' and then, in my enthusiasm (which has always focused on origins of gender identity, not transsexualism), I did not adequately stress—did not fully realize—how rare were the people I was describing. So those using my earliest writings find me talking of ''transsexuals'' as a synonym for ''true transsexuals.'' As such efforts to be clear were in fact confusing people, I began underlining that these cases are different from those whom others call transsexuals.

If my aim—to understand masculinity and femininity in anyone—is clearer, then we might enjoy working on the more interesting question: if too much mother and too little father helps make a boy feminine, and too little mother and too much father helps make a girl masculine, is there a continuum for such effects, one on which everyone can be measured? That is more important than fussing over the labeling of transsexuals, though I had to do that fussing (and keep it up in this book) in order to get the idea of a continuum—the matters of degree of strength plus the way the constituents are mixed—in place.

My hope, then, is to see if *all* boys struggle—some more, some less—over the temptation to stay at one with mother versus pleasures of mastery, of creating one's own separate sense of self; to see if *all* girls begin the process of femininity from what they draw in from mother's embrace. It was in looking at these experiences in the most aberrant cases that I first made out these factors and those in which father was crucial, and could then ask if and to what extent they are present in the rest of us.

Some colleagues bring up what is, for me, the more constructive criticism touched on in chapter 3: how can there be a symbiosis so gratifying that the infant is not traumatized and made to suffer primitive anxiety? I too find this the hardest part to believe in my description and so have considered the "nonconflict" explanation not only to be open to question but, even sadder, not available to firsthand test, since we can hardly read the mind of an infant in those early months.

Of those who question this "nonconflict" theory only Loeb and Shane (1982) have presented observations I would consider to the point of my argument. Other colleagues simply make generalizations, quote authorities, or give anecdotes taken from adult, nonprimary transsexuals, observations that to me simply confirm the hypothesis that such people do *not* suffer the constellation I described.

I would rather concur. It is uncomfortable to be out there alone, not only because I respect colleagues' arguments, but also because I have agreed with those arguments about almost everything else in gender and erotic behavior (for instance, the function of infant anxiety in guaranteeing gender development [Stoller 1975a] and in the etiology of perversion [Stoller 1975b] or the use of hostility fantasies in erotic excitement [Stoller 1979]. But I persist, for the issue is important. Must analysts believe that only unconscious conflict defines a psychic state as an object of psychoanalytic interest: "psychoanalysis is the study of intrapsychic conflict"?

Is pleasure a trauma? When is pleasure a trauma? Does developmental arrest come only from trauma? Is anxiety in the infant always massive? What precise observations—not generalizations—do we make that let us measure when, in an infant, a conflict is mild, severe, overwhelming, traumatic? To what extent is the start of infancy a time (or a period in which there are, from moment to moment, episodes) of nonconflictual, nontraumatic, nonfrustrating experience? Is the start of infancy especially a time of archaic, psychotic states of dread (for instance, "the paranoid position")?[12] Do states of high pleasure simultaneously contain, in the infant, states of dread? Would all infants, regardless of biologic endowment, equally resist the enticements of lowered pain and frustration? When there are no visible manifestations, how do we know that an infant is anxious? When, on hearing the report a few years later, should we rely on it?

I cannot answer these questions. Nor, I think, can anyone else.

12. The romance of madness, so appealing to many analysts.

5
HOW BIOLOGY CAN CONTRIBUTE TO GENDER IDENTITY

It helps our scientific impulses, we know, when we check the strength of an evolving theory by follow-up studies on patients with whom we work. The uncounted variables of behavior with which analysts deal and the nature of our relationships with patients, however, can make this endeavor uncertain, at times contraindicated. Then too, with the passing years, we change and our patients change, modifying our view of the effects of our treatment and causing our theories to ebb and flow.

Working on origins of gender identity, I have often had to give way before new data. Fortunately, because many of the patients seen in this study of masculinity and femininity (especially twenty or so years ago) came for evaluation or for catch-as-catch-can therapy, the less-than-intense relationship usually has made keeping contact with them uncomplicated. (I am not claiming, however, to have pressed adequately for follow-ups as would a scientifically scrupulous researcher. All I do is let everyone know the door is open.) The benefits—certainly for me—are beyond what one might expect for the hours spent. As we all learn, some things cannot be found or absorbed until we have soaked a situation in our heads for years. Others are immediately apparent but need the tempering of time to support, modify, or rid us of our first beliefs.

Twenty years ago, when research on gender identity was less advanced than now, I reported findings on a girl who insisted on behaving as if she were a boy and who in fact was found to be a male, born and reared by parents who thought the child a completely normal female (Stoller 1964). Since those days, we have learned more about the family dynamics that play a part in the development of masculinity and femininity, and so, as understanding grew, I kept talking with this family to see if the new hypotheses that developed augmented, changed, or negated the conclusions of this earlier time. I use the data reported herein to confirm the value of follow-up studies and to add a fragment to psychoanalysts' knowledge of biologic contributions to the origins of masculinity and femininity. Though none of what follows derives from analytic treatment, it still may serve us.[1]

CASE MATERIAL

Jack, born Mary, was the first of four children—later there were two boys and a girl—born to this couple. At birth, the doctor who delivered the baby assigned it without question as a girl, because the external genitals were unremarkably female in appearance. The mother, a feminine woman, wanted a girl and was happy to have had one. But the baby was difficult—too active, too forceful, too ungraceful, too struggling a feeder, too set, from the start, on living an existence separate from mother's body. These earliest activities were disappointing, and even more so was the child's unvarying development, in which these indicators flowered into full-fledged behavior that was the opposite of what the mother wanted. Mary refused to accept her mother's inducements to femininity. Because mother could not stop longing for a daughter feminine like herself, she persisted, a hopeless task that in time produced a steady sense of pain for both. The mother—as I know from occasional follow-up conversations over seventeen years—did not become enraged or otherwise openly hostile. She was, rather, long-suffering, persistent in trying to get the child to appear more feminine, never retreating from the relationship.

The father, a masculine though troubled man—he drank too much in Mary's late childhood—was present in Mary's first years; he was not a distant and uninvolved father, though he became so years later when moving toward divorce. In relating to this ''daughter,'' he was able (by his own account to me, by his wife's, and by Mary-Jack's as well) to enjoy the child. He was less distressed than his wife that Mary was not feminine. He went along more comfortably with the nonfemininity than did his wife, enjoying but not encouraging Mary's masculine behavior.

When this couple then had other children, the behavior of these children, from earliest life to the present, was free of gender disorder. Their true daughter is feminine and in this regard has been a joy to her mother and has relieved the guilt mother took on in her effort to ''explain'' her first ''daughter's'' aberrance.

At age fourteen, Mary's female secondary sex characteristics had not yet appeared. She developed a raspy, thickened voice, at first ascribed to a persistent upper respiratory infection. In time, however, the family doctor suspected an endocrine disorder, on the basis of this voice defect plus hirsutism of the extremities.

1. I am indebted to my colleagues Willard E. Goodwin, M.D., of UCLA School of Medicine, and Julianne Imperato-McGinley, M.D., of Cornell University Medical College, for their urologic and endocrinologic studies from which I have drawn in this report, and especially for all they have taught me regarding the disorders exemplified in this case.

The workup at our medical center revealed that "she" was "he," a male, not a female, suffering hermaphrodism: cryptorchid testes, a phallus that had grown in the previous couple of years to the size of a large clitoris but only 20 percent of normal penile size, chordee, hypospadias, bifid scrotum, and small prostate. Other than a rudimentary vagina, there were no female organs. Mary was a genetic male. On meeting "her," I found "her" grotesque as a girl; though "her" mother had attempted to have "her" dress properly for the doctor, it was a bad masquerade.

On discovering an anatomically wrong sex assignment one should not recommend that the patient change sex if his or her core gender identity—the sense of maleness or of femaleness—is that of the sex assigned at birth (see chapter 2). But it was clear that this child was living an impossible existence as a girl. Influenced by the naturalness of "her" masculinity and the believable lifelong history given by the parents and the child, I acted on the clinical impression (not attempting to "read" the masculinity as being a facade or a reaction formation, the product of penis envy, disruption in the oedipal conflict, early oral rage, or other explanations that make us rethink the meaning of observed behaviors); I told "her" to become a boy.

"She" did. From that day on, I was with a boy. He had immediately known how to be one, not just how to buy the appropriate clothes or get a haircut. Far more, he fit these accoutrements. To the present, he has been unremarkably, unaffectedly masculine.

At the time I wrote the first report on him, I had had limited experience with gender disorders; the psychiatric and psychoanalytic literature was pretty thin, too. One expected, in those days, that masculinity and femininity were heavily influenced by biologic forces. The idea was so logical that for some years I did not realize that Jack was an exception, not the confirmation of a general rule. What in 1961 seemed like the first of an oncoming series turned out to be a great rarity. From then on, almost all the patients I studied who had such complete gender reversal were transsexuals, in whom gender reversal could be accounted for on the basis of family dynamics, not biologic disorder.[2]

The control "experiment" for Jack is the transsexual female—a biologically normal female, correctly assigned at birth as a female, who, from earliest age on, acts in a naturally masculine way and wishes to be a boy. In all the cases studied by our research team, there had been in infancy and childhood a severe disruption of the mother-infant relationship. The mother was incapacitated by depression and other mental illness or by lingering physical illness in the daughter's first years. That broken symbiosis was balanced by a close relationship with father, though, unfortunately, he maintained closeness by encouraging his daughter to act like him and to identify with his masculinity. It was ten years after meeting Jack that I learned of these parental

2. The exceptions, those with biologic defects, were summarized in chapter 2.

factors in females transsexualism; only then could I test Jack against them. Might not his masculinity be the result of these family dynamics rather than of biologic forces?

FOLLOW-UP DATA

In the years since Jack and I first met, I (with more experience, more questions, and more explanations) have restated or expanded the inquiry on each encounter with anyone in the family. But the dynamics of female transsexualism described above have still not appeared. (I shall discuss certain similarities later.) Here, for instance, is Jack's mother in 1972:

S: How do you account for it?

M: I can't figure it out myself. He just was an unusual child. He was stubborn born; extremely stubborn by nature. He must have had the proper inherited traits to pull through. He had to in the first years of his life, with that defect.

S: You wanted a girl?

M: Yes. Surely. I wanted a beautiful daughter. I dressed her as a feminine girl. Absolutely, I wanted her to be what she was: Mary; it's a beautiful name. I wanted her to be a Mary Jane. And my husband was thoroughly thrilled with a girl; he was just thrilled. But he enjoyed her own personality [masculine] more than I did. Remember that I mentioned that was a cause of frustration on my part.

S: Did he encourage her to be masculine?

M: No, not masculine: he encouraged her to be herself. There are a lot of little girls who like to play rough. He never rough-and-tumbled with her as he would with a boy. He never encouraged her to play football or anything like that. [Since she insisted on dressing that way] he encouraged her in so far as he allowed her to wear cowboy clothes, but that was the way it was on TV in those days: the heroines were wearing cowboy clothes.

S: She was a cowgirl?

M: She was a cowgirl.

Or, in 1977:

S: She was an anatomically perfect child [that is, a normal-appearing female]?

M: Right.

S: Yet from the day she was born, she acted like a boy?

M: Right. Right. I couldn't turn that child into a girl. Almost immediately [after birth] she was never like the girl I expected. I was looking for her to come to my bed and to come into my arms. From the first moment that I saw her as a human being, after delivering her, the first moment I laid eyes on her, she pushed my breast away. The first thing she did was kind of a rejection. Yes. She was fussing at me. She didn't go warm and cozy or cuddly to me. Everything she did was different from what I expected. So I just cuddled her a little more, and she kind of settled down. But her every action was defiant, I mean the small things, not so much when she was a baby but when she was walking around. Barely walking. One year old. A table would be full of papers or books and—whew! All of them! Every action was violent. Every action was all this energy. Everything was active, not like a girl, never sitting down and looking at a book, never reading or ever coloring, never.

If I sewed for her, I would make a beautiful dress. Oh, yes, beautiful dresses. Also the regular clothes. But then on Sunday, there would always be a dress. And always, always a fight, always a fight. She was always rambunctious when you wanted to dress her, irritated with you for pawing her. I put embroidery on a little flannel sack, and she didn't want me putting her arms in the thing. Every time I'd touch her to dress her, she was a little irritated. Just an obstinate kid—very, totally different than I expected. There was one dress when she was two: it was gorgeous, a gorgeous pink . . . [sad]. The last thing that kid wanted to do was to sit around like a little vain girl who wanted to be looked at. But that is what I wanted her to do. And it never happened.

My daughter now, on the other hand, was another thing. She was a joy to have every minute, from the day she was born. She's a beautiful woman; she's in her teens now, and a woman, really. So I know I can raise a daughter. Oh God, it was so totally different. So the contrast makes me realize what I had.

What happened to Jack?

In the first year after his sex reassignment, he underwent several surgical procedures to masculinize his genitals. A one-inch blind vagina with hymen was removed. The phallus was freed from surrounding tissue and its chordee released. A urethra was created within the penile shaft, with a new meatus that opened in the normal male position. Exploration of the inguinal canals and abdomen revealed an intra-abdominal left testis, about one-third normal size, and a right testis in the canal, two-thirds normal size; both were brought down into the scrotal sacs (which had previously seemed to be external lips). Examination of the testes revealed no spermatogenesis. No female internal structures were found, but there was a full complement of male structures—prostate, vas, and so on; the prostate was small.

The family moved to another community where Jack's previous life as a girl was unknown. He fitted in immediately. He became popular, and his dreadful school record improved dramatically. What had seemed a severe, crippling, depressive, borderline personality disorder had been permanently cured literally in a day. He went on to college, where his record was so good that he was accepted in professional school, from which he graduated. He is now a dedicated, respected, and successful member of his profession.

Eager to go out with girls in high school, he was naturally shy about advancing sexually with them, but by the time he was in college he was managing sexual relations with women, in time coming to live with one whom he eventually married. His wife, whom I know, is feminine, intelligent, strong, without neurotic signs and symptoms or character disorder, and in love with him after some years of marriage. Both are regularly orgasmic in their sexual relations. He is tall, with manly physique and bearing, intelligent, steadfast, and also without neurotic symptomatology or character disorder. There is no trace of femininity visible, nor is his masculinity overbearing.

J: I've been fine. I'm doing pretty darn good.

S: You're a [profession] now. You went to X University?

J: Right. I went to X, and I graduated in 197-. I have been practicing now for almost four years with another fellow. We are talking partnership. And married, of course. My wife works near where I do. And we got a house and spend most of our waking moments on that. I am a handyman type, a novice—lay bricks, build retaining walls, projects like that.

S: Are you good at it?

J: I think so.

S: How do you account for your choice of professional training?

J: The only area that I really had any interest in, even back as far as high school, were the sciences. The only area where I got any decent grades was in sciences, and that was the only thing I really found that I wanted to apply myself towards [a radical change in learning ability that began immediately after the sex reassignment].

S: How did you do in college?

J: I did well enough to get in, and I was about a good B student in grades; not the brightest in the class; but I did all right.

S: Tell me again how it all happened; it is still astonishing to me.

J: It was like being born. I think it was fortunate for me that my parents never really pushed me in any one direction. They accepted the fact that I was just one hell of a tomboy; they were pretty good about it. Maybe it was because I was the first child. I was indulged to some extent. They were not insisting— other than a few times when I had to go to a party and was made to put a dress on. I remember going to church; I would just as soon be hung by my thumbs than dressed up in that getup and go through that. But I really had a pretty free rein, which obviously made it a lot easier. But I did not change. It was just like suddenly the rest of the world woke up. And I could get my hair cut and put on pants and act myself and not have to feel bad. One thing that really sticks in my mind is the ugly duckling days, when I was going through adolescence: when my voice started to change, when I sprouted hair on my legs, when I had to wear dresses—in those days, girls had to wear dresses—being ridiculed because I was different. That was the hardest, the worst part. It was so much better when I could finally cast off the female clothes and turn around and just act myself.

I met my wife when she was a freshman in college and I was a junior. I dated several other girls, but I just really became attracted to Sally. It was probably about a year after that I told her that things were different. [They had been dating and doing some lovemaking but not with genital touching.] I did not lay it all on her at once. She says she is thankful for that. I told her that things were not right anatomically: I did not have an average-size penis, and I doubted if I could have children. I hit her with that first; it didn't seem to make any difference. I forget how long after that I told her the whole story: that I had to go through a series of operations, that I was essentially born and raised as a female for the first fourteen years of my life and then had these operations. And again it did not make any difference; she of course only knew me as me. I was obviously slower in getting involved in a physical relationship with her than I would have if I had been 100 percent normal. I was very cautious. She was as understanding as anyone could hope. We took our time and did not push anything, did not try to set any goals or set any schedule. If things just happened, it happened naturally. For both of us it was—and still is—a beautiful experience. Things work well enough down there that we are equally satisfied. That was the biggest, that was the last question. It was in the back of my mind all along. I thought, if I found the right girl, I could make it work. And it does.

I doubt if I can have children. I really don't know. A number of things make me doubt it: the fact that the testicles [testes] were retained and brought down late in life; the fact that there is a very, very small amount of ejaculate; the fact that because of the hypospadias, the urethra is way down, and so I do not have an ejaculate discharge until later [the surgically constructed urethra is loose enough that the ejaculate remains in it and is not discharged extra-urethrally except by manual palpation]. My wife has not used any birth control in about three years, and nothing has happened. We take it as it comes. We are thinking of artificial insemination in a few years. But right now we are both working. These days it takes two to make a go of it.

s: Do you have psychological problems about your masculinity?

j: Well, someone with a short pecker has his drawbacks. Also because of shyness, I cannot just march up to a urinal next to four other men and start going to the bathroom. Something that everyone else takes for granted, I don't do. It is also not easy to meet a new physician for a physical examination. It bothers me to some extent, but most of the time I look at everything else I have got to be thankful for. There's so much.

s: How do you deal with your past history as Mary? You haven't forgotten it?

J: Oh no. You don't forget that. I have a lot of very good memories. There are the bad ones, that ugly duckling stage; those are the bitter memories. But that was for a few years only [as puberty approached and on until the change]. But before that, being a model tomboy, I had a lot of playmates and not particularly bad memories. I still wore pants and cowboy boots and played army and did all the things I wanted to. I wasn't cheated.

s: What was your first memory?

J: My father took me to see a tugboat, a real tugboat named *Little Toot* or something. It was a very bright, clear, warm day. I remember the blue water and the blue boat, the green grass. I remember learning to ride a bicycle. I taught myself. When we played house, naturally I played the father. But even when we [Jack and the girl who owned the bike] did that, I would think of just about any excuse to get on that bike and ride. I said, "I'm going to ride around and go see some names for the baby; I will be back in a while." So off I go on her bicycle and come back an hour later. "I haven't found any names yet; I had better go back again." I was just riding her bike all around.

It was a big fad to have shoe skates. The girls' were white and the boys' black. When I went to buy mine and they didn't have mine in white, I bought black. What else? Swimming. I took to water like a fish. I was the best in the class, probably because there was nothing but a bunch of girls. We'd play kick ball, and I always did fantastic. Everyone wanted me on their team because I could kick the ball a lot farther and throw a lot better.

That caused problems. I envied one boy: he had the best clothes; he was intelligent; his father was a lawyer. I remember bugging him. Another kid said to him, "You don't have to take that from her; go ahead and hit her." The boy I envied said, "Naw, I'm not going to hit a girl." And I was jealous of his being a normal, healthy, happy guy. He could get away with the things that I really wanted to do, and people didn't look at him as though he was funny.

But I also had a crush on him. I don't know what my feelings were. I would say, "He's my boyfriend. I really like him. He's neat." There were a few people like that who I wished I could be like or be friends with. I wished they had accepted me.

s: Did you daydream in those days of being a boy or of growing up to be a male? When you daydreamed, did you picture yourself as a female?

J: I honestly don't remember. I can't honestly think that I thought of myself as becoming a mother or a grown woman. Toward the last, when I was in junior high school and had to wear dresses, there was a blond, good-looking boy, and I thought, "Gee, nobody like that would ever look at me." Those were the years when it was really starting to get mixed up; I didn't know what the hell I was supposed to do. On the one hand, I would think maybe I should try to make myself prettier. I bought lipstick. It never did anything for me, of course. Nothing would have helped. Before I really thought about boys, my legs were starting to get hairy. I was actually proud of it. They were more muscular than the average girl's. In gym I wasn't ashamed of having hairy legs until some of the girls started snickering. I didn't really think it was too bad, but then again I felt bad about it. I shaved my legs once. I was striving for acceptance. But I didn't know which side to be accepted by. It was getting mixed up.

I didn't like being around my mother particularly. She started to get to me after a while. My father was the one I liked. It hurt her feelings, and I felt bad about that, but I definitely loved my father a lot more. We would go camping but we didn't do the sort of things I see most fathers and sons do, like playing ball. But we were very close. I felt I could always go to him rather than to my mother. But later when, after my surgeries, he pulled away from the family, I started to hate him and had fist fights with him. He could have flattened me in a minute if he wanted to. But I got sick and tired of him.

With hypotheses available that had not been thought of then, I find the situation more complex today. I know more precisely, as I did not know in 1961, how effectively postnatal external influences can modify gender behavior. What in those days seemed evident to many—that biologic forces are peremptory in human gender behavior—is now for me in most cases less a rule and more an unlikely hypothesis. I still place Jack at the far end of what Freud called a "complemental series" (ranging a piece of behavior on a continuum from mostly biologic to mostly psychologic origins). But now I attend to interpersonal influences that contributed to what Jack brought biologically to his situation. The two factors found in the childhood of very masculine women also were present—but in different ways—in Jack's early life. First, though in his infancy his mother was not dismantled psychologically or physically, so that she could not offer and maintain a close and loving symbiosis for her "daughter," Jack's mother was nonetheless unable to encourage her infant to nestle. *She* was capable of establishing a close symbiosis, but it was nonetheless disrupted. In this case, the failure was the infant's; in the case of other very masculine girls, it was primarily their mothers who broke the contact.

Second is the father's part in contributing to strong masculinity in girls and women. In the transsexual cases I studied (Stoller 1975a), the father enjoyed being with this daughter but encouraged her to relate to him by means of identification rather than as a beloved, opposite-sexed person. He rescued her from complete parental abandonment but encouraged her to be masculine. Jack's father was both similar to and different from the fathers of these other very masculine girls and women: he went along with what he found more than trying to make his daughter be like him.

To this day, the greatest mystery for me is the naturalness of Jack's masculinity. That, coupled with his lack of other neurotic problems, his successful and creative life, his openness, and his honesty is unexplained. Perhaps a psychoanalysis would uncover the roots of his normality, but one does not get to analyze such people.

Interviews with Jack's wife, Sally, confirmed everything he said about their relationship. It was obvious, seeing them together, that they were happy with each other. In fact, their relationship was strengthened by the constant knowledge that they had been lucky, that the odds against their meeting and being compatible were immense. Having interviewed plenty of couples in which one member of the couple suffered a major gender disorder, I am not naive about the stories such couples tell in order to convince themselves and others that they are happy, normal people. And one does not need analytic technique in order to see their gross gender and nongender psychopathology. None was present with Jack and Sally. Nor were there hints, when they were either alone or together, that they were hiding disorder. Their state of happiness was confirmed by their families.

DISCUSSION

The biologic rules governing sexual behavior in mammals are simple. In all, including man, the "resting state" of tissue—brain and peripheral—is female. We can now demonstrate without exception, in all experiments performed on animals, that if androgens in the proper amount and biochemical form are withheld during critical periods in fetal life, anatomy and behavior typical of that species' males do not occur, regardless of genetic sex. And if androgens in the proper amount and form are introduced during critical periods in fetal life, anatomy and behavior typical of that species' males do occur, regardless of genetic sex. We cannot experiment on humans, but no natural experiments (for example, chromosomal disorders) are reported that contradict the general mammalian rule.

But humans, we remember, have far more complex roots to their behavior than do the other animals. As the years unfolded, I was surprised at the extent to which, in origins of gender identity, these postnatal factors can overpower the biologic.

When Jack was born, almost none of the rules that govern the development of behavior typical of mammalian males and females was known, and even when Jack was first seen for our evaluations—hormonal and psychiatric—our understanding of the prenatal and postnatal factors that influence gender behavior was rudimentary. Knowing even less than we do now about the chemistry and physiology of gender behavior, we could do no more than fit him into a wastebasket of conditions labeled male pseudohermaphrodism. And among these conditions were very few that lead to reversal of masculinity or femininity. Usually—I used to say almost always—the gender identity of hermaphrodites conforms to the sex assignment at birth and its confirmation in the endless messages reflecting parents' attitudes delivered to the child's body and psyche.

Until recently, we had no clues to tell us what made Jack so insistently masculine, in contrast to most hermaphrodites, whose gender identity conforms to their sex assignment, not, as in Jack's case, to their biologic sex. My belief that his masculinity was due to an androgen-primed brain was only a sensible guess (and so had been my comparable belief in the second case, where I was wrong).

But now, the argument, though still not complete, has a tighter weave. In 1971, a new class of hermaphrodism was described: 17β-hydroxysteroid dehydrogenase deficiency in man, an inherited (?) form of male pseudohermaphrodism (Saez et al. 1971). In this condition, there is a deficiency of one of the number of enzymes necessary to produce testosterone from cholesterol. Since maleness requires adequate amounts of biochemically normal testosterone during critical periods of fetal development, there results a female-appearing infant who is, naturally, raised as a girl. Of the eleven cases reported in the literature, ten were raised as girls and the eleventh, following proper diagnosis at one year of age, as a boy. All but one of those raised as girls did not have their sex reassigned following the diagnosis of maleness. (The reports are almost totally without descriptions of the gender identity, so one cannot judge to what extent these patients were feminine or masculine in demeanor.) But a recently reported case (Akesode et al. 1977) closely matches Jack:

A 28-year-old male pseudohermaphrodite with gynaecomastia [which Jack did not have] was raised as a female until the age of 17 years, at which time he developed masculine features (deepening of the voice, development of facial hair, male distribution of body hair and male body habitus) and assumed a male gender role. He had a small phallus with perineal urethra, absence of labioscrotal fusion, presence of vaginal pouch and undescended testes. The testicular biopsy showed hyalinization of the tubular basement membrane, lack of spermatogenesis and hyperplastic Leydig cells. Baseline peripheral plasma studies showed androstenedione concentrations ten times normal, low testosterone, elevated oestrone and elevated gonadotrophins. The *in vitro* incubation of testicular tissue showed no significant conversion of androstenedione to testosterone. However, two types of peripheral tissues, skin fibroblasts and erythrocytes, had a normal conversion, as did the body overall as measured by the technique of androstenedione constant infusion. These studies demonstrate that the 17-ketosteroid reductase deficiency of the patient was limited to the testes.

Because his clinical picture fit this condition in most details, Jack was run through the biochemical tests; they revealed 17β-hydroxysteroid dehydrogenase deficiency.

CONCLUSION

Then something terrible happened. Jack developed a nodule in one testis, and so he returned to us for an examination. It was an embryonal testicular cancer, highly malignant. Cancer is a significant problem with cryptorchid testes; it occurs twenty to forty times more frequently than in descended testes. He weathered, with great fortitude, the surgical procedures, the subsequent chemotherapy, and the dreadful threat to all he had accomplished, without denial or psychopathology. The chemotherapy remitted his cancer. But suddenly, a year later, he developed a perinephric mass and a radiologic "hot spot" in a lung. Surgical exploration revealed that he had indeed developed metastases, but, because of the chemotherapy, these metastases were totally without malignant cells. He has since returned to his usual pattern of life, the happy possibility of successful chemotherapy confirmed.

Jack's case cannot, however, prove that, as some researchers believe, gender identity is, in everyone, the product of biologic forces alone. People like Jack are crucial for understanding gender development, but so are those without demonstrable biologic disorders, such as primary transsexuals, in whom the repeated finding of those family dynamics cannot be simply dismissed. Why can there not be, as my effort at differential diagnosis aims to show, different conditions and different etiologies?

The most intense argument against the hypothesis is offered by those who are convinced that marked gender disorders are the result of prenatal hormonal influences. Because it is possible, in all mammalian species that have so far been tested, to reverse the animal's sexual behavior to that of the opposite sex, it seems logical to say that the same possibility must also hold for humans, there being no absolute break in mammalian development between lower and higher species. We need not doubt that if these experiments were done on the human fetus and neonate, the same cross-sexed changes would appear as in all other animals; the "natural" experiments point to that. Yet, even in these cases, the massive and persistent aberrant hormonal influences generally produce only mild to moderate shifts in gender behavior, not the profound reversal of gender behavior found in very feminine boys and very masculine girls. Even more impressive, there are *no* reports of animals in natural—nonexperimental—circumstances that, in the absence of obvious intersexuality, develop full reversal of sexual behavior. Why should such aberrations be naturally occurring in humans but unknown in all other species that have not suffered massive laboratory tampering?

6

DIALOGUES ON A SOMEWHAT FEMININE BOY

This chapter presents a fragment from what became a years' long[1] study of a feminine boy whose femininity was less intense than those who form the baseline for this study on gender identity. The hypothesis is that to the extent that the full dynamics are mitigated, the full femininity—primary transsexualism—is reduced. This case agrees with that expectation. Still, with so many factors to be measured and the techniques of measurement and clinical confirmation so vague, this study—and the technique of "research" it represents—can be only suggestive, not definitive.

A related problem is that of presenting in words the complexity of people interacting. One rarely reads psychiatric or psychoanalytic case reports that seem to be describing real people. Given the problem that even the author's interpretation of what happened is biased, research on psychodynamic issues is most difficult. Though there are techniques that increase verisimilitude—good writing, audio- or audiovisual taping, and transcriptions of text—these do not remove the need for the audience to share in the subliminal communications that make up most of human behavior. These techniques fail to give the audience crucial information contained in the subjective experience of each participant. When confronted with a working style such as mine, you are at my mercy, for you cannot know if I report truthfully. Even if I do, what I tell you can still be only my opinion; you will never be there as I was. And I am at your mercy, for, in trying to imagine you reading this—a "you" made up of how many different personalities and levels of experience—I cannot control how you choose to read my words. Hardly the stuff of science.

I know that this is true, but keep resisting its pessimistic implication: that, at the same time we believe we communicate, we hardly do it. So in this chapter I once more try to soften the problem, again turning to transcribed interviews in

1. The vagueness exemplifies devices necessary to protect the identity of the family.

order to give a better glimpse of what happened than might be possible were I to write a narrative description.

This chapter presents parts of evaluation interviews with the mother and father of a feminine boy. Though the transcriptions cannot convey the sense of our talking together, I use them in the hope that you will believe, at a more feeling level than intellectualized narrative can elicit, that the three of us actually talked, really experienced one another, and that the summaries of data I give in other places are in truth derived from events that occurred.[2]

Reading dialogue can be unbearable when it is literal transcription. I have mitigated that only by editing this material a bit. In the case of the father's style of speaking, I have removed some of the indications of his hesitancy and garbled sentence structure but left enough to show how his personality is reflected in his way of talking. For his wife, I have removed only a rare "uh" or other nonverbal noise; to read them all would not only reduce your concentration but would give an impression of uncertainty that was not present in her. The main act of editing, however, is that necessary to preserve the family's confidentiality; that editing has not changed the essentials of the dialogue.

As you read, you interpret. And in doing so, you will sometimes reach conclusions different from my interpretations. Some of these will not be minor disagreements. Suppose, for instance, you believe that a child—in this case a young boy—will turn out better (whatever "better" means) if its father is physically present all day in the household and if the household chores are shared "in a nonsexist way" between the parents. You will bring to your reading the expectation that the boy is fortunate if his father is home. And your opinion of this mother's attitudes about her husband and children will shift if you feel, in her accusations about her husband's passivity, that she is politically, religiously, or otherwise conservative and thus bigoted. On the other hand, you may read the same words and feel that she is fighting bravely to save her son from an ineffectual, destructive father. You may start your reading with the belief—expressed by his father—that the boy is not feminine, not about to become homosexual, and not in need of treatment, but rather is a sensitive, kind boy whose behavior already promises that he will not grow up to be a cruel, unfeeling man. Or you may believe that, should he become a feminine man—homosexual or transsexual—such an outcome is bad only in the eyes of a sick society, that whether males are feminine or masculine is really a psychologically and morally neutral issue.

---

2. This disclaimer may make sense to those raised on an unending number of data reports—newspapers, journals, magazines, television broadcasts, reports of friends, lectures, history books, and so on—that we accept easily enough at one level and somehow do not absorb in our depths: if pictures of victims of car bombings do not make us even delay our dinner, what other than reality—if that—can get to us?

To allow your biases full play, let me add that the following communications took place years ago, before the feminist movement made these conditions conscious in our culture.

I saw this family in consultation in order to do a friend a favor; I did not expect them to be part of the work on gender identity and did not expect that I would participate in treating them. Having by this time pinned down to my satisfaction the appearance of the syndrome of marked boyhood femininity and the family dynamics out of which it grows, I felt that objective corroboration could be left to others. This attitude changed after I talked with them. Now I was curious to see if, when one alters major influences, the outcome in masculinity/femininity is altered.

Knowing that there are innumerable variables that might be important in the family dynamics and that these variables cannot be tested as one would in a proper experiment, when we have only one family to study I still felt—and feel now, years later—that a first search, rough as it must be, is a fair start.

Chance brought this family and me together at a time when I was ready with the questions and with a schedule free enough to work with another case. To take a patient on means that I must make available four or five hours a week for treatment; fifteen, twenty, or more minutes a day to dictate notes; and a block of time likely to stretch over six, seven, or even eight years. (This problem with time massively limits how many people can be studied and guarantees that the work can never be scientifically adequate.)

The variables different from the ones found in the earlier studied families were: (1) this father, though perhaps—time in the family's treatment would tell—as ineffectual as were all the very feminine boys' fathers, was physically present almost unendingly, day and night, for his son; (2) though this is not clear in the following transcripts, husband and wife loved each other and wanted each other, a quality not present in any of the other families; (3) this mother, in addition to some strong boyish qualities in childhood, was also—and wanted to be—feminine in many characteristics; (4) though this mother, like the other mothers, was desperate for a son and almost overwhelmed with joy at having one who was, she felt, beautiful and gratifying in their symbiosis, she did not need the skin-to-skin, relentless intimacy the other mothers had; (5) this mother did not enjoy her son's feminine behavior and interests and did not encourage it when it appeared; and (6) the boy, though beautiful and cuddly, did not have the startlingly feminine appearance and behavior the other boys did, and his feminine behavior was far less complete and started later (age four). He seemed to me more like some boys who will be homosexual, with less intense transsexual impulses than the very feminine boys I had been studying.

Whatever the loss in convincing data, I leave the details of the mother's past and present life vague for reasons of confidentiality and because an adequate report would require hundreds of pages. I shall note only that her parents resembled, in their relating to her in childhood, the first family I studied (Stoller 1968a).

Interview with Mother

M: My son[3] is eight and I have thought that it was peculiar that he liked to dress up in Betty's [his sister's] clothes. She's six.[4] Joan, my friend, kept suggesting that maybe he shouldn't do that when he was little—when he and Betty played together. Joan suggested that [the way they did so] was a little strange. It began to bother me. I noticed recently that he has a funny way of walking—very feminine—and his hand gestures and way of talking really disturb me and make me mad at him. I end up saying, "Don't act like that. You're a boy and you walk like a girl." It's a game that he and his sister play. They play house, but he always wears women's clothes.

He likes to draw. He's very artistic. He's very interested in what women wear, their makeup and fingernails. He likes to play with girls. He has a hard time playing with boys. He's not very physical and he can't or won't defend himself physically and he ends up crying.

I've been concerned for a long time by the way his father behaves towards him. He doesn't feel comfortable with his father. They don't get along too well, and I'm sure that has a lot to do with the fact that I don't like a lot of things about my husband. Rockwell picks up on that. Also my husband doesn't deal with him in a very direct way, doesn't take a very strong stance. Then I think about my own aggressiveness—what I call my strength—and how firm I am. It doesn't do me any good to get mad at my husband. He doesn't let me. He can't take it. He won't fight back. He won't discuss anything. He ends up feeling guilty and saying—you know, either getting mad and leaving the house or else he will say, "OK. I know you're right and I'll try to be different," but there's no give-and-take. I feel guilty because I feel like I'm being mean because he feels put down or else I feel mad because he won't fight back.

S: What's he do?

M: He's a painter. So he's home all the time. But he hardly ever paints. [She inherited money, so there is no demand that he make a living.] In some ways my husband is masculine. Yet he's home all the time and he does women things. Sometimes he'll wash the dishes or he'll help cook. He does a lot of things with the kids that most men wouldn't do, which I think is great because it lets me off the hook a lot. Yet at the same time he doesn't take a very masculine role. I don't know how that affects Rock. I know it affects me a lot. I'm very concerned that Rock is identifying with me instead of his father. He's developing a lot of feminine things instead of

---

3. He has a very masculine name. We shall call him Rockwell, Rock for short.
4. A third child, an infant, does not play a part in these interviews.

masculine things, and I want to push him out with the boys and make him play baseball and stop being interested in playing with girls and what girls wear and what he wears and how he looks. He's very beautiful, and people have always stopped him on the street ever since he was born and said, "You're a beautiful child," and "Is that a girl or a boy?" Every now and then, still, someone will say "your daughter." I don't think Rock likes that too much.

s: That's a question. If he's girlish, why wouldn't he like it?

m: Yeah. Well he *acts* like he doesn't like it. He thinks women ought to wear mink coats and have long fingernails and he's always bugging me about why I wear my Levi's. I've always been very affectionate with him and I will undress in front of him.

s: What contribution did your husband make to Rock's difficulty?

m: He's not firm in what he believes in and doesn't insist on making Rock behave the way he wants him to, whether it's right or wrong. He gives Rock the idea that Rock can do whatever he wants with his father and that Rock's strong and has some power over him. I don't think it is good for the boy to feel that. It scares him. My husband will get into a disagreement with Rock and hold his feelings inside of him, so that he can't stand it anymore. Then he gets really mad and just—he will just walk right out of the house. And Rock gets *terrified* of that—that something's going to happen to his father. I keep telling my husband that he ought to stay there and stand up for what he . . . I think my husband is like the man who climbs into the backseat and then punishes everybody else for not letting him sit in the front.

The other night we got into a fight because he was drinking. He drinks a lot and I don't like that because I don't drink very much. He is only mean, nasty, to me when he's drunk. He was being impossible, and I got out of bed and started hitting him on the chest with my fists because I was so furious. And he said to me, "You only do that because you know I won't hit you back." And that's true. He wouldn't hit me back. He doesn't do anything back. He deals with Rock in this same way. He doesn't give Rock any feeling of strength that he can rely on; that's scary to a kid.

s: With your now being scared about Rock, what are you afraid he's going to be like when he grows up?

m: I'm afraid he's going to grow up liking to wear girls' clothes, and I'm afraid from what I've heard and read that he'll grow up to be transsexual or homosexual, and I don't really want that to happen. I remember saying to a friend one time when we were talking about our sons, "I'm going to make my son love me so that he'll never leave me." That was kind of flip; I don't *feel* like I have any desire to do that. I'm kind of anxious that something's going to happen to my kids. I'm a little protective, although I've learned to be a lot less that way in the last couple of years.

He and his sister started dressing up in my clothes when he was about four, which was about four years ago, and they would play house and they've done it ever since, maybe once a month. Rock particularly liked to use silky-feeling things like scarves and slips, and in the last six or eight months, the few times that he has done it—fewer now because I bug him about it—he likes to put a scarf around his neck and high-heeled shoes and carry a purse and put my sunglasses on. I began to think that it was odd he always played the female role and I didn't like it. Then Joan [friend] said, "I don't think you ought to let him do that; you should let him know you don't like it." So I began telling him I don't like that about a year ago. Now I'm scared that when I tell him I don't like it he'll think that I really think there is something the matter with him, and it'll be a self-fulfilling prophecy. I don't know what to do. I don't know whether to let him do it or tell him not to do it. He hasn't done it now for I guess two months, except for one night ten days ago when we were out. He and the babysitter got all dressed up and she thought it was hilarious and really liked it. So he enjoyed doing it. But he didn't tell me about it. He didn't want me to know.

I've seen him do this and I've never had any feeling that it was sexually exciting to him. The other night I was sitting on Rock's bed talking to him and he reached out and started to rub my leg. I had my nightgown on. I just moved his hand away, and he said, "Don't. I want to feel your nightgown." I said, "I don't want you to feel my nightgown." And I got up and was walking out of the room and he said, "What's that made out of?" I said, "I don't know what that's made of. What do you care?" It bothered me. I'm sure I wouldn't have thought anything about it except that I don't like the feel of him rubbing his hand on my leg here, which he does often. He'll come up to me, and he'll put his hands on my legs, because I usually have pants on. And he just—you know—puts his hands there. And I move them away because I don't like that feeling.

S: Has he always been interested in cloth?

M: [Long pause] I don't—this was the first time that he's ever asked me, "What's that made of?" He really hasn't been interested in cloth, except that when he dresses up he likes a scarf. He went next door with his puppets the other day, and he wanted a scarf to wear around his neck because he was going to be the puppeteer and he picked out a red satin thing. He liked to have it around his neck; that's about the extent of his interest in cloth. He's funny about his clothes. He's never said anything about the way they *feel*. It's more he's more concerned about how they look. And he's very peculiar about his hair. He's afraid that one hair's going to stick up and when his new teeth came in he was horrified that they weren't as white as his baby teeth. [A constant fear in her treatment was that his elegance foretold homosexuality.]

He puts on his father's after-shave lotion, which really isn't all that bad, except that for a little boy going to school in the morning most kids don't even want to comb their hair or tie their shoes and he has to do all of that.

I was a tomboy up until I was fourteen. I had lots of boyfriends and lots of girlfriends, but even in high school I would rather wear my Levi's than a dress, although everybody wore a dress to school. I liked getting dressed up like a girl, but I also on the weekends and after school liked wearing Levi's. [This was years before they were a popular mode of dress for both sexes.] I remember when I was about fourteen or fifteen, I used to wear Levi's and men's shirts. I used to stuff the shirts down in the front of the Levi's and hope everyone would think I was a boy. I did that a couple of times, but then I felt embarrassed so I quit it. As soon as I started going out with boys, I don't ever remember feeling that I didn't want to be a girl. But even now I'm kind of tomboyish. I like sports. I like to play with girls too if they're good. I enjoy competing. I have a brother, and I'm sure that there was just enormous amounts of competition there. There isn't really competition now because I won. But I feel very involved with him. Sometimes when I'm fighting with Rock I feel I'm fighting with my brother and not my son. They're both named Rockwell.

One time, my husband was drunk and yelling at me. He said, "You bitches, you women, you're all alike." Now I don't feel like he reacts to me as if I were me. I don't think he gives a goddam what I feel or think. He can't talk about what *he* feels or thinks. He tells me that I should just be able to *intuit* what he feels, and if I can't there's something wrong with me. I think that's a lot of crap. When he's not drinking I don't get mad at him, because I'm scared he'll fall apart in little pieces, which I . . . which isn't true.

s: How did you meet him? Meaning: how come you married him?

m: I went to this party one night and I saw him and I said, "Who's that man?" and someone introduced me to him. He was very, very open and gentle and especially gentle and I loved that and about a month later, I left the crazy guy I was living with. I was just very tired of being harassed and unhappy. I was very unhappy. We got married four weeks after our first date. I kept saying to myself, "Well, you're just out of this relationship and this isn't the time to get married to somebody else." But I really wanted to. I wanted to get married to him. I wanted to have a baby.

But his whole attitude is to let things go and they'll take care of themselves. And I don't think that's true.

s: Both you and your husband observe the same things in Rock. Is that right? The difference is in your judgment of what's going to happen?

m: He agrees that we see the same things, yes, and I assume that he would describe them the same way.

When I went home after our first consultation, I waited for about three or four hours before saying anything, because he didn't ask me what had happened. I said, "Aren't you going to ask me what happened?" He conveniently forgets. He said he didn't realize that that was where I was going. And I said, "But I told you I had made the appointment and I told you a couple of times after that." Maybe Thursday morning I didn't say where I was going, but I assumed that he knew because we had discussed it a number of times. And he saw me getting dressed. He said, "I wondered where you were going," but he just forgot that I was coming here. So I didn't say any more about that. So I told him that I had talked to you and that you were going to see me again, that you really couldn't tell much from the first time. I told him that it might be possible that we would all be involved in treatment if it was decided that Rock really did have a problem, and I told him that you said that it sounded more homosexual than transsexual but that that was not a statement of fact and that's really about all that I told him. I told him that I talked about us and that's about it.

S: How did he respond?

M: He just listened. He didn't say anything.

S: How do you respond to his not responding?

M: [Pause] I felt kind of nothing. I didn't feel encouraged or discouraged. I didn't feel mad that he didn't want to talk, because this has happened so many times I just feel like, "Oh well—that's that." I feel like I should go off into the desert and cry for about a week, and then I could react to things in a more normal way.

Interview with Father

F: *Um*! I'm apt to resist this, I'm afraid. I . . . I . . . thought that the whole science is a . . . a marvelous thing, this research, psychiatric research. I'm not against that at all. And that it's terribly important. . . . [Nervous laugh] I think somehow I shy away when it comes to . . . right down to my personal involvement.

  She . . . her . . . [lots of pauses, mixed loud and low voice] her involvement about her son, about Rock, in his . . . it's . . . it . . . I talked to her a bit about it but for some reason . . . she was *so* . . . other . . . involved and passionate about this and that . . . I [long pause] felt discouraged from discouraging her or disagreeing with her and I . . . and after all, I know some of the indica . . . the indications that we both see, but I interpret them differently and feel that they're [long pause] reasonable and understandable and that . . . and if . . . I do believe that her concern for him and reading and talking about what can be done for him . . . that he needs other approaches than we've been giving him and so on. . . . I believe he needs more of my time than I've been giving him. Perhaps she feels that she was giving him too much of the female mothering and so on.

S: Did you feel that?

F: I didn't, no. She's . . . kind of very strong and . . . maybe, I think, probably feels that she's the boss of the household perhaps rather than myself. She . . . is *tenacious*. I think she had a rather lonely childhood in a way, and has pretty much done everything herself, and has done a great job. And her parents and the rest recognize her as sort of the head of the family. And she has developed a very strong kind of personality with this.

s: Tell me a little more, if you would, about her response to Rock's behavior.

f: We both had noticed before, sometimes the way he walks. He's . . . when he's ill at ease, when he's self-conscious sometimes . . . his . . . he's likely to dress up. I never paid any attention to . . . I still . . . you know, in girls' clothes sometimes . . . when they're all . . . they're all [very disjointed through here] . . . they get into the costume trunk and so on, and gets . . . puts on high heels and long dresses . . . crazy hat and parades around. I don't know . . . I used to do that, and . . . he likes making up [cosmetics]. He . . . he . . . uh . . . he's gotten away from it lately it seems . . . big mess . . . then it's hard to get out of his eyes, and soaps hurt him, and I think he's rather discouraged with it. But he used to say, "Can we make up?" and they'd go into the bathroom, he and his sister, and make up as clowns and all kinds of things. My wife's father is certainly masculine. But he has an odd walk, and sometimes, years ago, she would kid him a little about . . . it's a kind of a funny walk that he gets on every now and again that looks a little effeminate. But I think it's just the way his legs are hung or something. And all of these things I see in Rockwell, who is physically very much like his mother. But everything he thinks about is masculine in contrast to his sister.

s: What do you do for a living?

f: Well if . . . if I'm working on a painting or something, that usually is the sole concentration. But this comes and goes . . .

s: Could you be more specific? How often does it come?

f: Well I haven't . . . it's been a year. I haven't painted for about a year. Most of it is . . . is . . . I'm at home working around the house. With the recession and all, it's gotten increasingly tight and I think this is pressuring me a lot lately more than I admit to myself—worrying about it. If . . . I'm worrying about the way I handle it, you know. They say why don't you get out and get a job? Strangely enough I don't know what I could do unless I waited on tables or work in a men's store. Outside of painting I don't have any profession. It's not easy. You have to have skills. Or to be a plasterer's assistant or something like that. Physically I don't know whether I could do it anyway. We're weathering it out. I'm sad that I allowed it to happen, to get involved, to get in a position . . . immature, kind of, weak kind of handling, to drift into a thing like this. I suppose it disturbs me that I am not more successful as a painter, that I'm not working more. I . . . I . . . feel that I'm a good painter and have had certain successes and have been told by people who know that I am, but as far as the entire profession is concerned,

I've been on the outskirts of it and now as my life gets older and so on it's a . . . I realized it's kind of been wasteful as far as my painting is concerned and that's been important to me. When I left college that's what I decided to do, and I worked and studied with people and so on. And then I bought a gallery and ran it for about twelve years and . . . sold it.

s: Was it a success? Psychologically?

f: Well, uh—no.

Next hour—the two together:

s: How have the two of you responded as a result of this evaluation?

m: I like it. We don't talk very much about it.

f: No, I . . . [Long pause] I still don't see the need for it for Rockwell. You can always say perhaps everybody benefits by it—perhaps. If they're healthy enough anyway. But I don't feel since my wife has made me aware of the situation and possibility of it, I've become more conscious of it as far as he's concerned and more and more I'm convinced that he doesn't need this. As far as involvement for us, for myself, I think I resisted [unintelligible mumble] perhaps because it would be very good for me, perhaps because I really need it, I don't know. I do resist the idea of involvement. I feel I'd rather be involved in things that . . . if it meant . . . a really difficult thing between us, then I would perhaps not resist it. I mean, if it was something she felt so strongly about, the need of it for our relationship, and so on.

m: I don't know what you mean. I think it would help us if I were in treatment. I think it would help us if you were too, but not if you don't want to. I'm not going to say you'll have to get analyzed or I'll leave you or anything like that. I think it makes me feel better . . . makes me . . . I think something has to be done to help Rock. I don't think we can help him without some outside help, and the fact that it's possible that we can get help makes me feel a lot better about it. I don't know whether he needs it or not. I think he does. At least I think that somebody in our family needs help to help somebody else, whether it's you and me or you or me or all of us. I don't think that it can get any better without something happening. I just think we'll keep fumbling along in the dark.

f: Well, I don't know if you ever could . . . well, all I say is, I would resist going into analysis to solve his problem. . . . If we're convinced that it's necessary or else a great tragedy will follow . . . then of course we must. I'm certainly not convinced of that. I think that there are indications that our relationship to each other and therefore with Rockwell, at least his having his emotional problems and the more enlightened we are about them and so on, the better, but there are other ways that we can conscientiously investigate . . .

m: I don't think there *are*.

F: We could talk more than we do!

M: Of course! We talked about this before and we said this before: "We can do it ourselves." But I don't see how we *can*, because we say we're going to do it ourselves, and we try, and it doesn't get any better. And I don't like to see Rock suffering.

S: The two of you both see him under similar circumstances, but you feel rather different about what you're looking at?

M: I see his physical gestures as being very effeminate—sometimes his walking, his gestures with his hands and arms, and his face—and I don't like it because he looks like he's imitating a girl. I have a feeling it isn't something that he's seen and imitating, like an actor, but something that makes him feel good. I don't know if that makes any sense. That bothers me. It also bothers me that the—he is reluctant to make friends, that he stays a lot in the house, that he isn't interested in things that other boys do, like baseball and football. . . . It isn't so much those specific things as it is "Why don't you get outside and do things?" I have a feeling that he feels a certain way about his body, like he has to protect it. Like he can't go and run around and roughhouse and play contact games because something's going to happen to his body. And I feel like that's a feminine thing. I feel like he shouldn't be so concerned about how he looks and how things feel. And his father doesn't feel those things, or if he sees them he doesn't think they're important.

F: He's certainly not shy with the people he knows. He's a . . . the teacher said he's a leader in certain ways and I see him . . . the other day, he and this girl were riding bikes and he was riding down the hill just the way boys do. I was very glad to see this. This is the kind of thing he's a little careful of, but he's gotten used to the bike enough riding down the hill—skidding—whirrrrrrr! Just *screaming* around on a skid. [Laugh] Very dangerous and enjoying it thoroughly. It's the same kind of thing all the boys do.

M: Well, also he was with Marie, and I feel like he doesn't do that with boys, like the other day I took him to Billy's house, and Billy took off and ran like hell into the house and Rock started off after him and then he stopped.

F: He *has* a certain personality that some boys don't have and in many respects it's lovely. It is sensitive and he's got a kind of sense of humor and he sees things that I think other boys—some other boys—don't in a different way, but I see nothing feminine about him. If he acts like a girl he acts like a boy [joking] acting like a girl then.

M: [Irritated] Well sure! So let him act like a boy acting like a girl and grow up to be queer.

F: [Reflectively] No. [Pause]

M: "He acts like a boy acting like a girl." He *is* a boy acting like a girl! Not all the time but a lot of the time. All this business of wanting to know about eye makeup and trying it on his own eyes and all that stuff, I don't think that most boys do things like that.

F: I think one reason that I react, if not outwardly, at least inside, rather vehemently against her stand on this is that it almost approaches orthodoxy, and being concerned that he isn't orthodox like everyone else, and this I just kind of—it really bothers me—standardize him. Fundamentally this is what worries you.

M: What do you mean: fundamentally that's what worries me? That he's not like everyone else? I don't care if he's like everybody else. I know he's not like everybody else. He does everything, almost everything, ten times better than everybody else, but he also acts like a girl sometimes and that's what really bothers me. He's a lot smarter than most people. He's *very* smart. He's very talented. He's very sensitive. He's very aware.

F: I don't know—I used to dress up as a girl, for costume parties and things and enjoyed it thoroughly.

M: You said you did that when you were in high school. College or high school?

F: Well, I don't remember back to that. I suppose we certainly dressed up. And I'm sure I did my share of getting on my high heels and big hats and rings and all that stuff, I'm sure. And if [long pause] I kind of almost welcome it. A boy who is so masculine that he can't do those things would worry me more, I think.

M: [Angry laugh] I don't know. I feel . . . I feel . . . I don't know if I feel like laughing—I feel *defeated*. I feel like [laughs again] . . . I can't put it into words. It just makes me laugh. It's like you're up here and I'm down here.

F: [Genially] I know. [Laughs]

M: I think we've always disagreed on how to raise our children, and I think we've got into a lot of arguments on what should be done in regard to Rock's behavior that bugs me but doesn't bug you—the dressing up and the . . . the . . . too feminine . . . stuff. . . . I don't think *that's* changed. We have over the years gotten to be able to talk about things, but I'm not sure that we really get anywhere. My feeling is that if I didn't ever say anything that you wouldn't ever say anything and we would just go . . . gliding along. That's the way I feel and I don't . . .

F: Of course people say things to each other without specifically talking about the psychology of the thing. You say things to each other constantly by what you're doing, by what you bring up, by . . . how you treat each other. If all you can do is to continue to *talk*, somehow [slight laugh] you destroy some . . . you destroy some very nice things that you say to each.

M: I feel like I'm in some sort of experiment in sensory deprivation. You just accept utter passivity. You try to keep me from rocking the boat.

F: [Quietly] Well, it's true enough. I . . . I . . . I think she's right.

M: But when you say that you think I'm right . . . you've said that before . . .

F: Yeah. I was about to say, uh—uh—[pause] we, we have different ways of going at our relationship. I'm sure that over my years, you know, right from [when I was] small to now, I probably developed a kind of isolation of certain things from myself. This is the way I get along, and she won't accept that; and that's right. . . . It would be wonderful if we could enrich our relationship without professional analysis. It would be wonderful if we could sit down or talk this way, but she says we probably wouldn't. We probably haven't tried hard enough. At least I haven't. [Silence]

M: I think it's too hard to do all by ourselves [low voice]. I think it's . . . I don't think it's possible. I don't think . . .

F: Sometimes it may even be better. If you can accomplish it by yourself [laugh] you accomplish a better thing. [Starts to say something, then gives up into silence.] Sometimes I wonder if . . . if . . . maybe I said it [laughs] . . . if she wants too much.

M: I don't think that's true. You told me the last time we had one of these big discussions that I should be able to intuit and interpret how you feel and act accordingly. I think that's too much to ask of anyone. I can't read your mind especially when you're so skillful at keeping your feelings to yourself. As a matter of fact, I don't know whether you keep them to yourself or if yourself even knows them. I want you to react to me, to react to what I say and do, and I feel I want to know what you think and feel, and that I don't know enough of what you think and feel. And you say that I should be able to intuit and just know. I feel like maybe that's what a mother's supposed to do to little kids sometimes, but I feel like that's too much of a burden to put on me and I feel reluctant to do that. I feel like I can sense as much as I can sense but that I can't sense everything and I think that's unfair. What I'm really saying is that I don't think that you react to me so that I feel *me* in relation to you and I don't think that you let me know anything about you. [Pause] Your reaction to that has been that I want too much, that I want everything spelled out for me and that I should know things without having any spoken words.

F: It isn't that you want to know too much but that you ask too much of a relationship. I don't know whether that's being cynical—I don't mean to be, but [pause] hidden in all the subtleties of a relationship—if you want Shaw-Terry letters kind of relationship or Heloise and Abelard, this depends upon the individuals, their extraordinary ability to express themselves, also the limitations of the relationships but . . .

M: I'm not saying that I want it like somebody else has it. I'm just telling you how I feel. And I feel you know. . . .

F: I agree, as I already have, there's certainly room for expansion, room for deeper feeling that would come from further understanding.

M: The point isn't the need for deeper feelings. I feel like what I want is for you to let me know how you feel, and you just said then that you *were* telling me how you feel, but I don't think you were telling me how you feel. Or maybe you are: you're telling me that you feel that I ask too much.

F: Maybe if I put it this way, you'll get a sense of . . . this is even doing it for myself. I'm trying to put words in it for myself, of why I seem to resist. It's a question of [struggling] . . . that nothing is black and white ever, and therefore I can't ever quite take as seriously these things, and I've got feelings about myself, my feelings. I can't say, "Well, this is the way I feel" and so and so and so and so, and insist on it to someone else because I don't necessarily feel that way, certainly not all the time. Another time I'll feel quite differently and smile. Therefore when it comes out to expressing myself to other people and being serious about it, it always gets a little diluted because I know how I'll feel tomorrow and how I felt two days ago. I can't accept your reality because it isn't quite real.

M: Well, it's real for the moment. Nothing is black and white, but nothing is all gray either. You do this to the kids, you know. They say something serious to you and you make a joke out of it and it takes away their—you know: what's serious to *them*! and it makes them absolutely furious. And you do that [helpless laugh from father] to me as much as you do it to them.

F: [Rather sweetly] Well, I know. I feel that she's exaggerating this that I do it all the time.

M: [Interrupts] I take certain things seriously.

F: Well, I should hope I do it once a day.

M: I felt very optimistic after you came home on Thursday after your visit with Dr. Stoller. I don't know why I shouldn't feel that optimistic now, except that I'm scared. I feel afraid. I feel that you agree with me too easily and that you don't really . . . I don't know what scares me. I'm afraid that I didn't get at you enough, shake you up enough to make anything happen. I don't know if that's true or not. I don't know. I don't like these words that I'm using. I don't know what kind of proof I've got. I also feel guilty forcing you into this kind of situation. I know—I *feel* that you didn't want it, don't want it. Just because I think that I'm right and you're wrong doesn't mean that that's so. I don't really know. One thing about our being here and from what I know about you, I assume that you think something else, and when you say you do like it—when you don't say you hate it, I'm suspicious. [Big laugh from husband]

Fragment of Interview with Mother

M: I don't like him for being—for not being stronger than I am. I would like to sit back and stop having to take charge. I want him to do it. I'm not sure that I would let him do it, if he could. Maybe he can't, I don't know. We went to Europe one time and I had forgotten how to speak French and every time I tried to I spoke Spanish. So I let him do all the talking. He was very much the leader of that excursion, and I really liked that. I felt very much that I could depend on him and that he was doing what had to be done. On the way home on the airplane I saw him start biting his fingernails again and I thought, "Oh shit. Here we go again." I don't know whether *I* took over or he gave up or what, but once we got back home it was the same thing again.

Fragment of Interview with Mother

s: Tell me about the delivery, the first moments with him and how it went then after that.

m: It was great. It was just a fantastic experience. I wanted a boy. I think I would have killed myself if I hadn't had a boy. That's a stupid thing to say because I wouldn't, but I really wanted to have a boy. I don't have any idea why. But it was just absolutely perfect for me. I wanted him to be little so he would stay little longer [laughs] and be more babylike. He was a giant baby, and to me he seemed—tiny. He was very beautiful. I would have a baby every day if I could. Just—it was absolutely *the* thing that I wanted. Everything was just fine. He was a great eater, just gobbled up everything in sight. He was very active, very alert. He slept all night. He was up all day. Little tiny naps.

s: You know I have a research interest in Rock. I don't think it will interfere with our analytic work as long as we're both alert to it. . . . Now for that reason, to get some of that information—you have been contaminated; you've read some of my ideas, at least of a few years ago—how would you compare yourself with these mothers of the transsexuals as far as the way you've dealt with him?

m: I never had any skin contact with him like they talk about. It was just straightforward changing him and bathing him. When he was a baby I didn't carry him around a lot because he didn't want to be carried around. He wanted to be running and crawling. It seemed to me like he couldn't have been better. I know that's what they all say. Nothing was wrong. He was just perfect. He was a very good, healthy, active baby.

s: Your feeling is that you weren't, either in physical contact or the amount of time you spent with him, comparable to these other mothers that I have written about.

m: No. I would go out and leave him in the daytime or take him with me. I didn't feel that I had to be with him day and night or all the time. I never let him sleep in the bed with me. He never seemed to want to. I didn't have more contact with him than—I don't know what to compare it to. I came and went, and I took him or didn't. I felt like I should take care of him. I didn't want to hire a maid to do it or anything like that. I fed him, put him to bed, bathed him. If I had a babysitter, she did it, but I didn't want to hire a baby nurse for him. When he was first born we took turns feeding him at night for about a month. I've read those things and try to figure out where they fit in. I don't suppose I'll ever know all of the things that made him feel the way he does. I sure would like to.

Rock, reluctant, was treated by a child therapist and by his mother, who, responding in her treatment, needed and adored him far less intensely. Her fear that he might become as ineffectual as her husband motivated her highly. Rock today is not a feminine or homosexual man. His father refused treatment of any sort and slowly sank into a passivity beyond repair. His mother and I succeeded in analyzing her;[5] the sense of worthlessness at being female, which she shared with the mothers of very feminine boys, was replaced by her becoming peacefully and happily female and by her finally using her formerly dormant creativity.

5. I am embarrassed at using the uninformative *succeeded* for the outcome of a process as remarkably complex and unquantifiable as an analysis, another reason for suspecting the word *research* when used for clinical psychoanalytic reports.

7
A Child Fetishist

Here is another family with a boy who cross-dressed. But this boy has never looked or acted feminine. I would expect to find, then, that the mother-infant symbiosis and the father-son relationship were unlike those in the very feminine boys. And that was the case. There were, nonetheless, a beautiful infant and too-close symbiosis, but—different from our paradigm—one in which the participants were also combatants.

Though it may be doubted that a genuine perversion is possible in a small child, the following report lets us imagine that it is. In drawing such a conclusion, we must be careful. First, we may be facing a problem with no more substance than a matter of definition. Second, there is the question of whether a rarity is simply an inconsequential event or hides generalities, as is usually the case in biology (including psychology). Third, we should not use *perversion* loosely, as is often done in analytic theory: *perversion,* with its strong connotations of willful badness, becomes something else when made synonymous with any and all erotic or gender aberration. That is too un-dynamic a position; if there is one caution that analysis has given to those who study behavior, it is that behavior should be judged not only by its surface but by its meaning, at all levels of awareness, to the behaving person.

This little boy, two and a half when his fetishism first appeared, was frantic to put on his mother's stockings. I shall say he is perverse because he was so preoccupied with the act, became visibly erotically excited, and developed his fetishism as the result of specific traumas imposed, from earliest infancy, on character structure emerging in his relationship with his mother. There are those who, following Freud, say that perversion is not possible until one has passed through oedipal conflict (A. Freud 1965; Bak 1953); for in the perversions of later childhood, adolescence, and adults, one finds clear evidence of (perversion-related) damage from oedipal conflicts. The recent consensus in the literature, however, is that preoedipal issues also count.

A second problem in definition must also be faced before I report this boy's dilemma. Take the word *fetishism*. Let us ignore its common meaning in anthropology. Though my usage may share some dynamic and etiologic features with the anthropologist's, undue focus on an inanimate object such as a piece of cloth is very different if it is or is not accompanied by genital excitement. To use the same word to label experiences so different subjectively and dynamically is to invite confusion.

I wish, then, to show that this little boy was truly erotically perverse from age two and a half. He did not just have preoedipal precursors of perversion; but because of a precociously induced, erotically soaked, mutually needful, ambivalence-loaded relatedness between himself and his mother that led to his developing an erotic fetishism, he deserves to be assigned as perverse. Nonetheless, we cannot say that his disorder is the same fetishism as in the adult perversion.[1]

CASE MATERIAL

Mac and his parents were first seen for evaluation when he was three and a half. Here is my interview with his mother, Lorraine, at our first meeting:

L: About a year ago, my little boy was under some pressure. He was two and a half then. He had a six-month-old brother, and we had just moved him into his bed out of his crib, and I had started him in nursery school. He was not happy, because he is very shy with strangers; he doesn't want to be too far from me even now. He started pulling my legs and my feet and my stockings. I didn't pay too much attention to this at that time. I was nursing the baby, and I thought he just wanted to touch me. He really liked my hose and my stockings. He did not put them on, but he would always feel my legs. One day, my mother was visiting me; he started rubbing up against her legs. He was aroused, and it bothered me.

I thought at the time it could be just because of the baby; maybe if I paid more attention to him, he would find more creative things to do and it would stop.

So I tried that, and it did. Then a year later—two months ago—one day I saw him with my pantyhose with his clothes off. I was shocked. I told him to take them off, that they were mine, that girls wear them and he wasn't a girl; he was a boy and wore socks like Daddy did.

It didn't happen again until two weeks later. I was tired and took off my slippers with no stockings on. My baby came in; he is now a year and a half, and he grabbed my slippers and ran off with them. My oldest son, Mac, saw me without my stockings on, and he started rubbing up against my leg and

---

1. The diagnosis need not have heavy prognostic significance: children's psychic structure is more malleable than that of adults, and should the dynamic process we call "family" redistribute its forces, the perversion may no longer serve any of the parties.

feeling my feet. I turned around and said, "Stop it, Mac." He wouldn't stop. I turned around and whacked him and said, "Stop it." So he did. He went off, and later on he said he wanted to go play in his room. That's kind of funny because he normally does not ever say that. He likes to be very close to where my husband and I are, with the family. I was putting the baby to bed, and I thought, "He is very quiet." I did not understand. I went into his room, and he had a pair of my stockings. He had hidden them under his bed. I asked him what he was doing, and he just said, "What?" So I took them away from him and said, "These are my stockings. They don't belong to you, and you are not supposed to play with them." The next day I was tired and said to the boys, "Come on; let's go lie down and relax." My baby was jumping up and down on top of me, and my older son all of a sudden became very aroused. I could tell. I got up and tried to change the subject or whatever he was thinking, and it stopped. The next morning I woke up later than usual. He came in bed with me; he doesn't usually do that; I don't allow that. He was touching me where my nightgown was, and I said to him, "Go play in your room, Mac. I'm trying to sleep." So he went in his room, and I fell asleep—I normally don't do that.

When I woke up, I found my nightgown, my underwear, and my stockings all in his room. He had gotten them from a pile of clothing. He had hidden them—not really, but he thought they were hidden. Behind his chair.

Since then, he has been in my drawer and into my hose. Finally, I became so upset that I just took them and hid them. He would not listen to me. One day, I was sitting in the kitchen, and I thought he was taking a nap. I was concentrating. I got up to check if he was asleep. He was in my bedroom. He tore the whole place apart looking for my stockings, and he found them and he had them on with my boots, this time not just my stockings but my boots. Now I finally realized that he is aroused when he puts them on. This time his sexual organ was aroused. This time I saw it. He had my stockings, and he had no underwear on. He takes all his clothes off, and he puts on my stockings. He had an erection. . . . The very first time I ever saw him aroused was when he rubbed up against my mother's legs; that was the first, the very first time [two and a half].

s: You say that after that, you got him interested in other things; and it died away for a year?

l: Yes.

s: During that year, you didn't notice erections in regard to legs or stockings?

l: Only once in a while. I just assumed that he did when I went to the store with him. Then he sees mannequins, and he sits there under the mannequins, rubbing them. It's embarrassing. In fact, the saleswoman said to him one time to stop it. Perhaps I don't wear stockings enough.

s: It isn't that simple.

So that the reader can get some sense of the precise form of the data, I shall use direct quotations from tapes of the treatment hours rather than a narrative style. This, I hope, will put you a step closer to the clinical experience. I shall assemble these excerpts so as to represent categories that organize my understanding of the onset and nature of the boy's fetishism.

Let me quickly summarize these findings. Mac was adopted three days after birth. His adoptive parents had been unable to conceive, and my patient, Lorraine, the boy's mother, had been hungry for a child. The very fact of adoption stirred in her an intense process of identification with the infant, the result of her sense of having also been abandoned in childhood by her parents. A fiercely felt symbiosis was thereby set in motion, both mother and son responding to each other with intense love, frustration, and rage. By nine months, Lorraine reports, her son was already sensually focused on her skin, perhaps her legs, since he could reach them easily and since she at first allowed him his pleasure.

At a year, a circumcision—traumatic to them both—was performed. Following this, he never was seen to touch his genitals until at two and a half he was observed sexually excited, rubbing on his grandmother's (Lorraine's mother) foot.

Lorraine conceived and delivered a son when Mac was about two. This, of course, threw pressure on the Lorraine-Mac symbiosis.

When Mac was two and a half, he and his mother were traumatically separated in a restaurant. Immediately after, the fetishism began. It went underground after some weeks, to emerge a year later, again immediately following another traumatic separation when he was lost in an elevator.

Circumcision

Each number below indicates a different and later—sometimes months later—therapy hour.

Interview 1

L: Mac was circumcised when he was a year old. He should have been circumcised when he was first born; I did not realize that he wasn't circumcised. The adoption agency didn't tell me, and I was in such a state of shock: with a brand-new baby, it didn't occur to me that he wasn't circumcised. When I went to the doctor and he was six weeks old, the doctor said, "You realize he isn't circumcised, don't you?" And it just hit me. By the time I could get an appointment at the hospital with the urologist, he was three months old. It was too late for him to have it done in the office. They said they couldn't do it. Well anyway, he was circumcised when he was a year old; we went to the hospital for the day. After, it was very painful.

It wasn't healing correctly somehow, and I went back to the urologist.

He recircumcised him in the office. Without an anesthetic. With me hold-ing him down. With the baby screaming. And me, I was hysterical. I was. I didn't expect it. And I was mad as hell; I really was. I thought he should have had a nurse to hold the baby. He just said, "Hold the baby." When I turned around to look, he had a knife in his hand. Then he was cutting him, and it was very painful to him. I had to keep pulling the foreskin back. And he was screaming.

Interview 2

L: The circumcision. The first one [at one year]. He came out of surgery very groggy. He finally woke up and started to cry. I started to pick him up, and the nurse ran in and said, "Don't touch him! Don't touch him! He's still under the anaesthetic." I couldn't lift him up so I didn't. He had to urinate, and it must have been excruciating, because he went into a screaming, bloody fit, which is only natural. I know it must really, really hurt.

And we took him home. It was pretty hard for a couple of days. Every time he would urinate, he would really, really cry. I would change his diapers right away and put Vaseline on it to protect it. They never told me what to do. The doctor never said a word to me. And three weeks later, we went in for the checkup, and I said to the doctor, "It looks funny to me; it just doesn't look like a circumcision." I was standing, holding Mac. The doctor looked at it. And he went over to the side. And I was looking at Mac. And he came back and he was holding a scissors. I looked at him, and it didn't dawn on me what was going to happen; I just blanked out. I stood there, and he said to me, "Hold him"; I should have opened my mouth and said something to him; why I didn't, I don't know.

I don't know whether it went too fast or whether I was scared or whether . . . I should have opened my mouth and said, "Let the nurse do it; I don't want to be in here." But I didn't. I held him. And he cut him. I didn't look. I was sobbing. And Mac was screaming. In fact, I looked out of the corner of my eye, and I couldn't believe that he was doing that in front of me. So . . . I was hysterical. I couldn't believe that he would do that. Mac took it better than I did; he stopped crying after a couple of minutes. I was still crying. The doctor said I should have pulled the foreskin back [during the weeks after the first procedure] and I said, "Why didn't you tell me that I was supposed to do that after the circumcision was over?" The skin had just grown back.

So I left. I was really upset. I called my husband and said, "Come and get me; I can't drive home." I was hysterical. I couldn't get myself to-gether. I said, "What the hell is going on around here? I don't understand what he's doing. I don't know why he did it. He never told me a thing." When I got home, I called the doctor. He was very terse, saying it had grown back and he had to do it. I called him a butcher. He didn't do a normal circumcision; he did some new type. I said, ''Why?'' and he said, ''After a man becomes fifty years old, they lose their sensitivity there; by leaving more skin there, he won't lose the sensitivity.'' I don't give a damn about his sex life when he's fifty. I said he just doesn't look like he's been circumcised. He went through all that, and he doesn't look like he's been circumcised.

I didn't understand why he hadn't told me what to do. I had to continually pull back that foreskin, and he would go into a screaming, bloody fit every time I did. I had to continue that for two or three months. It hurt him every time. Well, I don't know if it hurt him every time, but I think he just expected it to. So he cried. I was supposed to pull the foreskin back every day, but I didn't. I was so upset by having to do it that I would avoid it. And I would try to do it when he was in the bathtub playing in the water. I would sneak it in. Pretty soon, he never thought about it. But one thing I can really say: he has never played with himself, never touched himself too much. Much less than Billy [younger son]. Maybe that's why he is so attracted to my stockings. Because the only time I have seen him with an erection is with my stockings. It felt good. He never otherwise has shown sexual interest in his penis. I think maybe he would have come out of it if the nurse had been there, if I hadn't seen it, if I hadn't been so hysterical. He must have known my reactions. He was only a year, but gee whiz.
I was leaning over him, holding him down, and I was sobbing, just absolutely sobbing, sobbing when I left the office.

Interview 3

L: When he gets hurt, that's another thing altogether. He would get into a state of absolutely going hysterical when he got hurt, when he bumped his knee or saw blood or fell down or the baby hit him. I think about the circumcision and how much that hurt him, when the doctor redid it. When he is hurt now, he becomes uncontrollable, absolutely uncontrollable, just absolutely screaming at the top of his voice. I try to calm him down and end up getting angry with him. I know it's a terrible reaction, but I can't help it. And then he will cry and cry and cry and cry and cry. I try to comfort him again, and it goes round and round and round in circles: I feel bad that I got angry, and then I try to comfort him. Then he keeps going, and then I get angry at him. And it will stop. I tell him he has to be a big boy because he likes firemen, and firemen don't do that. Even just a little scratch, he isn't able to accept at all. [But before the circumcision] he would fall down, and I would say, ''Boom, boom,'' and he would pick himself up and go toddling on his way.

With the baby, I don't do that at all. With Mac, before the circumcision, I could see myself clear about what I thought of how he should react. Later on, after the circumcision, I changed too.

Precipitating Events

Interview 1

L: When he was a year and three months, we moved to our new house. All of a sudden, I had lots of things to do and I pushed Mac into the background: "Mommy wants to do this, and now you have to play by yourself." I don't think he was prepared for that. All of a sudden no Mommy—not all day long. And I was pregnant. When I went to the hospital, he went to stay with my mother. He had never been to my mother's, he had never been away from home. Then all of a sudden there was a baby, and all of a sudden there was not very much time with Mommy. [He was two years and one month old.]

The day after the baby was born, I developed a migraine headache. [She did not have a spinal.] It lasted a week; I had never had a migraine before in my life. No matter what they gave me, I could not get rid of that headache. I know what it was from: I was so worried about Mac being at my mother's. I would call her on the phone, and I could hear Mac crying in the background. Here I am having a baby, and I adopted another one. I felt I betrayed him. A month after we were cleared by them [permitted to adopt] and were just waiting, my gynecologist said he can do an exploratory on me. And when I came out of surgery, there was a 100 percent chance of my getting pregnant; I never used anything to not get pregnant. I didn't get pregnant until Mac was fifteen months old. And I feel guilty. I feel he should be a pampered child. I had another baby; I don't spend that much time with him [Mac] because of the other baby. But he [Mac] is whiny, and I dislike whininess intensely. I am not whiny, and I dislike it in others.

Interview 2

L: The time when he was two and a half really started it. We were separated. It wasn't for hours, only for maybe fifteen minutes. But it seemed hours. And I'm sure it did for him, too. It was horrifying to me and to him. Before that, he had never been interested in pantyhose, except maybe to touch them while I was getting dressed, but he wasn't interested in touching me anywhere else or touching me intensely.

It was a big community party, hundreds of people. We went into a restaurant and waited an hour. Mac was having a good time with the other kids. Then we went outside, and I turned around to find Mac. And I couldn't find him. A little boy said that he went around the building. So we went around the building, and we couldn't find him at all. There was nobody back there. We went to the front, and there must have been a hundred cars in the parking lot. People were coming and going on a huge highway on the other side of the parking lot. And my first thought was, "My God, he's going to get killed. He's going to go out in that parking lot, and he's going to get hit." We all fanned out to try and find him. I went back toward the restaurant and heard this horrendous screaming from the inside. And he ran through all these tables and all these people. And he ran toward me, and he cried hysterically. He was crying at the top of his lungs, "Mommy, Mommy!" I grabbed him and hugged him and kissed him. And he calmed down. He didn't cry continuously after that, but he was petrified. I felt guilty as hell. I was terrified he would be hit by a car or someone would take him. This was a beautiful child. There are lots of nuts in this world that would just pick up a child like that and take him. I felt—because my mother has told me that for years—"Stay near me; stay close to me because someone might take you." I can remember that distinctly. It was a terrible feeling to ever have gotten lost from her.

I ran toward him with my arms open: "Here I am, Mac." Because he was so hysterical that he did not see me at first. I ran toward him, and I picked him up, and I hugged him and kissed him, and I said, "Where did you go? Why did you leave me? Why didn't you stay by my side?" Because I am always telling him, "Stay here beside me." I didn't say it that day because I was distracted.

It was right after that that he masturbated on my mother's foot and started with the clothes. Within a few days. A week prior to that he had been moved out of his crib and put into a bed. In a room separate from us. He was very excited about that, but it was a great strain for him too. That's why I delayed so long. I waited until Bill was six months old to make the transition as easy as possible. And that same month Bill was baptized. So there was a lot of attention for the baby.

And for two and a half months he was excited about the pantyhose. Then it went away. It died away for a year.

It began again the next time we got separated; that was a year later. We were in the hospital for Bill's eleven-month routine appointment. We came out of the office, walked down the hall, and went to an elevator off to the side. We waited and waited for that damn elevator. I sat Bill in his carrier. Mac was standing by my side, the elevator door opened, and Mac walked into it. I had turned to pick up Bill. And the door slammed shut. There was no one else in the elevator, and I could hear him screaming all the way up the elevator shaft. It was—my blood was curdling—it was horrible. Honest to God, there was nothing I could do to stop that goddamn elevator. Then it went down; I don't know where it went. And I pushed a button, and I waited and I waited, and I began to cry. Like I am now. I could hear him all the way down that elevator shaft, crying for me. And when the door finally opened, it was empty. It was empty! It was like that goddamn dream I had with doors opening, and I walking down the hallway and that dreadful thing was trying to suck me into it. I got on the elevator with Bill, and I didn't know where to go. I didn't know where he could have gone. My first reaction was that it went down to the main floor and that he had gotten off and gone out to the parking lot. I'm always afraid he's going to get hit by a car.

I went down to the first floor and walked over to some people and said, "Did you see a little boy who got off the elevator?" I said, "He got lost from me." And everyone said, "No." I felt like the earth swallowed me up; I couldn't figure where a little boy could be. I just stood there. I was beginning to get hysterical, not screaming and yelling, but I must have looked panic-stricken. Then the elevators opened, and a nurse came off. I said to her, "Have you seen a little boy?" And I said, "I can't find him; he got lost on the elevator." She said, "He may have gotten off on the second floor." So I got back into the elevator and went up to the second floor. And there he was sitting behind a desk on a nurse's lap. He wasn't crying, but the minute he saw me, he came to me, and he was crying, and I was crying, both of us were crying.

I know what it's like to be lost. I know the feeling.

Interview 3

L: One morning when he [Bill] was about two months old, I wanted to cut his fingernails. I took my husband's clippers and cut a little flesh on each finger. I looked at it and—you know—part of his finger was gone. I was so absolutely hysterical my husband had to stay home from work. I was just so hysterical; I couldn't believe it—that I would act that way. Bill wasn't crying; I was crying. It was bleeding. It was like I took a little portion of each end off his fingers with the clippers. It grew back right away. I never react that way about anything except with my children.

Fetishism

Interview 1

S: What's his preference: to touch you or to hold stockings?

L: Putting them on. And when he was a baby and I was getting dressed—nine months or following—he would come into the bathroom and crawl around my legs. (My eighteen-month-old does that; they hug your legs. And they put their little head there. So I never thought much about it.)

And he started doing this to me when he was two and a half years old, and he wouldn't leave me alone—for an instant. We went out to dinner one day. He was under the table the whole time—it was a nightmare—rubbing my legs. I couldn't believe it. And then it stopped a few weeks later. Only one time has he been interested in my bare legs. If it is cold and I am wearing slacks, he will say, "Do you have any stockings on, Mommy?"

And I will say, "Yes, I am wearing them because I am cold." I tried to explain that stockings are to keep me warm, like men's pants to keep them warm.

s: He knows something about stockings that we don't know.

L: Obviously. He is so bright. He said to my mother, when he was rubbing up against her that first time—she said, "Macky, you don't know what you are doing." He said to her, "Oh, but Grandma, I do."

Interview 2

L: These little occasions [pantyhose episodes] occur when there has been—not upheaval but tension. He and I had been sick for weeks on end and we never left the house. I was talking on the phone; he was in bed for his nap. I was on the phone for ten or fifteen minutes, and I saw him go back to his room, sneaky like—not crawling but low so he might have thought he was out of my vision. When I went into my bedroom, my whole closet—all my shoes—were just a shambles. Everything was completely ripped up. I went into his room. He was awake but he had his shorts off. I wondered: why does he have his shorts off? Then I saw underneath the bed were my ballet slippers from high school. Then I realized he had had an erection. Not then, but he had had—it looked very red.

There was another incident two days ago. I was sitting bare-legged in my shorts. All of a sudden, Mac turned around, and he looked at me very peculiarly. Nobody else sees this but me. I don't know if it was in my head or whether it's really there. But all of a sudden I just felt a little stiff [pause]. He walked between my legs, and he looked at my legs funnylike. He didn't touch me. I think it's sexual. To me it is. I've had that look before, from men. And from my four-year-old son! . . . After that he touched himself. He had on shorts, but he had taken his underwear off, I don't know when. Later, when I took his shorts off, he was all red.

Interview 3

L: He exhibits no femininity at all. That's not the problem. It's the pantyhose. He touches me or looks at me peculiarly: lustful. He does that to my mother at times. Today she had on Bermuda shorts. She was sitting there, and he was stroking across her legs. Mother gave me a look like: "What's going on here?" But he loves my mother very much, and I know he loves me. I know that. He's very verbal about it too. He'll come over to me and say, "Oh, Mommy, I love you." The other day, we were at the grocery store, and he saw, way down the aisle, the pantyhose advertised on TV. And he's yelling at his brother Bill, "Oh, Bill. Pantyhose! Pantyhose!" And Bill doesn't know or care what pantyhose is.

So Mac grabbed one, and I said, "Put that back, now!" He was giddy and laughing, and I was trying to get at the core of what he was saying. He said, "Let's buy pantyhose; let's buy pantyhose." And I said, "Oh, I have lots of them; I don't need any." And he said, "Well, we need some." And I said, "Who?" and he said, "Baby and me." And I said, "Oh." And I said, "You're a boy. You don't need pantyhose." And he said, "Oh, no. I'm a girl." And he kind of looked at me, and I just completely ignored that statement. I wasn't going to give him an inch to go on that. So I just turned around and said, "Let's go."

But it's there; something's there about that. I had some clothes piled on a couch. One was a pink silk dress. Mac was playing with the tie on it. I wondered what he was doing with it, if he was just horsing around. But in actuality he was playing it was a fireman's rope, tying it around his waist and saying, "Put me on something so you can hoist me up." Like firemen do.

s: Is other cloth stimulating for him—whether for his penis or not—other textures or garments?

L: No. The only thing is the pantyhose and my shoes and boots. I caught him once long ago in the pantyhose with my boots on. He's not interested in my underwear, just the pantyhose.

s: Does anything else turn him on?

L: No. I would say not. No.

Interview 4

L: I'm thinking of when I used to be getting dressed, and he was just standing there, like babies do. But I had stockings on. He was just caressing me, saying, "Mommy, Mommy." He was about nine months, just starting to stand. He could already talk. And he had a vocabulary of maybe twenty words. It scared me because he was so smart. He's so intelligent that I think to myself, "How am I going to cope with it?"

I can remember one incident specifically. I was getting dressed to go out. It was the first time I had a babysitter. Naturally he didn't know that, nine months old. Anyway, he crawled into the bathroom. I was standing there in my nylon slip, and I had my pantyhose on. He sat there and played with my feet for a little while. And then he had my leg. He just kind of felt it for a while. I was putting on my makeup, and I didn't pay any attention to him. I thought it was just sort of normal. Most babies touch their mothers. Then he stood up—managed to pull himself up—and he managed to stand there for a while, just touching me. I thought maybe he just wanted my attention, because he was all the time babbling, saying, "Oh, Mommy; oh, Mommy." I picked him up, gave him a hug and a kiss, and I talked to him. I always brought toys with me, wherever I was with him. But no. He'd never play with the toys; he always wanted to be closer to me. He'd sit there and touch my legs.

s: Now this is at other times as well?

L: Yeah. At other times. But this one I am remembering was the first. It would happen anytime I would get dressed. The other times around the house, I wore pants or shorts. If he touched me then, I don't remember it as well as when I was getting dressed to go out in a dress and pantyhose.

S: Excuse me: I want to get it right. The first time it happened, he was nine months old. He comes in and is feeling your legs, and you gradually realize that it goes on longer and is more intense than you expected. From then on, whenever you were in your stockings, he would try to touch them. And while doing this, from the start, he would say, "Oh, Mommy," as if he were having a glorious experience?

L: Yeah. And especially when I was going out. I wear pantyhose only when I go out.

S: Suppose you had pantyhose on and were not going out when he was nine or ten months old; would he still be interested?

L: No. I don't think so. But he has developed an eye for it. Say, for instance, I've gone to the grocery store and have pantyhose underneath my slacks. He will come by and make sure. He will just touch. He is checking up on me. And then at two and a half years it became different. He had on a very wet diaper that I should have changed and didn't. It was exciting to him, I suppose. He was laying across my mother's foot and moving up her leg, masturbating on her foot. And I thought to myself, "What is he doing?" I knew what he was doing; I don't mean to say that I was dumb. I knew what he was doing, but I didn't want to realize what he was doing. I should have picked him up and changed his diaper, but I thought it was good that he was having a good feeling, because, prior to that time, he had always been afraid of himself from the pain after the circumcision. That is the first time I had seen him get pleasure from his penis. The "Oh, Mommy" pleasure was not with an erection, only after this time with my mother. Before that he was avoiding touching his penis.

Interview 5

L: He hasn't been interested in pantyhose for a long time. Then yesterday, he pulled a chair up to my dresser and got into my pantyhose. Because he was away from school for two days and did not want to go back. He wanted to stay home with Mommy. "I don't want to go to school. I'll stay home, Mommy." It's my problem, too. He wouldn't go back to school with the car pool. So I took him. He toddled off and waved goodbye. When I picked him up, everything seemed fine. But when we got home, he was in my bedroom a long, long time. It did not occur to me he was in the pantyhose. I called him, and finally he came; he looked a little sheepish. He had pushed a chair against the dresser. So I said, "When I kept calling you, were you in here with my pantyhose?" He said, "No." "What were you looking for up there on the dresser?'' He said, ''Well, I did open your hamper up there. I touched them.'' I tend to think it was the crisis of going back to school.

Interview 6

L: We went to this restaurant. Mac got under the table and he was rubbing his hands up and down my stockings till I was ready to—not kill him—I was ready to lose my mind. I really was. . . . Yesterday I was wearing stockings. I was wearing a dress. Mac found any possible way to get near me. He'd joke and go around the table and touch my legs. Or he'd go under the table and say, ''I see a toy'' and make all kinds of excuses because he knows that it gets to me. And I cannot hide it.

Interview 7

L: I picked up his pillow, and my pantyhose dropped from inside the pillowcase. He no longer hides them under the bed; now he hides them under the pillow. Today I said to him, ''Mac, I found my pantyhose in your pillow the other day.'' And he said, ''Yeah, Bill is doing that now.'' I said to him, ''I don't think Bill is doing that. I think you're doing it. Why do you hide them in there?'' He said, ''I put them there so I can put them on.'' And I said, ''Why do you have to put them on?'' He never really answered me. He went back to saying it was Bill who got them and put them in there and that he—Bill—was wearing them. I said, ''I know Bill wasn't wearing them; you're putting them on.'' And he said, ''Oh, I never put them on.'' I said, ''Well, one day Daddy caught you with them on.'' And he said, ''That was only one day.'' I said, ''I would appreciate it if you'd leave my pantyhose alone.'' Which I'm not sure was good. But at least he and I were talking about it; he opened up that much about it, where before if I would even mention the subject, he would scream at me. We had a nice conversation.

Masculinity

Interview 1

L: He never had had a lot of pain before in his life. Then he did [circumcision]. And now, all of a sudden, he realizes he has a nice sensation. I am confused. I feel threatened. Here is my son, my adopted son at that. He is making—not really—sexual advances toward me. Maybe it is—I don't know—but it's not right. And it frightens me that I don't know how to stop it without . . . because I am angry. I am angry at him. I don't understand what he's doing. And I don't think I'm controlling the situation correctly. I have tried to think what I am doing wrong in my reactions toward him: maybe I am angry at him too often. I know he is much too dependent on me.

My youngest isn't that way at all. Because Mac is so smart, he gets bored easily and that makes him more dependent on me. He has a lot of toys and creative things. I will put his things on the kitchen table, and he will paint for five or ten minutes. Then he is bored. He loves books. I read books to him a lot. But lately he is smothering me. He wants me to kiss him all the time, and he wants me to carry him, and then he gets mad at me. Then he talks to me in a mad tone of voice all day long, very angry with me, and I get angry with him because he is bored and underfoot. He follows me around the house and gets into whatever I am doing. Then he won't play; he won't go out and play unless I really tell him, "Go outside and play."

I could understand that if he didn't have a good father who didn't spend a lot of time with him.

Interview 2

L: When my husband is home, he will go with him to the garage together. He loves tools. He will work on the truck with my husband. He will work in the yard with my husband. He loves being with my husband. When Jim [husband] is home, I could be long lost; but when Jim isn't, then I'm the one who he sticks around with. Other three-and-a-half-year-olds are more independent than he is. I have never tried to push him. I know he will go at his own speed, like playing in the yard or in the park. He never gets into anything dangerous at all; he's very careful about himself. He wouldn't climb up the ladder to go on the slide until he was with another boy his age who did it. Now he does it and goes down stomach first. I am happy to see that. I want him to be a real boy. He doesn't have any feminine characteristics, though: he doesn't want to play with dolls; he doesn't want to play with girls. He doesn't like girls really, except his twelve-year-old cousin. He loves her dearly and will sit and pet her in the same way he does me.

S: With excitement?

L: I have never really seen it. I think it is more subdued, although I am not sure. There is always a lot of commotion when she is over. He bothers her a great deal. I don't think excitement has really come to his mind until this happened again.

Interview 3

L: He was beautiful physically. Gorgeous. I never saw a baby with such a head of hair in my life. He never lost it. Beautiful features. Very fine skin. He looks very much like my husband. I think he is going to be a very handsome man. I don't think it is a homosexual thing, but I have heard of men who cannot get aroused with women because they have fetishes. I want him to be a normal man. I don't want him to . . . I cannot figure it out. I have finally just taken and hidden my stockings in the closet. He shouldn't go to my clothes like that, although he hasn't touched my nightgowns or any-thing else. It's just my stockings and my shoes, my boots. He doesn't like girls' clothes. In fact, he is very interested in firemen and fire trucks. He likes his one red shirt because he thinks it's a fireman's or a ranger's. He plays with fire trucks a lot, and he's a forest ranger; and he has never played with feminine things. I have a doll, and I gave it to him one day, and I said, "Would you like to play with this?" And he said, "That's dumb."

Interview 4

L: Mac [age five] said something odd to me yesterday. It took me off guard; I didn't know how to take it. He said, "I have a great dream, Mommy. That I will marry you." That night before, he had had a nightmare. Sometimes, when he has a nightmare, he climbs into bed with us for five minutes and calms down. Then I put him back in his own bed. But this time, because Jim was having a hard time sleeping, I told Mac, "Let's be quiet." And instead, I got into his bed with him. It was just going to be a couple of minutes, but I fell asleep and woke in the morning. Mac had had a night-mare. I don't know about what. After Jim left for work, Mac came back to bed with me. I was so tired I just fell asleep and he fell asleep. And when he said, later on, that he wanted to marry me, I thought of that. I shouldn't let him do that; I shouldn't have gotten into bed with him. Not that it's sexual; maybe it is a little bit with him that he's taking Daddy's place. He kept saying to me all day, "Oh, boy! Tonight I'm going to have a nightmare, and you're going to sleep in bed with me." I said to him, "No nightmares tonight; if you have a nightmare, I'm not coming to bed with you. That's it!" When I went to check him the next night, he said, "Hey, Mommy; no nightmares." I said, "You're a good boy," and he went to sleep.

He never slept a whole night with us, never even stayed a long time in the bed. I never wanted to start that business. But Jim has a new schedule, and he gets up so early. It wakes Mac, and he comes into bed with me. I'm half asleep, really. Really, that time of the morning I'm very, very deep asleep and sometimes don't even know he's in bed with me until I awake later. I don't think that's such a wise idea. It's been off and on for three weeks now.

S: When he was a baby, how much, if at all, did you have him in bed or hold him?

L: I always made it a point when I gave him his bottle to never prop it up. Even when he was a year old, I still held him. I don't even remember putting him in his crib and giving him his bottle. I always held him, walked him, and sang to him, and held him. He would climb into bed with us if he had a nightmare, but it would never be for long. I always held him and cuddled him an awful lot. That's not so with my baby now. I always held him and rocked him when I was reading to him when he was little. Now we sit on the floor in his bedroom propped up against his bed next to one another; and I read to him. He's getting to be a big kid, and I don't think he finds Mommy's lap helpful unless he really hurts himself.

Interview 5

F: He is a very inquisitive boy; he is always inquisitive, always wants to know why things work. And I encourage that. I think it is good. He is always trying to help me. Like, today I was in the garage. I needed some textbooks for the office and was going through the books. He wanted to go through the books. He was looking at the photographs of the buildings and architectural details. He is just interested, and I let him look at it. I have a bunch of boxes; he will go through them and pull stuff out and scatter it around. He is with me when I am working around the house with tools; he will be with me until his interest runs out. Sometimes I'll go after him, because he'll leave the tools around and drag off stuff. They lose interest and go out and play. I can see where it would be easy to tell him, ''Don't bother me; go play'' when you really had to get something done right away. But sometimes he will come back and bother you, hang around. Just hang around until you are forced to say it a half dozen times. His mother doesn't have the patience I do. She is home all day and has to do the work. I can come home; it's easier. Sometimes I lose patience with him, too. When I come home, I just want to sit there. But it's easier for me, because I look forward to seeing the kids. I play with them for a half hour or so; it's kind of new with me and takes my mind off things. I enjoy playing with the kids and get a kick out of it. But with her: you are there all day long. There is a difference.

Interview 6

L: When Jim's home, Mac leaves me alone. He only wants Dad. He only wants to be in the garage, in the car, or working in the yard, down the hill, across the street, just Dad, Dad.

But not when Dad's gone.

Adoption

Interview 1

S: How did you happen to adopt him?
L: My husband and I had been married for some years and no baby. I had taken birth control pills for the first years. Then I stopped and had no period for years and finally had surgery, became regular, and my obstetrician said I could get pregnant. That was two months before we applied to the adoption agency. They said we would have to wait nine months. I never told them that I had the surgery. Six weeks after surgery they called and said they had a baby boy and gave us twenty-four hours to make that hard decision: should we wait and see if I could get pregnant or should we take this baby? I

said maybe I'll never get pregnant. So we adopted him when he was three days old. We were very lucky. He was a beautiful baby, very healthy.

Interview 2

L: Thursday was one of the most horrendous days I ever had. Not only as a mother but just as a person. My day started at 6:00 A.M., and the boys were into everything all day long. My husband wasn't coming home until midnight. Billy was sick, I couldn't get out of the house—I was stuck with two kids. I was an absolute, total, unbelievable bitch to Mac the whole day. I never felt that way before. I really recognized that I hated him. That day, anyway, I did.

I didn't handle them well. I was lousy. I yelled at them all day. I called Mac a little bastard all day, not to his face but to myself or when he walked out of the room. And I don't think I have ever said that about my kid before. Because he *is* adopted.

S: All right, let's hear about that.

L: He was conceived by a bastard. And that's the best I can think about him. His father was married twice. Not to Mac's mother. I guess they had an affair—he found out that she was pregnant and he took off. Then she fell in love with someone else and decided she wanted to start a new life without this baby that she was still carrying, which I think is shitty.

When I think of their having an affair, I don't even picture it was in a motel. It was in the backseat of a car, something like that. I figure that because what they told me about her—that she—I don't know how they got that information—but somehow I have the idea that he was the first man she had ever gone to bed with. From what they told me, he was very, very, extremely handsome, and she was beautiful . . . a very sensual relationship. And she got pregnant. She was Catholic and so she wouldn't— very dumb—she wouldn't have an abortion. So she gave the baby up. She had the affair because she was in love with him. Because he wooed her. All I can say is I feel extremely sorry for her. He was a bastard.

S: "He was a bastard; she was a virgin; he was a handsome guy who really didn't care." Isn't that right?

L: Yeah. He didn't give a shit about her. He just used her. She was used. She had more guts than I did.

S: So she's abandoned. She has to go to the hospital. She has to go through the delivery alone. And she has a baby. And he takes off, which—incidentally—not at all incidentally—recapitulates your childhood.

L: Yes. My father [see pages 117–19].

S: What about the baby?

L: He's my baby. It's just as if he is, and what I imagine happened with his father and mother is what I always imagined would happen to me if I had had an affair before Jim.

s: But the baby. Why do you get enraged at the *baby?*

L: I was just thinking that he was left like I was left.

s: Why would you get angry at him? What's he done wrong?

L: He was my baby till Billy came. Then he was no longer my baby. Then I abandoned him.

s: Then you're like your father?

L: Uh huh. [Dead pause] I've lost my train of thought.

s: Don't look for it. What are you feeling?

L: Horror. . . . I feel sick. I feel like a bad seed. That's what I feel like. I feel like I'm getting back at him [Mac] for what they did to me. I want to get back at him. I really want to get back at him. I really want to make him sick and scared. And I feel unloved. Because he's a boy. I don't know why I said that. Because he's a boy. I'm scared that he's going to turn out like his father. He's going to abandon me; so I'm going to have to abandon him first. He's going to find out that he's adopted, and then he'll take off. That's what I'm afraid of. He's going to take off and leave. Because I love him too much. He was the most beautiful thing that I ever saw. Jim and I had a big fight the night before. I had had surgery [ovarian wedge resection] six weeks before, and I went back to work. I was back to work three days, and I got a call from the adoption woman. She said that she had a baby boy. . . . She said we had to come down the next day and make up our minds if we wanted him. I talked to Jim, and he said no. He said that the doctor told us we could have our own child, so let's wait and have our own child. I thought maybe he was right, maybe.

I just cried and cried and cried. I said I wanted the baby. I didn't give a damn if I ever had any of my own. At that point, I didn't think I ever would anyway. Finally, he changed his mind. Because he knew how much I wanted that baby. So why did he not want it? Well, we got to the adoption agency, and she came in with him. He was absolutely gorgeous. He was the most beautiful baby I ever saw.

But his face was all red [indicating to her that he had sheet burn and therefore had been abandoned by the hospital personnel]. They said he had been laying on his stomach, turning back and forth. And they said he had a caul [that is, was completely enclosed at birth by intact fetal membranes and therefore, she once said, isolated from the world]. I always thought about that [his being taken immediately from his mother, who never saw him] because when I read a lot about those first hours [of newborns], I knew he was so alone. Nobody to nurse him or come in [to visit]. He was there three days.

He was so beautiful. A very serious little boy. Didn't smile or laugh. My period came that day—the first period I had had in five years. I was in agony, like I was in labor. [It was] the first period I had after the operation. And . . . we went home, didn't have anything for him but a blanket.

And . . . I laid down on the bed with him beside me, and Jim went to the store. And it was like I had [given birth to] him. I was in such pain. That's why I feel that he's mine. He *is* mine. And I don't want to tell him who the doctor was who delivered him; I don't want to tell him. Because when I do, he's just going to look his mother up and go back to her. He will; I know he will. I know he will. Just as I went back to see my father's family years later and my mother didn't want me to. But I did. I wanted to see them. I wanted to know them. I wanted to hold them. I know that he wants to do that, too. He's going to want to look at them. And after I saw my father's family, I liked them better than my own; I like them better than my own family. And he's going to do that to me. I know he will because I've been so awful to him.

Interview 3

L: I always thought I was adopted. . . . I felt alienated, different. . . . My mother said that it was because of the incubator [she was premature; Mac's caul equals her incubator], which was a bunch of hogwash. I would sit and think about it for hour upon hour when I was a child. I really wasn't my mother's child. I was my father's. . . . I think I felt that my [dead twin] sister was my mother's child but that I wasn't: by some fluke, she was the real child and I wasn't.

Symbiosis: Ambivalence

Interview 1

L: I felt so sorry for him [Mac] Tuesday. [He was very ill.] Wednesday, when I took him in to the doctor, when I saw he was in such pain, and he was so good, he was so good. And I knew what pain he was in, I knew what pain he was in. And he was so happy, he was happy, really happy. I have never seen him like that in a long time because he had me in that reception room by himself. He and I were together. And I knew what kind of agony he was in, and I held him and loved him and . . . [pause].

S: Then we are left with the paradox: you love him so much that it is almost supernatural and at the same time you're turning on him and thinking, "My God, what a fiend I am!" What happens to the impulse not to turn on him?

L: Where is it? Oh, it's lost. It's like I'm an enraged animal. The rage is absolutely, totally uncontrollable. I could kill him. I could literally kill him. Not beat him or stab him or shoot him. But shake him, shake him, shake him. Just shake him. I've only done it a couple of times to where it's been enough to rattle his teeth. I never slap him across the face. He's never gotten slapped; it's been on the fanny or maybe on the hand. That doesn't mean I haven't had the urge to slap him across the face. Tuesday I had that urge. I know mothers who have done that, but I think that's totally degrading. I have spanked him pretty darn hard on the ass. I shook him Tuesday. I wanted him to leave me alone. I wanted him to go away. I wanted to call up the adoption agency and tell them to take him back.

I'm frightened that I love him. So why not do it first? How can I love somebody so much and hate them so much at the same time? Is it possible for two people to be like that? I've never done that before. My mother said as a kid I would go around the house leaving her little notes: "I hate you, I hate you, I hate you." But I never told her to her face. I remember that. I hated her because she left me every day to go to work. When I was little, I was alone, alone, lonely. I had nobody to play with. Just my grandmother in the house, who would yell at me and scream. But my hating my mother was not very sharp. More dull, more . . . not that she would ever leave me, but that she would die, up and die on me. Her and her goddamn Kotex [see pages 119–20].

s: What are you waiting for Mac to do to make it all all right?

l: I don't know. To tell me that he really wants me, that he loves me. I hate him because he's hers [natural mother's] and he's not mine: He's not really mine. He's a fantasy; it's a horrible, horrible, horrible, horrible, unbelievable fantasy. It's because I took those goddamn [contraceptive] pills [before discovering she was sterile]. He'll go back there, and he'll find her.

Interview 2

l: I just love Mac; I love him passionately. I love him like I would have loved my father, I suppose. I know I did love my father. I saw him until I was five. I was the same age as Mac is. It makes me so goddamn angry, because I feel Mac knows me better than anyone else does. I feel that I am never faithful to him, that he has seen me in all kinds of horrible, miserable, terrible moods. I know this because I hate him so much for this. He has seen me at my worst. My husband never does. When Mac and I get into these things, we're alone.

When I get angry at Bill, he jolts back when he sees me that way. But I never get angry that way at him; it's that he sees me that way with Mac. When Mac gets that anger thrown at him, his eyes get big. Most of the time, he comes at me with his own anger, or he'll joke around or he'll tease me. But he does not pull back the way Bill does.

s: He is more your equal than anyone else on earth?

l: Yes. But I feel he is that way because he has lived with me. He knows me better than anyone does.

s: But there's no dishonesty in the relationship?

l: No. None at all. He lies like all kids lie at five. But that is completely different.

Interview 3

l: Last night I was with Mac and Bill, in a bookstore with them, and they were sitting and reading. I was across the room, hidden by a bookshelf, and Mac came out and called to me. And I moved from behind the bookshelf and said, "I'm right here, Mac." And he said, "Oh, don't move from there. I want to make sure that you're there." Ten million times—when I *was* there. I did not move—he'd come back and check on me. Bill couldn't have cared less; he was so busy looking at those books. We were there half an hour with Mac continually asking, "Where are you, where are you, where are you?" And I tell you—continually: "Are you there?" It drives me batty. I swear to God it does. I don't know what I've done to do it but . . . I remember when we first got him, he was very unsmiling, a very serious baby. I always tried to make him happier. I always talked to him and cooed to him and sang to him. I don't mean that I held him every minute, because I didn't do that. I was thinking, the other day, that whenever I picked him up, I kissed him, and whenever I put him down I kissed him. Up and down into the crib a million times, to change his diapers, to put him into the crib. I probably did it just to pick him up, to kiss him. I love him—a truly dear, dear baby. Just give him a hug and a little kiss on his cheek. You know, kiss him. I always kissed him that way. I always kissed Billy that way, too. I think I kissed Bill more, because I nursed him. I held him more than I did Mac. With Mac, it was less touching him, because I was holding the bottle. And holding him and holding the bottle wasn't easy. With Bill, it was just I was nursing and I had a free hand. I could touch his hand, his little arm, or his face. But with Mac, I couldn't manage both. And I always felt I wish I had a third hand to touch him more. But I never propped a bottle with him. I always held him until he was fourteen months.

When I wasn't feeding him, I put him in his playpen or in the infant's seat. I didn't carry him around all day. I didn't want him to get into the habit of that. But he was always near me, because he always fussed if he wasn't. I don't mean right next to me but in the same room. Sometimes when he got older, he would come and crawl into bed with me. But he always had his own room, and we had ours.

Interview 4

L: The intensity came not with me but with him. I can remember when he was maybe nine months, a year, sitting in the car with him. I would be driving, and he would grab me and he would put his arms around my neck and he would hold my [slip] head very close to my chest. He always did that to me.

Interview 5

L: I'm afraid I won't do it—treat Mac the way I can Bill. Because I'm unable to: to push him away. But I don't mean totally. I feel that I have hurt him so much that the only way I can make up to him is by not pushing him away. Not in the slightest. The way I can with Bill. Do all children grow up feeling abandoned? I don't think Bill does.

Yesterday I took Mac for his five-year-old physical exam. The nurse came in and gave him a shot. . . . He's a big kid now, and here he was crying, every inch of the way, and I had to help her hold him down. It was just like I wanted that. I wanted that sensation. He didn't see my reaction, he was laying on his stomach, but I could . . . and immediately afterwards, I felt this horrendous migraine headache. It was so bad I could barely focus. Then they were going to take blood tests. He was sitting on my lap. That kid was so good, but he was so scared. And I was angry, because any time anything happened to me like that when I was a kid, I was always alone. But with Mac, I was always there. And it seems that I'm angry with him for my having to take the brunt of what's happening to him. I don't mean that I don't want to be with him: I want to be with him, and I want to share things with him. But it's almost that I've taken too much. Do you understand? [Crying] I'm putting out for him what I never got myself.

Symbiosis: Separation Anxiety

Interview 1

L: He went to nursery school for the first time this week [age four]. A big boy. I said, "I'm going now, Mac." And he said, "Bye." You know, like, "OK. I'm OK. And I'm safe." But every once in a while—we went to the county fair yesterday, my husband, the boys, and me. And I sat down on a bench, and Mac walked a little far away from and didn't see me for a couple of minutes. He screamed bloody murder. "Mommy! Mommy!" It was just half a yard away from me. And I thought to myself, "Holy cow, he really is afraid of being lost."

S: He does not feel lost in nursery school, and so he can just wave you goodbye, but he is lost when an unexpected break in the contact between you occurs?

L: Very much so. Yes. He spoke to me this morning. "What would happen if you forgot to pick me up at nursery school?" And I said, "Well, I don't think I would ever forget to pick you up at nursery school." And he said, "Well, what if you did? Would I live there forever?" And I said, "No, if something happened and I was late, I would call them and they would take care of you until I got there." But he worried; he worried about that in the back of his head.

S: How do you know?

L: When we go to strange places, he will always hold my hand. I don't have to ask him to hold my hand. Bill won't; he's a little rascal, that one. He is extremely independent and he'll just take off and: "Bye Mom." But not Mac. He'll always be there to hold my hand, I can just see him thinking, when we go to some place far away, he just never really goes too far from us. It's just something I know. I can't really explain it to you. It's just something I feel, I don't know. He's always been that way since a baby, very close to me more than Bill. I nursed Bill for almost a year, yet Mac has always been more physically close to me. Holding on to me or clutching me or . . . he never let me out of his sight. I couldn't leave him in the front room in his playroom. He would always want to be where I was, in the kitchen. This was at six weeks, three months. Yeah, sure; he just didn't want to be alone. I always had to bring his playroom into where I was so he could see me working. Not physically wanting to hang onto me all the time but just to know where I was.

He was always a very serious child. I never got that kid to laugh. I was looking through his baby book and every picture I have of him is serious. Whenever I took him to a photographer, he would never give them a smile. It was a terrible thing; he would scream and cry and never want me away from where the photographer was in order to get a picture; just was always very glum.

s: What if you were separated from him around the house?

L: He'd cry. Well, he could stay by himself for maybe a total of fifteen minutes or something like that if I was out of sight. I had to keep all kinds of baby toys in the crib so he would be busy and occupied. He'd be quiet for ten or fifteen minutes, and then I'd have to bring him in to where I was. But Bill played for a long time by himself; not Mac. But I don't think I ever treated them differently.

s: How long would he keep crying?

L: It was not a question of how long he would keep it up but it was how long I would let him keep it up. The longest was probably ten minutes. Not sitting there screaming his lungs out but just fussing.

And when he grew older, maybe eighteen months, he would whine because he couldn't follow me around the kitchen or from room to room. It drove me up the wall. Maybe some mothers can take that but . . . I could never do any work until he went to bed. Like if I was cleaning the bathroom, he would get into the tub-scouring powder; that stuff's poison.

Interview 2

L: Jim and I are going away for a few days, and Mac was a little worried. Perhaps he thinks I won't come back. The last time I was gone for a few days was when he was a baby and Bill was born. And what I did to Mac was something awful, so Godawful. I left him. And I had a baby. I wasn't supposed to have a baby. When we signed up to adopt a baby, we had been married for so many years and couldn't have a baby. That was why they let us sign up. That was why they let us have Mac. So I had promised them—and it was like I had promised *him*—that I would not have my own baby from inside me. I promised the adoption agency, or Mac, or whoever, that I would never have a baby of my own. He would be the only baby I could ever have. And the day after Bill was born, I developed a migraine headache, and it was horrendous. I couldn't move my head off of the bed. Mother called me at the hospital. She had Mac. He was crying on the phone. She told me she was having a terrible time with him. He would not do anything she said; he wasn't eating and he wasn't sleeping. She managed to lay it on me right there: why wasn't he doing what he was supposed to be doing. Here I am, just six hours after having Bill. And she pulled that. I just wanted her to stay home and take care of him. I wanted someone to just stay home and take care of him. But no one would listen to me.

After I came home from the hospital with Bill, Mac seemed so forlorn and lost. Two days later, he came down with a herpes virus; his entire mouth was filled with sores. He was so sick. God, he was sick! He couldn't eat anything. He cried and cried and cried. And when I came home from the hospital, two days later Mother left and Jim went back to work. And there I was. Mac was sick, and I was trying to learn how to nurse the baby. It was awful; it was horrible. And it continued like that for months, months, and months. I never left the house. I was angry at Mac. I was tired. Sick. It was horrible, horrible. And I handled it absolutely awful. Mac took the brunt of it. I didn't want him to. It was like I abandoned him; it really was. I was caught in between—one son who was adopted and one who wasn't. I couldn't decide if I should love my natural-born son or Mac. I was thinking that I loved Bill and that I didn't love Mac. After all those years, I had Bill, my own.

I would be nursing Bill, and Mac would hang around. He would hang around every single minute. And I'd think, "Why doesn't he leave me alone; why can't I be alone with my own baby?" I just wanted to be alone with him. "Why can't he just stop it; why can't he just go and play a little bit?" And then I would feel horrendously guilty for feeling or thinking that. Mac would be around continually. He wouldn't leave me alone, not for an instant. I was trying to sort out how I felt about him, and I couldn't. There was no time. All the time I had no time, no time to be away from him, no time to be alone with my baby, no time to understand, no fun. No time to love him or care for him. Every time it went wrong, I'd just pile up the guilt on top of me. When I yelled at Mac, I'd go in the bathroom and cry because I didn't want to do that. But I wasn't able to control myself.

But when I put him to bed at night, I'd touch him and read to him, and I would love him greatly. Or he'd be asleep, and I'd go in and look at him. And I'd feel that I really loved him in spite of everything he had done during the day. But the thing during the day—that he was on me so much, yelling and screaming and crying. It wasn't that I didn't love him at those times. I was only angry at him. Horrible anger. I just wanted to . . . I just had to leave him alone. So I'd just be silent. I can only remember once losing my cool: Bill was lying on the couch and Mac was standing on the couch, jumping up and down. I told him to stop or he might fall on Bill. But he kept doing it and he fell on Bill. I thought he had crushed the baby's head in. I went really nuts. I spanked him, and I put him into his bed, yelling at him the whole time.

Interview 3

L: I dropped a can of cream on my foot and thought I had broken my toe; I was in absolute agony. So I lay down and was crying. I couldn't stop. Mac became so upset. Bill just stood there and looked at me, but Mac became so upset that he went into his room and he cried. After he finished crying, he came back in and got ice and put it on my foot. And he sat there for half an hour and kept putting ice on my foot and kept saying, "Is that better?"

Interview 4

L: A bee bit me on the face—it didn't sting me. And Mac became very upset. So Jim said, "If I die, I'll never have to worry about someone to take care of you, because Mac will always take care of you." That's very nice for a mother to know about her child; I want him to love his mother, to be responsible for me. But I don't want him to live his life worrying about me. My cousin remembers what Mac was like when he was little. She remembers that he never left my side, never let me go anywhere without him.

Mother's Relationship with Her Parents

Interview 1

L: And he's [Mac] going to leave me. And there's going to be so much heartache for me. It's going to be just like my Dad did. He's going to grow up and leave me. Because I've been a crappy mother to him. Because I've wanted to leave my mother's and find my father's family, Mac must too. He must. He must want to know about them. Because I wanted to know so much about my father's family. I know that feeling. I know it desperately. I know that he's going to know it. I wanted to know them. I wanted to leave my family and go to them. But there was no way when I was young. They hated one another. My mother hated my father's family. To this day, she hates them, and they hate her.

When my mother married my dad, she married him! She stayed home, and she was his wife. If anybody did the running around, it was Dad. He took off six months after they were married and went on a job far away. He took off for a year and left her. My mother's version was that he went because of the good pay. I don't know my father's version. But he was an adventurer. He was truly an adventurer. He took off and did what he damn well pleased. When he was thirteen, he joined the merchant marine and did not come back until he was eighteen, and his family did not know where he was for five years. He moved all around the world. He could do anything he put his mind to. And he made money at it. He was good. And he was sneaky as hell. Either he was not sneaky and my mother was dumb, or I can't understand how she managed to go from place to place with him and not really understand . . . she must have. Either that or she just didn't want to understand. But *my* husband wouldn't cart me around unless *I* knew what the hell was going on.

Interview 2

L: I was always by myself for everything. My mother was there, physically, but I don't remember her holding me. It's like I've taken all the pain of my children upon myself. I don't want to do that but I have to, out of my own misery. I don't want to go through that anymore. I'm mad as hell at my mother, because she didn't go through it for me.

I'm thinking about when I was five. My mother took me to the county clinic, because I had bad tonsils, and they were going to do a tonsillectomy. There must have been twenty-five or thirty other kids in the room, and they were just sitting there [that is, abandoned also]. It was early in the morning. I remember my mother taking me, but I don't remember her being there. The nurse and doctor came in, looked at all the kids, pointed at me, and said, "Let's take this one; she's little and so skinny." So they took me first. And she wasn't there. Mom wasn't there. She took me there, but she didn't hold me. She wasn't there when I woke up from the ether.

And I can still remember the dream: of being in a tunnel or hole—black—and calling for her. And I can remember around that age playing on the ground. The wind was blowing very hard through the trees. And it blew a beehive right down beside me. I can remember screaming for my mother. And she didn't come. Daddy finally came. I don't remember him coming any other time but that time. He got me out of the bees. It seems that I have always called for her. And she has never been there. Never been there. I've always been there for her, always taken care of her, always. [Crying] As a little girl, I sat by her bed when she was sick. I sat by her bed hour after hour and never went out to play. I always stayed with her and brought her water, took care of her. It was like I was the mother, and she was the child. All my life like that. I feel I was taken away from him by my mother, always taken away from him. He never abandoned me. Not till the end. But it was always her. She had to run back to her damn family. And her family would always say to me, "You're lucky you have a good mother." Saying, I suppose, that a mother is better than a father.

When I leave Mac and Bill with my mother to come here, I look at them: he's so afraid. And it's me all over again, waiting for my mother, looking out the window, feeling a horrible knot in the bottom of my stomach until she came home, so afraid that she'd never come back. I think of that every time I leave Mac. I do. It is like I was left again all over again. That's why it's so hard for me. With Bill it isn't hard, but with Mac it is. [Crying]

s: Your feeling transmits itself, doesn't it?

L: Yeah. He's so damn perceptive. Sometimes, in my brain, I think of coming and going on airplanes and ships and never staying in one place or being in one bed for long enough. I've always worried about where the kids are going to sleep, are they going to sleep well. Now I know why; because I've slept in so many beds myself.

Interview 3

L: I can remember standing every night at the window when I was little, waiting for my mom to come home, thinking what if anything happened to her . . . it was bad. . . . I was scared something would happen to her and I'd be left with my grandmother.

I already had feelings of being abandoned by my father; so feelings of losing my mother were horrible. I don't know why I was so afraid to live without her; your mother's your mother. I love my mother very much, although she's acted very stupidly in many ways. She puts her heart before her mind.

She was always bleeding heavily. Extremely. All the time . . . one night I woke up, and my aunt was there. And she [mother] had gone into the hospital and was losing blood by the gallon. They did a hysterectomy.

I don't want to think that she abandoned me. Well, I think I felt that when I was little. I would go to bed and cry, feeling that Daddy didn't love me and that's why he left me. Mother had to work and support us but didn't abandon me. I was always with her even on vacations. There was never a physical abandonment, just in my stupid little mind, and I think just her going to work every day was an abandonment. I was left alone with my grandmother. I was always terrified of Mother being in an automobile accident, or someone hurting her, or her dying.

She was terribly sick. She told me that she was so sick when I was four or five that she would lie in bed for days on end. I would never leave her side—hemorrhaging. I knew she was sick. I dream about that in myself: if I die, what would happen to the children.

Fear of Traumatic Abandonment

Interview 1

L: I can remember when I was a kid my family's joke about my mother's Kotex. My uncle would say that if he grabbed a box of Kotex and threw it out the door I would be enraged because they belonged to my mother. And she needed those [pause] . . . or she would die. I was always afraid she would die. When I was six, we had twin beds and my mother always slept in one. But this time my aunt was there. I don't know where my mother was. I said to her, ''Where's Mommy?'' And she said, ''You'd better be a good girl because Mommy went to the hospital and she was hemorrhaging.'' My mother had had surgery six weeks before, a hysterectomy. The night before, she picked my big baby cousin up, and she ripped her stitches. And I guess during the night she started hemorrhaging in the bathroom. And they didn't wake me up until she was at the hospital. They stuffed a sheet between her legs. I can remember seeing the sheet . . . it was in the kitchen. And it was—they couldn't stop her bleeding and rushed her to the hospital. They got her out of the car, and she fainted from the loss of blood. And the sheet was loaded with it. I never saw so much blood in all my life, and it was my mother.

I can't imagine my aunt saying that. I wouldn't say that to my child. It scared the shit out of me. And for all of my life I was afraid that she would die—not so much when I was growing up. . . . I was with my grandmother. . . . I was an only child, the only one in the neighborhood, and all I had was my grandmother.

I'm just sorry about my twin sister [who died at birth]. My mother named me after her dead sister . . . pretty tough to take. She died at eighteen of leukemia. And I never thought I would live past the age of eighteen. I thought since she named me after her that the same thing was going to happen to me. All of the children in my family are named after dead sisters and brothers.

THE TREATMENT

Data are, of course, the product of the treatment, and so theories and explanations are at the mercy of what happened in treatment and what we decide is worth reporting. So let me say a few words about the treatment. Lorraine was in treatment with me for about three years. It could not be analysis for logistical reasons, such as the long distance between her home and UCLA and the difficulty and expense of getting regular babysitters. Instead, Lorraine saw me twice a week, sitting up. She would have been a good analytic patient and in fact allowed me to work with interpretations that were effective; she had no difficulty in associating freely, so that I felt almost always immersed in a comfortable and creative analytic atmosphere. A transference neurosis developed, and it was dealt with via interpretations and reconstructions (though I was more restrained in this work than I would have been had she been seen more often). There was, therefore, interpretation of resistances and other unconscious dynamics, investigation in depth of her oedipal situation, but less exploration of her earliest life. There was far more to the treatment than Mac; that material is not pertinent here.

Though she first came because of Mac's fetishism, her relationship with me converted almost immediately, because of her needs, from an evaluation to treatment. The greatest part of our time was not spent on Mac but flared out into all the other areas of her life. Unfortunately, her therapy was effective; she changed so much that her marriage was thrown out of balance. Her comfort in accepting the role of wife and mother, as drawn and commanded by her husband—to whom she had been grateful for rescuing her from an unanchored life—gave way as she discovered how much more she needed and was able to seize from the world. His demands that she break off treatment became so dangerous that she had no choice. And unfortunately, from the start, he stated that he not only had no interest in joining the family's therapeutic process but found the whole effort absurd. Mac should simply be told to stop his behavior, and if that failed, he should be properly disciplined. It was only Lorraine's failure of nerve and toughness, he felt, that allowed Mac to persist in this dirty habit.

Mac was in treatment for a year and a half with one of our child fellows, supervised weekly by a child analyst on the faculty. They confirmed Lorraine's descriptions of Mac in every way. His treatment failed to change the fetishism, though his therapist and the supervisor felt that in other ways Mac was coming along very well.

When his therapist left our training program, Mac was referred to a behavior modification program. That treatment seemed to have failed, for Lorraine reported at the end of her work with me that Mac had not changed. But now, years later, when she read this report, she told me that she saw no evidence of the fetishism after the behavior modification procedures and now believes it is gone. (It is, however, too soon to be sure.)

On reading this manuscript, she added: "Going through the report, I still feel the loneliness of waiting for mother. I suppose I still haven't worked it out or I wouldn't act so scared inside when I am an hour late getting home and the boys are alone. I wish I could be rid of that horrible anxiety. I cried a lot when I read the report for the second time, as I am crying now while I write you this. I think the one line, 'She loves him the way she feels her mother could not love her and hates him the way she hates herself,' is very true, yet devastating. It says it all."

Can a two-and-a-half-year-old be perverse? Erotic fetishism has been an important subject for psychoanalysts, containing in its structure mechanisms of defense that are central for understanding all human relationships. The capacity to substitute part for whole, nonhuman for human, inanimate for animate helps make life bearable—even enjoyable—when intimacy, insight, and lovingness would be too intense. So it does not surprise us that adolescents and adults turn to this complex construction. But that a child of two and a half can also create the symptom full-blown is impressive.

A child may get genitally aroused, but can it be sophisticated enough to fill the excitement in the ways one uses from later childhood on? Such behavior in a small child should not be; in fact, we must question—as has Anna Freud (1965)—if it can be: "Diagnostic categories which cannot be used outright for children are perversions such as transvestitism, fetishism, addictions. In these as in the case of all *perversions,* the reason is an obvious one. Since infantile sexuality as such is by definition polymorphously perverse, to label specific aspects of it as perverse is at best an imprecise usage of the term, if it does not imply a total misunderstanding of the development of the sex instinct. Instead of assessing certain childhood phenomena as perverse, as even analysts are apt to do, the diagnostic questions must be reformulated for these cases and we must inquire which component trends, or under which conditions part of the component trends, are likely to outlast childhood, i.e., when they have to be considered as true forerunners of adult perversion proper" (pp. 197–98).

Here is a problem: "Infantile sexuality as such is by definition poly-morphously perverse." Though this statement has been a classical position in analysis from 1905 on (S. Freud 1905), it confuses me. (Glover too [1933, p. 496].) First, knowing the history of the word *sexuality* in the development of analytic drive theory, I just am not sure to what experiences it refers. It can mean such things as "erotic," "masculinity and femininity," or precursors to these; "sensual," "life force" (as in Eros), or defenses against all these. It can mean pleasure or pain, activity or passivity, love or hate, excitement or boredom. With such a load of meanings the word scarcely has meaning. What, therefore, is "infant sexuality"? Or perhaps we should ask what is not.

Second, sucking fingers or playing with feces are, in this view, examples of polymorphous perverse behavior because mouths and anuses may be part of adult conscious erotism and may play an unconscious part in later neuroses; there is too much slippage in a theory built on such logic.

Third, "polymorphously perverse" is part of the language of a clinically incorrect theory that, in regard to body parts or body functions, equates *awareness* ("cathexis," "hypercathexis") with *erotism* ("perversion") in the infant/child as if it were all the same if that awareness is consciously erotic, becomes erotic only in later life, is sensual but not erotic, or is simply an aspect of relations with others. One thereby manages both to call infants perverse when they do what comes naturally and, as above, to deny that perversion can exist in infants.

We are well warned that, as is found daily in work with children and adults, precursors are not full-blown pictures, and a full-blown picture in a child may be gone by adolescence. (Freud 1905; A. Freud 1965). Yet I have trouble with the idea that a boy of two or three or four or five who gets erections from his mother's stockings and who is masturbating while fondling or putting on these stockings is not perverse. When a behavior starts in childhood and persists into adult life—a not so rare occurrence—is it perversion only from adolescence on? For instance, over half the children with significant gender disorder in childhood—some starting as early as a year or two of age—are found still to have a gender disorder in adolescence (Green 1985). And if a psychotic child grows up to become an adult psychotic, we do not question that the child was truly psychotic.

Should "perversion" identify only those excitements that result from a failed passage through oedipal conflict?

With regard to manifest behavior some clinical pictures in children are almost identical with those in adult perverts. Nevertheless, this overt similarity need not imply a corresponding metapsychological identity. With adults, the diagnosis of perversion signifies that primacy of the genitals has never been established or has not been maintained, i.e., that in the sexual act itself the pregenital components have not been reduced to the role of merely introductory or contributory factors. Such a definition is necessarily invalid if applied before maturity, i.e., at an age when intercourse does not come into question and while equality of the pregenital zones with the genitals themselves is taken for granted. Accordingly, individuals under the age of adolescence are not perverts in the adult sense of the term, and different viewpoints have to be introduced to account for their relevant symptomatology. (A. Freud 1965, p. 198)

Again we have the problem of those whose aberrant behavior carries through from childhood to adulthood. To what extent is the behavior, though behaviorally the same, "metapsychologically" different at six and twenty-six?

Another who denies that a child can be a fetishist is Bak: "According to a strict definition of the clinical concept of fetishism, it is a male sexual perversion and belongs to adulthood. *Formes frustes* may appear in childhood from the age of four or five, with experiences of diffuse sexual excitement, but they do not necessarily lead to adult fetishism" (1974, p. 193). I cannot call Mac's fetishism a *forme fruste*, nor is it an experience "of diffuse sexual excitement" (whatever that is).

There can be a childhood—but not an infancy—fetishism that is transitory. . . . Genetically, the *sine qua non* of fetishism is its phase-specific castration anxiety during the phallic phase in an oedipal setting. . . . It is absolutely necessary to emphasize the phase-specific position of fetishism in order to clarify its relation to aggression. The destructive and castrative wishes of the male child reach their peak at the phallic-oedipal phase with their consecutive retaliatory fantasies of heightened castration anxiety. In contrast, the so-called pregenital fetishes defend against separation, object loss, deprivations, and total loss of body integrity, at a phase when the destructive wishes toward the parental objects play a different and less important role. (pp. 194–95)

An essential feature of perversion for Bak is regression: "This regressive feature is common to all perversions and involves the denial of heightened castration anxiety and marked bisexual identification" (p. 195). It is regression for Mac if we feel he crawls into his mother's skin when he puts on her pantyhose, but it is not regression if we grant him the genius to create such a dynamically rich neurosis when so young.

Though we must heed the warnings of Miss Freud and Bak that we look beneath surface phenomena to underlying structure,[2] theory should suggest, not command. Can we not say that Mac is perverse and a fetishist and still not consider him identical to an adult fetishist? (Freud [1919], p. 192, is vague on this issue: "A perversion in childhood . . . may become the basis for the construction of a perversion having a similar sense and persisting throughout life.")

What do analysts mean by "fetishism" and how do they explain it? Another problem arises when we turn for help to the rest of the analytic literature. Some use *fetish* to refer to an object that is erotically exciting, some to an object that is not. For instance, some feel a transitional object is a fetish (or prefetish), and some do not. Though erotic and nonerotic fetishes may share similar origins and dynamics, there are also great and wonderful differences between a state of erotic excitement and one that, though intense, does not feel erotic. Once the definition is open to include the nonerotic fetish, one's explanations can go anywhere. Many psychoanalytic authors contribute many theories (few testable). I shall list them here without pause so that the reader can sense how many there are, how they often contradict each other, and how far we have to go to make order out of intellectual license.

These are direct quotes or, in a few cases, undistorting paraphrases: pregenital identification with the phallic mother, separation anxiety, anal erotic fixation, scopophilia, symbolic representation of the female phallus, identification with the mother with the penis, identification with the penisless mother, castration anxiety, compromise between separation anxiety and castration anxiety, intense submission to castration, father's penis fantasized in the female genital, the last object (for example, a piece of clothing) seen before the recognition that females do not have penises, congealed anger, splitting of the ego, displacement of the female penis onto another body part, interference with the distinction between self and nonself, physical trauma in infancy, the fetish as representative of the feeding function, suffusion of the entire body with aggressive stimulation, diffusion of aggression resulting in frozen immobility, susceptibility to active irritability, a kind of automatic reversal of reaction at a psychophysiological level, topical unreality, flowering of protective screen memories, prolongation of the introjective-projective stage, nasal congestion, turning away from the primary object, annihilating sadistic love, the unresolved wish in the male to have a child plus the consequent fear of pregnancy, persistence of attachment to a transitional object, fetish as a substitute and/or symbol for mother's breast (good or bad) or mouth or uterus or vagina or anus or swollen pregnant abdomen plus their products, early motility disturbances, illness in infancy, illness in the mother, inconsistent mothering,

---

2. I think, however, it is closer to the facts to say "meanings" or "fantasies" rather than "structure."

envy, seeing female genitals too frequently in early childhood, very close visual contact [type undescribed] with a female, a state of primary identification with mother or sister, blurred sense of one's own body's dimensions, hypertrophy of visual activity, subjective sensations of sudden changes in body size, defense against homosexuality, substitute for criminality in cowards, depreciation of females, the female genital as a wound through which a woman could empty herself out, dentate vagina, denial of parental intercourse, defense against suicide, defense against homicide, defense against psychosis, defense against incest, focal disturbance in sexual identity, infarct in the reality sense, the fetish as a substitute for excrement, passive homosexual submission to one's own sadistic and castrating superego, fetish as a symbol of one's own castrated self, defense against rejection, splitting of the object, weakness of the ego structure that may be inherent or may come about secondarily through physiological dysfunctions or disturbances in the mother-child relationship that threaten survival, the mother's body, oneself as pregnant and at the same time as mother's fetus in the womb, defense in homosexuals against heterosexual impulses, invented oedipal relationship with the father, passive anal relationship with the phallic mother, oral sadism, anal sadism, unsuccessful olfactory repression, erotization of the hands and predilection for touching, an exquisitely sensitive body-phallus equation, observing the primal scene, inborn weakness of ego integration, an executive weakness of the sexual apparatus, defense against a fear of annihilation, respiratory incorporation, respiratory introjection, alien smells that stand for archaic superego elements, massive overstimulations (such as frequent body massages) that throw the infant into states of extreme excitement with abrupt termination, the conflict between anal giving and withholding, pleasant tactile sensations, to find the object identical with one's own fantasized penisless state, transferring of sensual sensations to an indifferent object by association, bisexual splitting of the body image, witnessing a particularly mutilating event in childhood, the mother's unconscious need to resist separation from her child, a deprived or violent family atmosphere, mothering that is not good enough or at least not quite good enough, inability to accept weaning, mother's consciously or unconsciously encouraging the child to take a fetish, all the significant instinctual part-objects of the prephallic years, mother's abdominal skin which the fetishist penetrates, identification with the maternal feces, identification with the bad mother and at the same time feeling the elation of the introjected good object, the fetish as symbol condensing breast-skin plus buttocks-feces plus female phallus, identification with the partial object (the breasts) of the total object (the mother), the fetish as a symbol of mother's milk devaluated and subsequently commuted into excrement, a replacement of a combination of breast and penis, an effort not to avoid castration anxiety but rather outcome of pregenital disturbances, fixation not regression, disturbance in formation of the body image in infancy, the fetish undoes the separation the mother, the fetish creates an independence from the love object. And more. (I spare the reader and printer the citations for this long list.) Almost any guess goes and is expressed with no regret that no data (often not even a well-honed anecdote) are given.

Though these explanations do not each contradict all the others, it would take some artistry in theory making to shape them, even after debridement, into a synthesis. Besides, we know that most of these have been used to explain many conditions examined by analysts and that many are so nonspecific that they fit the description of the genesis of almost any behavior of almost anyone.[3]

Nonetheless, and less disheartening, *these experts tend to agree that the fetish—erotic or nonerotic, in child or adult—stands for some aspect of the separated mother and that the precipitant to creating it is castration anxiety.* At any rate, a fetish is a thing that has become a story.

Having now immersed myself in the data and thinking of ethnography, I join with those who wish we analysts would temper our *furor theoreticus* and at least muse on other societies. If a glimpse of pudendum—the cause of fetishism in classical theory—is enough to derail a boy for life in New York or London, why does the same not occur in primitive societies? For instance, despite intimate observation, Herdt (1981) knows of no perverse fetishism in the Sambia (though all men turn onto boys' mouths the way heterosexual men do to, say, breasts in our culture). The skeptic also wonders why, when the trauma of seeing a female without a penis occurs in childhood, the overt perversion first occurs shortly thereafter in a few boys, in latency, puberty, adolescence, and for decades after in adults, or—as is almost always the case—never.

Fetish can as well indicate either an erotically exciting or nonerotically exciting object. I shall, however, use it to refer only to the former.[4] Bak (1974) is especially helpful here.[5] This not only sharpens the clinical description leading toward theory; it also highlights how unusual was Mac's behavior.

3. Other than the psychodynamic, there are two general types of explanatory systems for fetishism. ⁓t is the learning theory model, in which the aberrant erotism is said to result from an otherwise ⁓ect (such as a shoe) being by chance perceived at a time of high erotic excitement with the drive then fused. The second is an organic explanation, as exemplified in the following: ⁓eased organismic excitability is considered the primary disturbance in fetishism. This ⁓ a product of cerebral pathophysiology. Some of the major manifestations of this ⁓ated to seizure and other episodic phenomena found in temporal lobe dysfunction'' 7).

the clearest possible clinical definition is the best approach in looking for ⁓iish between objects that themselves erotically excite and those that only clear ⁓bject. The latter include such things as amulets held in the hand or looked at, ⁓otent in erotic use. The shared psychodynamic features of the two types should ⁓nces.

⁓ositions, compare, S. Freud 1927, 1946; Gillespie 1940, 1952; Friedjung ⁓1953, 1955, 1960, 1968, 1969, 1970; Winnicott 1953; Weissman 1957; ⁓; A. Freud 1965; Roiphe and Galenson 1973, 1975; Silverman 1981.

There are mighty few fetishists like Mac, in age and form of the fetishism. We can legitimately use *fetish* for erotic or nonerotic objects so long as we appreciate the clinical differences (compare, Roiphe and Galenson 1973, 1975).

Mac had a security blanket, used only in early infancy and held only while he nursed. He gave it up easily. Disagreeing with Sperling (1963), I feel it is clinically inept to call it a fetish (especially, as we sense, the fetish—different from the usual transitional object—is such a densely compacted tangle of sadomasochistic fantasies).

Early childhood fetishism is very rare. In some reports of fetishism, the interest in the fetish goes back to childhood, but rarely before age four or five.[6] (Of course, we cannot be sure the need did not start further back with the failure of patients' memories keeping us from knowing of a very early fetishism.) However, in almost none is the object reported as erotic for the adult erotic in early childhood.[7]

If we restrict ourselves now to preoedipal children with a clear-cut erotic fetish, there are few reports. (I have not attempted a survey of the nonanalytic literature.) To what extent, when we are dealing with adults talking of their childhood, we are dealing with a childhood amnesia or with a truly absent behavior cannot be determined. At any rate, I am not surprised to hear transvestites report that their earliest memory of erotic cross-dressing is in childhood, though none remembered before around age six.

I am not familiar with the detailed report of erotic fetishism in another child as young as Mac. In fact, the analytic literature has few reports even of adults who remember early childhood erotic fetishism (see Garma 1956; Socarides 1960; Wolf 1976). In addition, I have reported (Stoller 1968a) on a man with a fetish for women's stockings who remembers excitement when he was three or four (his father reports seeing the boy in nylons at age two and a half). I also evaluated a very feminine boy whose mother said she saw him at age three with erections while fondling his *father's* clothes, never his mother's (Zavitzianos [1982], who says this homeovestism is not fetishism); this behavior disappeared spontaneously in a few months. (See also Socarides [1960].) These reports are clinically thin, and when the child is reported to be sexually excited, we are not told enough to be sure what was experienced. Even the next report, more explicit than most, could tell us more: "Around four or five, the experience of being left alone at home when his mother went out shopping had been unbearably frightening, and the patient recalled seeking relief through creating a state of sexual excitement by running into mother's bedroom and excitedly feeling her smooth, silky underclothes" (Wolf 1976, p. 109).

The following case suggests that other cases have been around for a long

6. See Friedjung 1946; Sterba 1941; Lorand 1930; Idelsohn 1946; Wulff 1946; Hopkins 1984.

7. Dickes (1963) tells of a woman with a nonerotic fetish that had been erotic in childhood. It is not clear in this case to what extent the object—a teddy bear—was in itself erotized; we know only that it was used for rubbing the genitals, which need not be the same as being a fetish.

time: "In a case reported by *Lombroso* ('Amori anomali precoci nei pazzi,' 'Arch. di psich.,' 1883, p. 17) . . . a boy of very bad heredity, at the age of four, had erections and great sexual excitement at the sight of white garments, particularly underclothing. He was lustfully excited by handling and crumpling them. At the age of ten he began to masturbate at the sight of white, starched linen. He seemed to have been affected with moral insanity, and was executed for murder" (Krafft-Ebing 1906, p. 254).

The synergy of trauma, excessive and focal identification, and separation anxiety. In line with Greenacre's observation that marked physical trauma may contribute to fetishism, we can note that Payne (1939), Peabody et al. (1953), Hunter (1962), Hamilton (1978), and Socarides (1960) report on the significance of circumcision in a fetishistic patient (as was manifest in Mac's case). Lorand (1930) links his patient, who had a nonerotic interest in shoes, to a circumcision at age two. Though we cannot build a case for childhood (not postnatal) circumcision as an expected feature in erotic fetishism, a more careful study might show that the conjunction sometimes is not coincidental.

Putting aside the question (because I cannot answer it) to what extent the transitional object, the nonerotized infantile fetish, the erotized infantile fetish, and the adult erotized fetish are related, we have unanimous agreement, based on observations, that these objects stand as a bridge between the infant's wanting to stay merged with mother and to become an independent person. No one writing in recent years disagrees that "the background of the development of the infantile fetish is a chronically disturbed relationship to the mother, with individuation delayed and incompletely achieved" (Greenacre 1970, p. 452).

The second common feature with which most concur, one that can help explain why erotic fetishism is unreported in female infants/children, is castration anxiety.[8] "The fetish . . . is the product of need for reparation because of the persistence of an illusion of defect in the body, which has become fixed through its association with certain concomitant disturbances invading self-perception. The adoption of the fetish makes it possible for development to proceed though under a burden" (Greenacre 1970, p. 455).

No one has suggested as strongly as Greenacre (1953, 1955, 1968, 1969, 1970) that severe physical trauma in infancy, as was the case with Mac, can precipitate fetishism (though the absence in most reports of a history of such trauma cautions us not to generalize):

It is my impression that early fetish formation does not develop unless the accompanying disturbances have been so undermining as to produce a severe pre-oedipal castration prob-

---

8. I hesitate to use *castration anxiety* here because that term has historically implied an oedipal (as Freud felt to the end [1940a, p. 190]) rather than preoedipal-stage danger. But in these infant erotic or nonerotic fetishists, castration threat *in the classical sense of threat from father* is not part of the picture. In addition, if we did not use the classical term, we might more easily sense connotations of more profound danger—separation anxiety, dissolution of self, loss of existence (Roiphe and Galenson 1973, 1975).

lem, whether through illness, operative procedure, or severe parental mishandling. It is significant that at the early age of one to two years there is a general body responsiveness to discomfort or physical insult, and discharge of tension may occur through whatever channels are available at this special time. If the disturbance is so severe, however, that ordinary discharge mechanisms are inadequate, premature genital stimulation may be induced. This is most likely to occur during the second year. (1970, p. 30)

In Mac's case we have, as in no other reports, his mother as an articulate witness. She not only dates and describes the circumcision and separation traumas but also lets us know how she maximized Mac's trauma by her shocked, terrified, and enraged behavior (perhaps heightened by her own experiences in childhood with her hemorrhaging mother). Recall the ambience of their relationship and contrast it with the way, from birth on, she related to Bill, her younger son.

Mac's mother is—barring good luck or good treatment—permanently stamped with grief and fear because of her abandoning mother plus the remembered terror during her mother's bloody, life-threatening episodes. Her father was literally a deserter of the family. Mac, as an adopted child, is, in his mother's eyes, another creature abandoned by mother and father, and so he and she resonate to each other, fears and rages locking them into an excessively close though jittering mother-infant symbiosis. So now she sees herself treating her child as her mother did her, leading her to more self-hatred. (Greenacre [1953] talks of "those infants who are held in a state of appersonation—especially guilty, hostile, or anxious appersonation—by the mother, who may touch the child little, and when she does so, handle it as though it were a contaminating object" [p. 90]. This describes only half of the ambivalence Lorraine laid on Mac.) She experiences herself as a fusion of an unlovable child and a failed mother. She hates herself in the body of herself and herself in the body of the son with whom she identifies. Therefore, she must undo that hatred and its visible effects on Mac. Powered by her identification with him, she tries to prevent his being mother-abandoned as she was, but the effort to save him from suffering as she did exhausts her, as do his efforts to separate himself, alternating with his nestling in to her intermittent engulfments. I hope you can see in the transcript material, as was powerfully present when she talked with me, the anguish Lorraine suffered as she kept failing to come close to her maternal ego ideal, she, a woman who felt that was her most important aspect (Blum 1981).

He was to be her eternal cure. Now she would no longer be alone, abandoned, anatomically incomplete, and endangered (as her mother was by her father). It was to be just the two of them, but after promising him symbiosis forever, she became pregnant and had a different sort of infant, one she could only define as "normal," a complex of lovely qualities that intensified her sense of the frenzy in her self-Mac relationship. To make the ambivalence more wonderful and more awful, Mac really was a beautiful, intelligent, precocious child, who in those ways lent himself to her being drawn to him as her equal, a part of herself that, though outside, she was constantly drawing back into herself. As if all this were not enough, she is the person who left behind at birth—or was left behind by—her dead twin sister. (Incidentally, with the present interest in bonding as an innate mechanism, Mac and his mother show us how even in the absence of a chance for bonding in the first three days, a fiercely intense symbiosis can occur with an adopted infant.)

I do not think, however, that she actively and consciously helped him choose his fetish or encouraged its use (Sperling 1963). Mac did not need her to assist him in creating his fetishism (compare, Dickes 1963).

I want to note, without elaboration here, the fantasy of parthenogenesis. It is probably at work in the pregnancies and postpartum periods of all mothers—an aspect of Winnicott's "primary maternal preoccupation" (1956, pp. 300–05), I suppose. Its more intense and prolonged forms put children at great risk, whatever its roots (for example, a mother's thought: "I don't need you anyway, Father," where "Father" means her father, her child's father, and her child-as-father). This fantasy can be so intense that it swamps children's development. Though it harms gender and erotic development, it may, depending on a mother's needs, lead to precocity intellectually and artistically (Stoller 1968a, 1975a).

Let me suggest, as a further twist to parthenogenesis, that women not only get themselves pregnant by themselves but also with themselves—that is, with themselves as infants. The issue, as we see in Mac's case, is not that the dynamic is there but how powerful it is.

We cannot get into Mac's mind; he could not put in words the signals arcing between him and his mother, and his therapy was not psychoanalytically illuminated. Still, we can imagine how her silky smooth, skin-like pantyhose—a garment closer to being her than any other can be—fit his needs to have her with him, part of him, covering him, protecting him, and comforting him more reliably than she, a full person, did. The garment, as is true for fetishes,[9] was better than his real mother in so many regards that it was really delectable. Pantyhose are infinity (as long as he could keep the adults from meddling). Once in his possession, they were always available; he could control their presence. They did not scold, become enraged, threaten with abandonment, go crazy, excite and frustrate, have a mind of their own. They did not have to be shared with father or brother. They could cover him as if he were still inside his mother. They did not complain when he put them aside. With them, he mastered the trauma of the symbiosis.

Perhaps we should emphasize more the function of mother's skin as a recognized, perceived, wanted part of an infant's relation with its mother and not just equate skin, breath, belly, face, hair as all—for the sake of theory—being "the good breast." The same oversimplifying makes the fetish equal

9. Gillespie 1952; Greenacre 1953; Mittelmann 1955; Socarides 1960; Bak 1974.

mother's phallus, thereby keeping us from seeing that other parts of mother (skin, breast, voice) are also incorporated in the fetish.

Yet we are left with the same question we have with all psychic constructions, neurotic or other: who/what put together all the pieces so that the perversion resulted? That boy who experiences himself as Mac did not do it, nor did Mac's "self" or "ego". (I find the usual analytic answer that "the unconscious" does the work begs the question completely.)

Nor do we know—it is no slight question—why and how he connected her pantyhose/skin to his *erotic* machinery so that he not only got comfort, safety, and peace from his fetish but that much more highly experienced, focused, uncontrolled, tight, hard tension that a *motivated* erection has for a child, who does not have the physical means for gratifying it or the psyche for dealing with not having the means.[10]

Why, at that age, does his need involve his genitals? To reach at this point for a brain–spinal cord explanation, as we do with vague biologic explanations such as "constitution" and "diathesis," is premature. Such explanations may have value, but we do not yet know how; we do not even have procedures for testing them. (Still the old question: how is the mind connected to the brain?) Let me guess: the physical trauma—which was certainly terrible psychic trauma as well—was to his penis, that most primary erotic apparatus. And the psychic trauma—the jolting symbiosis—threatened his developing sense of separateness as a male. The cure he invents—fetishism—should therefore be directed to the anatomy of maleness and its consequence, masculinity.

DISCUSSION

This chapter, unlike other writings on fetishism, is presented more from the point of view of the mother than of the fetishist. Partly this is because the data from Mac's treatment were thinner and not filtered through an analyst-therapist. However, I want to emphasize a point of research methodology not available when the analyst has only the patient—adult or child—as the partner in the search for childhood experiences: though the analyst fills up with and interprets the transference, we still do not get a full picture of childhood, though it may be good enough for therapeutic success. For studying the events—external and psychic—of childhood, transference data must be augmented by information from parents, the deeper the better. In joining those

10. Nor can the physiologists tell us how his still unformed body could mobilize its response so efficiently. Colleagues recalling that hearty erections are available to infants from birth on will wonder why there is a question here. Perhaps there is not, but—no more than a hunch—I think these mindless erections of infants are little more erotic than the reflex erections of "spinal preparations" such as quadriplegics. I do not belong to the school that believes a nursing infant with an erection wishes—let me use the most evocative word possible—to fuck his mother. (Or even the good breast.) Mac did, sort of, *but not in infancy.*

who believe this, I also repeat the position (at times forgotten in the heat of theorizing) that some of what is intrapsychic starts from the outside world. In other words, what mothers and fathers and siblings and others actually do to an infant/child counts in the psychic structure that develops. Fetishism is not due simply to castration anxiety, splitting, fantasies of the female phallus, separation anxiety, symbolization, fixation, identification, or fantasized good and bad breasts—the view from inside the infant. We should see those mechanisms as defenses raised to deal with traumas inflicted by the outside world. What parents and others really do really counts. I gingerly quote Ferenczi: "Having given due consideration to phantasy as a pathogenic factor, I have of late been forced more and more to deal with the pathogenic trauma itself" (1930, p. 439; see also Glover 1933, pp. 490–91).

In Mac's case, Freud's explanation of fetishism (1927, 1940b)—the conjunction of the boy's seeing female genitals and later being threatened with castration by his father for masturbating—does not fit. That being, Freud believed, every boy's experience, it does not tell us why every boy is not as fetishistic as Mac.

How interesting that Mac's masculinity developed in the face of traumas strong enough to produce fetishism and was not grossly eroded as time passed (Scharfman 1976; Katan 1964). He is not a feminine boy and will not, I think, become transsexual. Will he become a transvestite, a nontransvestic fetishist, or a homosexual? I would guess not. Will he exchange his erotic defense for a nonerotic neurosis? I dare not predict. From Freud on, our theory of fetishism says that the perversion serves males to protect their sense of maleness against the threat of castration, but no report gives data making clear why in one case the outcome of that threat is fetishism and in others homosexuality, narcissistic personality, fear of flying, Don Juanism, voyeurism, a successful career as a painter, masochistic heterosexuality, or a need to kill prostitutes. One cannot even decide from the reports why one boy will grow up to be a fetishist of the transvestic type while another's fetish is rubberized garments or dead bodies.

There are two clues to why Mac is masculine. First, his father, though tough, taciturn, and unempathic, was masculine, present, admired, and supportive of Mac's being masculine. Second, his mother encouraged masculine behavior. (The mothers of some very feminine boys also have an excessively close identification/symbiosis with the son who will be too feminine, but those mothers—opposite to Mac's—try to encourage all behavior that society reads as being feminine.) Yet most present-day theorists do not argue, as does Freud, that the fetish is used to protect masculinity but, rather, that its primary purpose is to prevent traumatic disruption of the mother-son symbiosis. At least in Mac's case, inventing the fetish seems a matter between mother and son, without father's playing a major part in the interpersonal dynamics.[11]

---

11. I think, however, that there are fetishistic cross-dressers—transvestites—for whom the damaged relationship with father is powerfully important, something like "If I were a girl, you'd

Perhaps this helps: Mac is not repairing castration anxiety, the result of observing a castrated object—mother, but is repairing his own direct experiences with terrifying separations and literal castration: circumcision.

Renik et al. (1978) report the case of an eighteen-month-old boy with a bamboo phobia. This child has much in common with Mac, though phobia and fetish—even infantile phobia and infantile fetish—do not intuitively seem connected. In both boys there is intense genital erotism (pp. 262–63); a markedly premature erotic relationship between mother and son (p. 262); disruption of "the orderly and sequential unfolding of psychosexual phases" (p. 262); mothers who are intensely interested in their son's masculinity; mothers with a great need to identify with this son, who is to repair traumas of their infancy (p. 256); intense and precocious motor development (p. 258); direct or indirect fear of the genitals being literally cut off—in Renik et al.'s boy, on observing his father trimming bamboo (p. 260)—not just castration anxiety from observing absent-penisness, that is, femaleness; mothers each of whom "reenacted situations in which she considered herself stranded and left behind by an adventurous and self-centered male. The pleasure she received from her identification with [his] aggression and confidence was denied by her ostensible feelings of being neglected and victimized" (p. 257); a boy in whom "the particular emphasis on his penis led to a dominantly phallic organization of . . . sexuality at a time when conflicts pertaining to the oral and anal impulses had not yet been resolved or mastered" (p. 262); each boy with a mother who, "out of her own needs, met the wish for increased closeness with a certain impatience and rejection" (p. 276); each boy with precocious sexual and cognitive development, "while the development of his *object relations* was not [precocious]" (p. 277).

We have a clue that can fit the clinical facts of Mac's perversion with the insistence by Bak and A. Freud that perversion cannot occur before oedipal development:[12] he is cognitively and genitally erotically precocious, so that he moved into a full-blown phallic phase—"premature genitalization" (Roiphe and Galenson 1973, p. 152)—epigenetically out of kilter with the rest of his development. Then, because his mother was excessively identified with him—treated him in many ways as an equal—a precociously "adultified" relationship was established between mother and son. This poor, crazy little wise man was driven, by his inner—innate and learned—precocities and by his mother, beyond what his body, his experience, and his phase-disrupted development could handle. Renik et al. (1978) hint at this in saying, "Considering the sophistication of Ted's phobia, his case demonstrates that capacity

---

love me; so I'll be one even if I am also, and will always be, a male." Probably we ought not to look for identical explanations in the fetishism of a child as young as Mac and the fetishisms that surface later.

12. They would be more accurate, I think, if they stated that perversion cannot occur before a fully experienced phallic stage, with or without triangular oedipal conflict.

for symptom formation is not easily correlated with level of psychosexual development'' (p. 267). In treating their sons as equals, these mothers encourage the boys to identify with the aggressor (mother), that process becoming a part of the symptom. In addition, by being mother's equal, the generation difference is obliterated in deeply telling ways, complicating the oedipal dynamics even more.

Renik et al. feel that the mother of the boy they studied ''actually treated him in many ways as a phobic object'' (p. 265). Perhaps we could also say that such mothers, who try to cure their own lifelong unhappiness by overidentifying with a son, use the boys as a (nonerotic) fetish. Recall how, in extremely feminine boys and men, their mothers handled them as *things,* the mothers' lifelong sense of worthlessness as a female repaired by having brought forth this penis from their own bodies. As adults, these transsexuals are more like things than people capable of interpersonal relationships (Stoller 1975a).

Though I do not believe that neurosis is the negative of perversion—I believe, rather, that perversion is an erotic neurosis—there is sense in a similar idea: phobia is the negative of fetishism (Glover 1932).

I see Mac's fetishism, then, as a frantic precocity (Greenacre 1970, p. 452). His mother treats him as an equal and wants him too much, but she also cannot bear him. She hits him and then hugs him. He is to undo her infantile trauma, but she feels him to be just like her and so not to be trusted, respected, or found lovable. She loves him the way she feels her mother could not love her and hates him the way she hates herself. Every day he is thrown from one extreme to the other—merged with and extruded by his mother—hardly the best ambience in which to develop a stable body image and sense of self. Driven by these unmanageable demands, Mac does what everyone does: without training or experience, as if for the first time in the world's history (he certainly has no genes for pantyhose fetishism and no center for it in the limbic system), he invents neurosis. He condenses his problems and their solutions in one efficient, ever-ready, exciting, gratifying act. Themes that are loving, hostile, defensive, and reparative to himself and to his mother now exist in a fiercely intense instant, a wondrous collecting of unconscious and yet purposive—logical, effective, creative—elements that give mastery of formerly uncontrollable traumas, frustrations, threats.[13]

What we do not know is how he ever managed it. The rest of us need years more of development, experience, and conscious and unconscious intrapsychic experiments in childhood and beyond, before we can impact such scattered debris into the densely massed experience we call erotic excitement.

---

13. ''This way of dealing with reality, which almost deserves to be described as artful . . .'' (Freud 1940b, p. 277). Or: ''One is impressed and almost awed by the degree of condensation—the literal putting of all urgent needs into one durable pot [the reported fetish]—by the two-year-old boy'' (Greenacre 1970, p. 449).

CONCLUSIONS

Is Mac so rare a case that he does not tell us much of anything? I must be careful not to overstate his value for theory or to extrapolate freely from him to fetishists in general and beyond that to what seems a whole race of erotic minifetishists: most males of most cultures (Stoller 1979). Yes, in a way, Mac's case is too rare to be a model for fetishism in general. On the other hand, the reasons he is rare contain clues for wider application. We do not know enough yet to make firm statements on the causes and dynamics of fetishism. Here are ideas of which he reminds us.

1. When the word *fetish* is used loosely enough, it fits any interesting object (or theory).

2. Though identification with each parent is inevitable and essential for identity development, a mother's excessive need (for example, in a parthenogenetic fantasy) to encourage that identification in her son is dangerous for both.

3. Mothers with a badly damaged sense of worth about their femaleness are likely to misuse a favored son as a cure to their lifelong sense of defectiveness.

4. Castration threat is not just father's prerogative.

5. The combination of intellectual and libidinal precocity can upset the natural pace of gender and erotic development.

6. A true perversion—a true fetishism—can develop in very little boys, though perhaps only if the boy is erotically and intellectually precocious.

7. The perversion of fetishism at any age is not just an oedipal matter in the classical sense but is especially a consequence of a mother-infant symbiosis in disarray.

8. Erotic fetishism in a little boy is as much the result of a primeval separation anxiety as of the more sophisticated, more cognitively recognized experience of castration threat.

9. Intense physical trauma, especially when augmented by a terrified mother, can be a precipitant to fetishism.

10. Early boyhood fetishism is the consequence of a constellation of events, not a single event. It is therefore very rare since few boys are exposed to the whole constellation. To explain any case, much less all cases, as a splitting of the ego in the effort to substitute the fetish for mother's absent penis leaves out too much.

Though he is statistically rare because so young, Mac paradoxically confirms the belief of A. Freud and Bak that perversion does not occur in so young a child, for, in his intellectual and erotic precocity, Mac was as if much older. But in their saying that perversion—by which they mean erotic and gender aberrance—requires triangular oedipal tensions they are wrong, for lifelong disorder in either or both of these spheres is found as early as the first year to two of life. Also, we do not want (nor do they) their emphasis on oedipal matters to obscure the fact that, as has been described by most recent workers, the preoedipal relationship between mother and son—with father not playing much of a part—is crucial.

8
ORIGINS OF MALE TRANSVESTISM

If a man is a transvestite—a fetishistic cross-dresser—his childhood can be expected to differ from the constellation described for very feminine boys. So far, I have never interviewed a transvestite or his family where the constellation was present, nor has it been reported in any case of transvestism I have read of or had presented to me by colleagues.

For instance, for about twenty years I have had a friendly, more than therapy-oriented relationship with a transvestite man. In that time, we have often talked of his childhood, his parents' personalities, and the relationships among the family members. The constellation was not present. Our conversations, though the years have increased the richness of my impressions, could not possibly provide the information one gets in a psychoanalysis with its development and illumination of infancy and childhood via the transference. And without the power of therapeutically successful probing (the better the treatment, the richer the data), I have not gotten a satisfying view of those early days. Nonetheless, I have learned a lot about transvestism.

To collect better observations, I worked with the mother of a transvestite—an early adolescent boy at the time the analysis began—in an analysis. My nontherapy goals were to see if, under the microscope of analysis, the constellation was or was not present and, if not, what was happening in the family that would help account for the fetishism. I never really—only sort of—found out; or perhaps I did but the truth is hidden in the stupendous mass of detail that makes up a psychoanalysis. (I have experienced that often in the past, when it took years, countless repetitions of remarks, and working with a number of cases before a wayward observation suddenly emerged as a significant finding.)

When first seen for evaluation, the family consisted of the parents, in their thirties, the transvestite boy, aged fourteen, and his sister, three years younger. The mother was feminine—if one is allowed such brute summaries—in appearance, carriage, and fantasy life; her husband (to whom I spoke in person only a few times but about whom I, of course, heard continuously through the years) was as masculine as his wife was feminine. The daughter did not participate directly in either the evaluations or the treatment. The father did not want treatment, the boy had a year's psychotherapy, and the mother was in analysis with me for many years. The son was seen again, at that point a young adult, in evaluation toward the end of his mother's analysis. (As always, I shall in spots be vague, falsify insignificant facts, and delete material to preserve confidentiality. The reader is at my mercy when I say these alterations are unimportant.)

Because the focus of this chapter is on origins of transvestism—and, again, to preserve confidentiality—I shall not report on this mother's treatment and its outcome or on how each family member has fared through the years.

What findings in this family do not fit those for very feminine boys? The mother was not of the bisexual sort. She was not consumed by a desire to be a male or by a hatred and despair of her femaleness. Though she says this baby was beautiful when he was born, she rarely talked of him in her analysis and in no way perceived him as the mothers of the very feminine boys perceived their sons—as marvelous, as a cure for hopelessness. She had no need to create a blissful symbiosis and therefore did not stay in constant physical and psychic contact with him. Her husband, though too passive for her liking, too much absent from the family, and an increasingly heavy drinker as time passed, was not the object of a disappointment as raging as that I heard from those other mothers. On the other hand, a severe febrile illness that was followed by a permanent personality change and a traumatizing surgery (as was also noted for Mac, the boy fetishist reported in chapter 7) assaulted this infant's development. And this boy (like Mac) is fetishistic to stockings, though it didn't stop with that.

On first seeing this family, I guessed—an idea that had struck me before and that has been confirmed often enough in the years since—they would report that Tim, the boy, had (1) been first cross-dressed by another person (2) in a circumstance that started with a feeling of humiliation but in time became erotically pleasing. This process differs from that in the very feminine boys, whose cross-dressing comes on spontaneously as a manifestation of their feeling feminine; they could not be traumatized by being put into females' clothes.

But neither the evaluation interviews nor, for years, his mother's analysis revealed that Tim had been cross-dressed by someone else. Her analysis simply could not convince me—disappointing as that was for my gender identity study—that she was a proximate agent in his disorder, as are the mothers of very feminine boys. Then, late in our work, came a finding that, as you shall see, reduces the mystery a bit.

Here now is an edited transcript of some of the interviews before treatment began. (The same rules for editing hold as previously described.)

M: Tim was born with a partial cleft palate, the soft palate. It was cleared up at eighteen months, and we have had touches of speech therapy. He's been dressing up like this since ten, and at the time I didn't . . . it had been a gradual thing. I wasn't shocked or anything. They had been imaginative kids, and they had always dressed up but not particularly in women's clothes . . . cowboy. Tim is fourteen and his sister is three years younger. When they were little they dressed in cowboy clothes. Tim continued with this. . . . We had a dress-up box, and he liked it. The other child lost interest, and I also got rid of the dress-up box because of this [cross-dressing]. But at ten years of age I became conscious of it, because he'd put on things that I didn't want him to put on, good things of mine. I mean my gloves mostly, and then as an adolescent . . .

S: Let me interrupt you. Were these things that were in the dress-up box?

M: At first. And then he started to go for my gloves. In the dress-up box were cowboy things mostly, and funny hats.

S: Were there feminine garments in the box?

M: No. I wouldn't have put women's clothes in there. There may have been gloves, old gloves I sometimes stuck in there because they said, "We need cowboy gloves." I didn't go out and buy them: I gave them old gloves. I got rid of the dress-up box and they kept hauling it out. I kept putting it out for the Goodwill [charity]; and then he started to use my clothes.

S: On his own?

M: Yes. Then I became concerned because it was going on quite often. I'd come home from a shopping trip, and there would be Tim dressed up. It happened quite often when his dad was transferred away, and we were living for three months without my husband being there during the week. Then it [cross-dressing] happened just constantly, just all the time. But even before that [transfer], it was happening often when his father was there. We were having a sort of a problem in the family between my husband and myself. I guess the kids sensed it. There wasn't any fighting, but there was all this dissension and lack of rapport. And Tim was doing it all the time. His father was not dealing with it at all; he didn't pay any attention to it. I'd say, "Let's do something. This is terrible. Get angry or something," and he'd speak to him. But we knew enough not to be too punitive.

Unfortunately, because of my husband's work, we've been transferred many times. Tim is very shy. He had the cleft palate surgery at eighteen months. Beyond that there was just nothing, except at age three he got this illness. He had to go to the hospital. He was home two weeks before he was hospitalized. Antibiotics had no effect; a temperature all the time. Then it started spiking, going way down and way up. It was very frightening. He was hallucinating. He would see bugs and all sorts of things. So he was hospitalized. He continued that for five days, and I stayed there with him.

We don't know what it was. But all the symptoms stopped. Anyway, Tim, we feel, had a personality change at that time. He seemed very subdued. Possibly he may have had . . . you know it was a frightening experience . . . and it may have cut down a lot of self-confidence. . . . I don't know what the term would be, but he was not the same, not as tough and little-boy-let's-go about anything. He became quite shy. It wasn't all that dramatic. But it was a bad illness, and he was weak afterwards. And then he seemed just subdued. He didn't play as well with his friends after that either. He might have suffered some brain damage during that time or something. He isn't testing very high in his IQ tests; he's not doing well in school. He isn't having any kind of a happy time. This may have affected his feeling about himself. See, he was three and a half at that time.

S: What was it like with the two of you before that?

M: All right. First of all because he had this cleft palate when he was born, there is a special feeling about him. My husband notices it more on my part than his. I suppose it can be covered by overprotectiveness or anxiety regarding him. When he was born, my husband was going to college, and we were having a difficult time with Tim. At the beginning, they didn't even know he had a partial cleft. They couldn't figure out why he couldn't drink milk and . . . and then we took him home, and he got thrush. He had a hard beginning. So our feeling during his babyhood . . . he became very healthy after we got him over this initial time. He was really a very husky child and very healthy and beautiful. Then my husband accepted a position which involved a training program, and he was separated from us for nine months, from the time Tim was just before he was a year, thirteen months on, it was a nine-month period. During that period [age eighteen months] we had his surgery [on the palate] done.

 We lived in an apartment after that, and I spent a great deal of time with him with a group of other girls; we spent all our time out with the children. The other girls all had little girls, and I had this little boy and we used to just let them play. . . . I suppose I inhibited him or something. Anyway, I treated him more specially than maybe I should have. Doing things for him all the time, like tying his shoes, feeding him . . . much more so than with my daughter, always.

S: Did you carry him a lot?

M: Well, when he was little. No. The problem with him was he was very aggressive. He ran everywhere. He was almost hyperactive. We lived in rolling country, and there were cliffs and he was always running off into the woods—I don't know, I would drag him back. I only spanked him a couple of times when he ran off. And when he pushed the little girls, I climbed on him for that. I notice other mothers ignore a great deal of what their little boys do: I never ignored anything that child did. I inhibited him or changed the direction [of his attention] if I felt he was going to be at all aggressive or hostile. I thought: this little boy mustn't hurt these little girls. But I didn't turn my back. I was just on him all the time as a tiny little fellow.

S: Your husband was completely gone for nine months because of this assignment. How old was Tim when that happened?

M: He was thirteen months, and we had the surgery done at fourteen months . . . we had the surgery done at eighteen months.

S: So you were alone with him from about thirteen months to about two years?

M: Yeah.

S: How close were you to him during that time?

M: I'm a smothery person, but I'm not a mothery person—I can't explain. . . . I read to him, I did spend a lot of time with him, and we took walks. Very close. I didn't have a great social life, nothing marvelous going on. So I spent a lot of time with him.

S: When your husband came back, he was still transferred around a lot?

M: Uh-huh.

S: Was he out of the house a great deal?

M: Yeah.

S: Because of his work?

M: He doesn't think so, but he is basically out of the house a great deal more than I think many men are.

S: Why do you feel that?

M: When Tim was very young, sometimes my husband had to stay away a [whole] day. He's a reserved person in many ways, not any more, he's changed quite a bit. But he withholds a lot and I still think there wasn't the exchange . . . there wasn't much of a relationship [with Tim]. I do feel this about him, that he wasn't like some fathers are, very anxious to make a man of this little boy. That didn't interest him. He's very athletic, very physically active, a very masculine person, and I just thought . . . that was one thing that attracted me. I thought he'd be a terrific father but he really wasn't interested in developing a little boy into a man. That didn't preoccupy him. He liked Tim, but he was really interested in what he [father] was doing more than anything else. We have a very intense relationship, too, and we get involved in each other. Maybe he just hasn't had enough [time] with Tim.

S: Would he see very little of his son during the seven days of the week or did he spend as much time, actual time, as another father does? Did his work keep him out at night, for example?

M: Uh-huh, occasionally.

S: Was he ever gone over the weekend?

M: Right, sometimes. That particular line of work involved a lot of time and irregularity, and when he would be home sometimes it would be when Tim was in bed.

S: Let me ask you one more question; then I'll talk with him. Have you had any impression that putting on clothes was ever sexually exciting for him?

M: Uh-huh. The very last time and his father . . . his father has never caught him. . . . When his dad is home nothing happens. The last time we had both been out. He had come home, and we weren't there. Then we came in and the drapes were drawn in the living room. He came home by himself, and he was masturbating with a petticoat of mine. So I assume . . . I found this happening before with my nightgowns and things.

Mother leaves and Tim comes into the office. He is slim, not effeminate, fourteen-year-old-boyish.

T: When I was little, I started dressing up a little bit and my mother never stopped me and then . . . I was about six. My sister and I were playing house, and doctor, and dress up . . . I guess I was wearing clothes. My mother's older clothes. My mother came in and she saw us sitting. And I guess she didn't get too upset. And then I start doing it because I had a weird feeling or something. And then my mother started telling me not to do it. And I just kept on doing it, and I guess I didn't stop.

S: I see. Your mother had old clothes. Instead of throwing them away, she gave them to you kids to play with? Any particular kinds of clothes?

T: High heels and an old dress or something. I think that's the first time it happened, but I'm not sure exactly.

S: Tell me more what the strange feeling was. Was it a sexual feeling? You know what I mean by that? Where your penis gets hard. Was it that when you were six or was it a different kind of feeling?

T: I don't know. It just felt like silky. It just felt a different feeling from what I wore. Soft and everything.

S: Exciting, very pleasant? I would guess that by now it gets you sexually excited. Is that correct?

T: Yes, a little bit.

S: At any rate, from the first time, you knew it was something special, that is, around age six. Right? And then you continued doing it regularly?

T: I started doing it sometimes when my mother went out, because I wouldn't dare . . .

S: You also did it when she was around, or she would never have known about it.

T: When I was a little kid, I did for a little bit, and then she stopped it. When I was seven or eight.

S: And then she never let you do it any more after that?

T: No.

S: Did she ever find you doing it after that?

T: She saw me doing it before.

S: How about your father? How did he respond to it?

T: He didn't want me doing it. He told me I shouldn't do it.

S: When you have this feeling, do you want to dress up completely, or do you just want to have one thing at a time?

T: I guess completely.

S: Have you ever dressed up completely?

T: Yes.

S: Makeup, lipstick?

T: Once.

S: What about a wig?

T: What?

S: A wig or something to make your hair look long.

T: No.

S: Have you ever thought you wanted to be a woman?

T: I don't know. I guess I always wanted a girlfriend.

S: You what?

T: I guess I always wanted a girlfriend or something like that, but I don't have any.

S: I'm not sure whether you understood what I asked or whether I understood you. What I asked was: have you ever wished that you had been born a girl and grew up to be a woman?

T: No, not really.

S: What do you mean when you say "not really"?

T: I don't think I really want to be a woman. I was born a boy and I guess I just want to be what I am.

S: Have you ever thought that you would like your body changed, that it should change to be more like a woman's body?

T: No, not really.

S: Have any girls ever put girls' clothes on you?

T: No.

S: Have they ever dressed you up or wanted to dress you up?

T: Uh-uh.

S: . . . and your mother didn't either. But it was your mother who gave you the clothes to put on.

T: No. She just put them in the box.

S: If you could, would you dress up every day?

T: I don't think I really want to that much.

S: If they were to leave you alone and there was nobody around, would you stay dressed all day or would you stay dressed just part of the day?

T: I guess just for a little bit. Maybe an hour.

S: OK. Some day you're going to be grown up. What would you like to be?

T: An architect.

S: An architect. How come?

T: I don't know. I just like to design motor homes and that sort of thing.

s: Anything else?

t: I like animals. I'd like to be a zoologist and collect animals.

s: And what would be your next choice?

t: Let's see. Oceanographer.

s: What's the best movie you've ever seen? The one you like the most?

t: Ummmmm. I guess *The Sand Pebbles.*

s: Why?

t: It's pretty interesting . . . in China. What they did. And I like the army type of things. [Discusses movie with enthusiasm. I ask about other interests—TV, books. His are unremarkable for a boy in southern California.]

Tim's father was also interviewed. He corroborated his wife's report in all particulars, adding no new observations, perspectives, theories, or clues; so I do not present a transcript.

The patient did not mention Tim very much during the analysis, but I do not feel she was hiding it from our work. She was focused on other issues, especially her relationship with her parents in the past and, in reality, a deteriorating marriage. Tim left home about halfway through her analysis; she was less grieving at his going than guiltily relieved.

Let me draw from her analysis in order to amplify issues brought up in those first interviews. I shall report these vignettes pretty much as we talked in the particular discussion that illustrates the issue.

1. *To have a baby.* I asked her how it felt to have a baby (wondering silently if she would report as did the mothers of very feminine boys). Though she had never imagined growing up to be anything but a housewife and a mother, she was never frantic about having her babies or when with them. She neither needed nor used Tim to fill an emptiness: babies cannot do that for her. She was happy to have him, but he could not—being an infant—give her the companionship, the closeness, the conversation for which she had been greedy all her life.

She said she did very well during her pregnancies and thought of herself as a good mother. She had wanted to be a good mother and was at ease mothering her infants. Her husband has felt she was a good mother. She gained forty pounds—too much—with Tim. She exercised during her pregnancy and had the baby by natural childbirth. Her deliveries were easy. What struck me as she talked of all this was her rather bland affect, as if there were nothing below the surface: though talking of mothering, she gave me no sense of her as a mother. After a while, I asked her how it felt to be creating a baby on the inside, but she spoke only of physical sensations, as if she had no creative maternal quality. Toward the end of this hour, my belief that the blandness was not a reflection of her state of maternity was confirmed. It was, rather, a reflection of the present state of the transference. I understood that when, with her now having filled me with her superficiality, she confessed that that was indeed what she was doing to me. "Your voice is so well-modulated," I said. She was amused: "That's what they used to tell me. That's the exact word they [her parents] used—modulated." Between ages ten and sixteen almost every day she was told she must learn to be "modulated" because they thought she talked too much, too loudly, and was too dramatic. She then recalled being afraid at the start of treatment that she could be heard outside my office: she was sure her allegedly loud, piercing voice could penetrate even the soundproofing.[1]

2. *When Tim was small.* The first year or so with Tim was, on the whole, good. The experience, however, was dampened by his cleft palate, which at first made it difficult for her to nurse him. That proved her inferiority since he came from her body. So she was angry at him from his birth on. She had wanted to be a marvelous mother and thereby cure her sense of inferiority. But he could not suck because the nipple slid into his cleft palate. She would then want to shove it into him in anger. (This came up as a transference association to feelings toward me and my intruding comments.)

Another hour. Part of a dream: "My cat is drowning. I can't get him out of the water because he's old, and I figure maybe it's just time he died. I left in order to get my daughter to help me, because I thought I really shouldn't let him die. When I returned, he was out of the pool and was getting around but was very weak and trying to live." Tim, who by this point had left home, was back for a visit and had gotten a bit drunk with his father. She fears that when she is out of the house, he will steal her clothes for cross-dressing. She wonders if the dream is about Tim. She can't understand how she turned out to be a rotten mother: "I was afraid of that baby. I am still afraid of him." In his first eighteen months, he was hyperactive, vigorous, beautiful. An uncle said Tim would grow up to be a football player. She thinks of the time when Tim was age two to three and, for about eighteen months, she restricted his playing only to little girls. She kept him from boys. "I inhibited him, because I thought girls were delicate. I didn't want him to associate with boys." Then came the spiking fever and the permanent personality change.

She recalls a fragment of a dream, the only one ever reported in which Tim appears: "Tim was painting a room. He is not right [normal]." Her first association is that she does not think he is "right" in reality. Over the weekend, she thought about him a lot, becoming aware that she was angry at him continuously from infancy on but did not recognize until now how much that is the case. Only now does she realize that the anger was strong and that it

---

1. Let this illustrate the unending difficulty in interpreting what patients tell us. Which is a correct explanation for her superficiality in this hour: that she is schizoid, borderline, was transiently afraid of me; was experiencing a transference affect toward me; or was manifesting a flawed maternal capacity, which I would now discover and report as a crucial factor in the creating of Tim's transvestism? Or something else? All psychoanalytic clinical reports should start with "Once upon a time."

influenced everything she did and said to him. She says she believes that she "overidentified" with him: his defectiveness touched on her inner belief that she was psychically—not anatomically—defective. (This quality is like what we saw in Mac's mother.) So, she feels, there was a special closeness between them, built not on sympathy or love but from her disparaging him as she does herself.

When he was three, his sister was born, a healthy, beautiful, satisfying infant.

She recognizes that she "took it out on Tim all the time" because he was difficult and "disappointing." He was born with a small penis. His masculinity was inadequate: "He just didn't come up to what I wanted when he was born; there was no question that there was something wrong with him." He had never been as close or loving as the next baby.

3. *The personality change after surgery and after the febrile illness.* When the surgery was done on Tim's cleft palate, during his second year of life, the surgeons instructed her not to visit for the ten days he was hospitalized. They said that he would cry and thereby tear the sutures. Then when she came to take him home, he acted as if he scarcely knew her. The doctor really cheated her. She should never have taken his advice. She did so because she is a bad mother who wanted to hear that advice: she did not want to be around the baby when he was suffering.

When she was a girl, she thought she could bear only girls, that she would be a failure as a mother of boys, and that she would somehow feminize sons. But when Tim was born, he was masculine and vigorous; she was amazed that she could produce such a child. Then came the change in his personality, first after the surgery and then after the febrile, hallucinating illness; following that, "his mouth has been turned down [beginning of sadness], and it's never turned up since."

She talks again of the surgery, of her not being allowed to visit, of her subsequent feeling that that was a terrible thing to do, that she abandoned him, and that his personality then changed. Then she abruptly stops talking of Tim, as if the faucet went on for a moment and then turned off. Her next association is to her dentist. Then a dream: "I called the dentist. I needed him, but he was taking his wife to the movies. There was something the matter with me. My blood wouldn't circulate."

4. *Unsettled living conditions.* From the time Tim was born and for eleven years thereafter, the family moved eleven times as his father gradually advanced in his career. In the first three years, father was twice gone for months at a time, related to his work. These uprootings were to rental homes, purchased homes, or living situations with relatives, each stay for a few months to two years, almost all to different cities.

5. *Transvestism.* She talks again of how Tim's transvestism started (from her viewpoint). He was fascinated with cowboy clothes, and because there were no gloves and because she wanted to discourage his tremendous interest in those clothes, she let him use her gloves. Gradually he proceeded secretly to use more and more of her clothes. Would it have been different, she wonders, if she had bought him gloves of his own rather than allowing him hers? She recalls once walking into the bathroom and finding him completely cross-dressed, with a wig and lipstick. She was horrified but did not know how to handle it. She thinks her husband shares responsibility for the behavior. When she saw Tim completely dressed up, she felt especially awful because she imagined he might have been trying to imitate her, and it was a terrible parody. She wonders if another contributing factor might be that a young woman who often wore a bikini or less was visiting at the time. At any rate, his cross-dressing reached what she judges was its "absolute peak" right after the woman left.

6. *A new clue.* Near the end of the analysis, she brings forth a new clue on Tim's cross-dressing. Speaking as if I already knew it—but she had never mentioned it before (and this is corroborated by no mention of it in my daily progress notes all those years)—she says that he had been cross-dressed by a neighbor girl. What she reports now is that some time in the months after she substituted her own gloves for use in the cowboy games (and these gloves, she always emphasized, were not feminine but neuter looking, old), there was a period of almost two years when Tim's closest companion was a girl his age. This child refused to wear girls' clothes. Even when they all went to church, the girl would wear her jeans until they got to the church door, at which point her mother would take her aside and change her clothes. Immediately after church, she changed again to boys' clothes. So, for two years, the two children played, each dressed in the clothes of the opposite sex. And that—the last time Tim's cross-dressing came up in her analysis—brought the clue I had in previous work felt was a significant finding for fetishistic cross-dressing.

Six or seven years later, a week after his mother finally told me of his cross-dressing with the neighbor girl (a report probably precipitated by his having an appointment with me), Tim came in again. After a few preliminary remarks:

s: You are now twenty-one?

т: Yes.

s: OK. Tell me about your cross-dressing.

т: I don't know how it got started really. I was talking to Mom about this the other night; the very first thing I ever remember was when I was about three years old, or about two years old, about there. I was on the way to the hospital with my dad, because next door this guy by accident hit me with a snow shovel, had about seventeen stitches. I was putting on my mom's white gloves. She has these formal and driving gloves. I was fascinated with them. I have this picture [image] of me putting them on. I suppose I could interpret it as looking up to [respecting] mother, somebody to look up to and want to be like, because at that time I didn't see much of my dad. So my mom was the only person I ever had to relate to.

s: Does any feeling go with the memory, or is it just a picture?

T: It's just a picture: standing up in the front seat and turning my hands with the gloves on and looking at them.

s: What's next?

T: Five years old. The first house we lived in. A friend and I were playing in a cart. I was pushing him. I had one of my mom's scarves, one of those wool-type things, hand sewn or something like that, one of those long ones you put around your neck to keep you warm. I can't remember whether my mom gave it to me to put on because it was cold out or whether I picked it. See, cross-dressing happened a lot during that time. I was doing it more as a habit then. I don't know how it got started being a habit, but by that time it was a habit.

s: Describe what you mean by a habit.

T: I remember something. Around third grade. "I'm going to go home and dress up," because this teacher had some clothes on that reminded me. The clothes looked nice, and so I had this feeling: I had to go and dress up. I would think about it at school, the last couple of hours at school.

s: By "habit" you mean it was happening regularly, a part of your life, not an exceptional experience?

T: Yes.

s: Always your mother's garments?

T: Yes.

s: What were the favorites?

T: Silky stockings, the ones prevailing throughout the whole time. I think the last time I did was a couple of years ago, the main fetish. My mom told me that it was a fetish. I would walk around with regular boys' clothes on with stockings under.

s: How far back do you recall stockings?

T: About eleven. I did a full dress-up. It didn't matter what kind of garments as long as they were my mom's. She had a dress-up box; now I think it was mostly for my sister. I would take stuff out of that, like a green dress.

s: How does the dressing up completely compare with just putting on gloves or a sweater?

T: It would be like stockings, part of the whole thing. It created a good, a secure feeling: having part of that with me at any particular time without having to walk into a room [?], a security type thing.

s: If it wasn't complete, why didn't you complete it?

T: At times my Mom would be home; I couldn't dress up.

s: While she was away, why didn't you? Let's say you are seven.

T: As a matter of fact I did then.

s: So it was earlier than age eleven. It started then [age seven] that you dressed completely?

T: Yes, I remember being scolded for getting caught because I broke a zipper on my mom's dress. I was about eight.

s: How long did she know about this?

T: I was about five years old. The only attitude I got is that they would scold, use rough language like, ''Don't do this.''

s: She continued to know about it and scold you and you continued to do it?

T: Yes.

s: What about your father?

T: He didn't have much to say about it except for scolding me for breaking the dress. It wasn't so much that I dressed up, but I broke the dress. He didn't condone it though. I don't know; he didn't really have much to say to me about it at all. Throughout my whole life, when I once started cross-dressing, it wasn't in control.

s: So then when you were seven or eight you can recall then that it wasn't just a scarf or a pair of gloves, but, if you could, you would get completely dressed up. Does that mean underwear?

T: Yeah, everything.

s: Did you want to look like a pretty woman?

T: Yeah, yeah. I would definitely do that, especially as I got older. Sometimes in my mind I could mostly imagine the legs as being girls' legs.

s: Legs were important?

T: Yeah. As I got older and wanted to have girls, I was really shy about girls. It [dressing up] was a substitute. After some tries, I wasn't able to get a steady girlfriend. So it was a substitute. I would pretend I had a girl. I played double parts.

s: You pretended you *had* a girl and you *were* the girl?

T: Yes.

s: Would you, when you dressed up, make up stories?

T: No. It would be mostly for the looks.

s: When you were looking in the mirror was it you, Tim, looking at her or was it you, a girl, looking at yourself, a girl?

T: Sometimes it was me, the boy, looking at this girl. And how pretty she looks. As things went on, it was me as a boy dressed up as a girl, looking at this guy dressed up as a girl and liking the feeling. What was exciting was the feeling of being close to the clothes. [This description is typical of the mirror experience of which other transvestites have told me.]

s: Not the looking?

T: Not particularly. It was the clothes.

s: Let's see if I got it right. There were two different excitements. With one you were looking at the girl you didn't have. That was a different experience from the second, where it was you, a male, wearing the clothes and knowing you were a male.

T: Yes, it was like visualizing myself as a girl—a male touching a girl through the clothes. It's Tim feeling the girl's clothes.

S: Now what happens if you were the girl and you feel her clothes?

T: It would be like me, another person, feeling a girl.

S: Let us say you are sixteen, seventeen, eighteen, or twenty or whatever, and you go out with a girl, not you dressed as a girl. Do her clothes excite you?

T: No. The stockings did. I found, when I go out with a girl, that I like to feel their legs. I don't get a feeling of wanting to put them [the stockings] on, though.

S: What about the rest?

T: The panties have an excitement. The rest doesn't except to look at. I like to look at girls with a short dress, or a low collar, or low neck.

S: So now when you go out with a girl, you like to feel her stockings but wouldn't want to put them on yourself? You'd rather that they be on her legs and be feeling her legs? But years ago you wanted them on yourself and to feel them on yourself and that was exciting?

T: Yeah, because it was using it as a substitute; like I imagined my legs as somebody else's, as a girl.

S: When did it become clearly sexually exciting?

T: When I was twelve or thirteen. Finally, I found a girl that I liked. I would go home and dress up and imagine it was her. The first time was when I put my stockings on, fully dressed up, and I was thinking of this girl, and I got really excited about it. I was feeling my legs and stuff. I didn't have any control over it, and finally I masturbated.

S: What about dressing up with other kids?

T: This friend. We would play *Bonanza* [television cowboy show]. He had a wig he would put on, his mother's. I remember a number of times going over there and dressing up with him. Full dress-up in clothes.

S: Did you ever dress up with little girls?

T: No.

S: If you had to choose one garment, it would have been stockings?

T: Or second it would be panties.

S: And then, what would be the decreasing order of importance?

T: It would be like: stockings, panties, a slip, dress, and shoes.

S: How important was the texture, the actual feel?

T: That was about the most important.

Though I do not have a tight argument regarding the etiology of male transvestism, I believe the following summary of Tim's case is more or less (the details will be different in each family) what has often happened.

A little boy who has already developed a male core gender identity—a conviction, an acceptance, a body knowledge that he is male—nonetheless has a developing masculinity more vulnerable to threat than other boys'. With Tim, the factors that weakened gender identity development were the cleft palate, which disappointed his mother and made her identify with him (and thereby build the sense of flawedness into him); inadequate mouth structure for normal feeding as an infant; the minor speech defect, which marked him as different in early childhood; the surgery to repair his palate; her not being with him for the ten days following surgery; the severe febrile illness that—perhaps producing minimal brain damage—left his personality permanently changed from enthusiasm to sadness and with a dull normal intelligence; his mother's continuous, usually covert anger and disappointment in him; his parents' gradually deteriorating marriage; his father's being passive and distant when he was around and often physically not present; the disruption by constant moves; the birth of a sibling, a girl who was desired and who made mother happy.

If a boy with a compromised sense of intactness and worth is then cross-dressed—especially for two years by a girl with powerful transsexual impulses—he is, I suspect, at high risk for transvestism.

9

NEAR MISS: "SEX CHANGE" TREATMENT AND ITS EVALUATION

Since 1953 (Hamburger et al.; see also F. Abraham 1931), a fantasy held for millennia—that one could change sex—has seemed to become reality. This solution to an unacceptable sense of bisexuality has pressed the light and dark sides of people's imaginations, as we know from the comedies and dramas, stories, myths, and visual portrayals of artists back almost to the beginning of preserved records. And in the dreams of ordinary people, in the agonies of paranoid psychotics, in the erotic behavior of all sorts of folks (diagnosable or not), and in the structure of identity, we find this ubiquitous effort to come to terms with impulses toward, or fear of, turning into someone of the opposite sex.[1] The issue for discussion now is the latest version of this struggle: "sex change."

I shall not, in this commentary, present data from a properly constructed piece of scientific work; my experience is too meager for that. Instead, I speak from a knowledge of the literature and from working with a scattered sample of patients selected, as you have seen, in an unplanned manner, as part of my study on masculinity and femininity (not on "transsexualism").

More than with most objects of endocrinologic and surgical interest, the desire to change sex reaches deep into most of us. But the elemental passions that result have invaded the medical procedures and also the research that surround the treatment. We should all wonder—and out loud, not secretly in the corridors—to what extent scientific exploration and medical decisions are adulterated by the personal biases of the experts. When, for instance, does high morality corrupt one's research?

These introductory remarks serve, then, not only to justify my lack of good

---

1. The most powerful investigation of the subject is that of Freud (1905, 1937), who found bisexuality and its permutations to be a bedrock of human behavior. In a more recent extended and lively review, Kubie (1974), oddly, writes as if Freud had not covered the same ground four decades before.

enough data but to suggest that those with more data may not really be more objective or, in certain important ways, more informed.

SUMMARY OF HORMONAL AND SURGICAL PROCEDURES

Most readers of a book like this are probably at least sketchily familiar with the procedures that lead to "sex change"; this review serves only to remind you of these practices in order to establish my perspective that *all* aspects of this subject are controversial. There are three main medical contributions to the treatment:

1. Secondary sex characteristics are to be reversed, primarily by hormones (and, in the case of males, by electrolysis for hair removal).

2. Surgically, in the male, the testes and penis are removed, with scrotum and penile skin preserved; perhaps a stump of the penis is kept to function as a clitoris; and a fascial plane is dissected to produce the space that, when lined with penile skin and skin graft (some surgeons use gut), will become a vagina. Labia are built from the scrotum. Surgically, in females, breasts are removed, panhysterectomy performed, and—though with little success, I think—a phallus is produced by grafts (but one that is nonfunctional erotically and often incapable of transporting urine).

3. The psychiatrist serves as the gatekeeper who decides which patients should receive these treatments. My impression is that most psychiatrists (in some regards, perhaps all of us) are incompetent for this task because the indications are unclear.

A LIST OF CONTROVERSIES

Most people think that there is just one controversy regarding "sex change" treatment and that it is a new one: There should/should not be "sex change" surgery because the results are/are not good. But actually, many controversies are intertwined with that one, and they add up to a situation that, to me, smells to heaven. Let us put our noses to it.

All the items below deserve some discussion and some a whole chapter; but I shall here settle for merely listing them or giving them a few words. Even so, you will at least be aware that a controversy exists. Though each of the following issues has both practical and theoretic aspects, let me arbitrarily divide this discussion into two categories.

A. Practical issues in the decision-making process
   1. Morality
      a. The libertarian position: The patients, most of the public, most physicians not involved in these treatments, and most physicians

(including psychiatrists) who participate in the treatment respond to "sex change" as if it were an over-the-counter nostrum: those who want it and can afford it can have it; let people have the treatments they choose; they will live with the consequences, good or bad.

b. The antilibertarian position: "Sex change" should be forbidden. Of the few psychoanalysts who have spoken on the matter, almost all believe that "sex change" procedures are wrong in principle because the treatments ignore the psychodynamic pathology at the bottom of transsexualism (Ostow 1953; Socarides 1970; Volkan 1979). (Transsexualism in these discussions is not precisely defined.) Transsexuals, from this perspective, create their transsexualism out of conflicts and defenses that hormones and surgery cannot overcome. The patients deserve the best possible treatment, and that is not "sex change," which not only does no good but also can lead to disastrous consequences. These writings often describe transsexualism as, at best, a facade that masks psychosis.

A different antilibertarianism is that of—surprisingly—the ultimate medical libertarian, Thomas Szasz (1979). Though he feels that people must have the right to determine their own treatments and that dangerous, even mortally dangerous, actions such as addiction and suicide are beyond our rights of interference, he takes the opposite position about the choice of having one's genitals removed. He finds that the term *transsexualism* is not just confusing or misapplied but rather is "like much of the modern psychiatric mendacity characteristic of our day"; "sex change" is a fake, is abusive, and is antifeminist.

c. The religious position (the Bible, canon law): "Sex change" destroys reproductive capacity and encourages homosexuality. It opposes natural law and therefore is a sin, since those who receive it do so responsibly, of their own choice, with free will.

2. Ethics: (If your positions are already set, you may not believe that there are people on the opposite side of these positions; or if you know that there are such people, you cannot believe their positions are ethical.) Which of the following groups are taking an ethical stance? Says who?

a. Surgeons who say that psychotherapy (including psychoanalysis) is not indicated, is not necessary, is useless, or is harmful.

b. Psychotherapists (including analysts) who believe that surgery is not indicated, is not necessary, is useless, or is harmful.

c. Psychiatrists who say that those who request "sex change" are either frank or disguised psychotics and that to change the body's outer form is collusion with delusion.

d. Those who say that though the surgery is "psychosurgery" in that no physical illness is present, the results are worth the risks.

e. Those who say that the procedures, hormonal and surgical, are still experimental and should be restricted to research institutions.

f. Those who say that the procedures are not experimental but are established, accepted treatment within the community's standards.

g. Those who say that the surgeons and endocrinologists are only technicians, are not the primary decision makers, are not—except for their technical skills—responsible agents throughout all stages of the treatment, whether at the stage when actively involved or not.

h. Those who say that physicians who promote themselves and their treatments in the media help patients by instructing them and the public.

3. Preoperative evaluations—to do or not to do? (You will not understand that controversy attends each of the following items unless you are informed that, for each, there actually are practicing physicians who, without feeling their work is incomplete, omit any or all of these next items.)

a. History taking back to childhood, with efforts at corroboration from families, friends, schools, and so on.

b. Extensive physical workup to determine if there are somatic contributions to the disturbed gender identity.

c. Complete routine physical examination before administering hormones or surgery.

d. Mental status examination to rule out psychosis (active or latent), severe depression, true psychopathy (vs. antisocial behavior secondary to the gender disorder), organic brain disorder, suicide risk.

e. Extended psychologic examination (by interview, psychologic tests) to determine the gender identity diagnosis.

4. Among those physicians willing to offer treatment, what criteria should be used for deciding:

a. Which patients shall be treated: primary transsexuals, secondary transsexuals, nontranssexuals, psychotics, children, family members, society?

b. Which treatments: which preoperative management, which kind of psychotherapy, which behavior modification technique, which established or experimental hormonal/surgical procedure? Exorcism?

c. If the indications for treatment are legitimately different for private practitioners than for university research centers?

d. If the indications for treatment are different for pragmatic treatment than for research (and its added costs)?

5. To do or not to do follow-up data collection—immediate and long-term—on the following issues:

a. Results effected by hormones, surgery.

b. Psychologic functioning.

    c. Social adjustment, including work.

    d. Effects on interpersonal relations.

    e. Complications, physical and psychiatric.

  6. What methodology to use in follow-up data collection.

  7. Follow-up in order to offer continuing management and treatment:

    a. Psychologic management, including psychotherapies, to improve and extend results.

    b. Treatment of complications, physical and psychiatric.

  8. Legal issues—the following subjects are still controversial in the law:

    a. Documentation of one's sex by means of birth certificate, name, driver's license, marriage license, passport.

    b. Marriage, divorce, annulment.

    c. Contracts (if one's sex is legally unclear, it is unclear who signed the contract).

    d. Estate planning (for example, if the will leaves a bequest to a son but the latter is now legally changed to a female).

    e. Community property.

    f. Medical (governmental or private) insurance and welfare payments; eligibility for rehabilitative services.

    g. Adoption and custody of children.

    h. A spouse's claim that "sex change" violated the marriage contract.

    i. Cross-dressing as evidence of intent to defraud.

    j. Cohabitation with people of one's original sex as evidence of homosexuality.

    k. Surgery as negligence, mayhem.

    l. Informed consent.

B. Theoretic issues

  1. Criteria for diagnosis.

  2. Differential diagnosis.

  3. Research techniques for discovering and measuring the strength of one's attitudes about masculinity and femininity, social adjustment, happiness and unhappiness, goodness and badness.

    a. Statistically adequate samples versus an in-depth study of a single case.

    b. Whose opinion do we use—patients', families', researchers', neutral judges', the treating physicians'?

    c. Influence of researchers' moral and scientific scruples on their conclusions.

  4. Hypotheses about etiology:

    a. Somatic (for example, prenatal hormones, X-Y antigen, diencephalic centers for same-sex erotism).

    b. Psychologic: psychodynamics, conditioning.

c. Social.
d. Reincarnation.
5. Origins of gender identity.

Let us now look more closely at a few of these items.

THE RECENT, VISIBLE CONTROVERSY

In 1979, Meyer and Reter published a paper that, coming from the most noted of all programs for "sex change," that at Johns Hopkins University, had great impact. They followed up fifty of a sample of one hundred patients who applied for surgery; of the fifty who were followed up, fifteen had had surgery. Of the remaining thirty-five, fourteen eventually had surgery and twenty-one were still interested in having it (making up, therefore, an oddly formed sample, from which conclusions should be drawn with caution). Hunt and Hampson (1980a) summarize as follows:

> The outcome criteria were based on residential change, psychiatric contact, legal involvement, Hollingshead job level, and gender appropriate sexual cohabitation choices. . . . The report did not separate male and female subjects or assess changes in interpersonal relationships, family acceptance, or psychopathology other than psychiatric contacts as outcome variables. The subjects who had had surgery showed a trend toward improvement, but the improvement was not significantly different from that in the subjects who did not submit to a gender-trial period and receive surgery. (p. 433)

To quote Meyer and Reter (1979):

> Socioeconomically, operated and unoperated patients changed little, if at all, with operated patients demonstrating no superiority in job or education. . . . five-year follow-up is certainly ample to demonstrate socioeconomic improvement and stability. The failure of the operated group to demonstrate [in that time] clear objective superiority over the unoperated is all the more striking. . . . Sex reassignment surgery confers no objective advantage in terms of social rehabilitation, although it remains subjectively satisfying to those who have rigorously pursued a trial period and who have undergone it. (pp. 1014–15)

Therefore, "sex change" was discontinued at Johns Hopkins, where, years before, enthusiasm for the treatment had been brought to public attention.

Rebuttals appear as fast as the laborious process of publication permits, focusing on the methodology of data collecting in the Johns Hopkins study. Hunt and Hampson, after reviewing earlier published follow-up studies and pointing to problems in them, examined the methodology of the Meyer and Reter work. They disagreed that the unoperated patients were really a control on the operated group, for some of the unoperated group eventually were operated, and there is reason to think that in time still more will try for "sex change." In addition, they stated:

Although it is certainly useful to know what happens to individuals who do not have surgery, it is not valid to use them as a control. An approximation of a control group might be those who are willing and able to go through the trial period but are not offered surgery because of overly masculine features. Those who are unable or unwilling to go through the trial period would appear to be so dissimilar from those who had surgery as to even raise questions about the diagnosis. (p. 433)

They then reported on their own series of seventeen operated cases:

The subjects as a whole improved in the areas of economic adjustment, interpersonal relationships, sexual adjustment, and acceptance by the family, which had the highest rate of improvement. There were no changes in the level of psychopathology, as judged by their criminal activities, drug use, and degree of psychopathology, that interfered with work or personal relationships. . . . None of the 17 transsexuals regretted the decision to have surgery. . . . In spite of the considerable pain, expense, and delay, they would all choose the same course. . . . In our study the strongest positive gains were in the areas of sexual adjustment and family acceptance, which were either not recorded or not evaluated in earlier studies. (pp. 434–36) (See also Hunt and Hampson 1980b.)

In a more recent editorial, Fleming, Steinman, and Bocknek (1980) say, in regard to the Meyer and Reter study:

The major variables used to assess adjustment before and after the surgery were arrest records, cohabitation with members of the "appropriate" or "inappropriate" sex, psychiatric records, and employment history. Perhaps the most serious failing of the study has to do with Meyer's selection and definition of these as his only major outcome variables. (p. 452)

They disagreed with the method used to rate adjustment:

For example, it assigns the same score (-1) to someone who is arrested and someone who cohabits with a non-gender-appropriate person. From this same set of cryptic values comes the assertion that being arrested and jailed (-2) is not as bad as being admitted to a psychiatric hospital (-3) or that having a job as a plumber (Hollingshead level 4) is as good ($+2$) as is being married to a member of the gender-appropriate sex ($+2$).

On what basis are these values assigned? Should we infer from a score assignment of (-1) that anyone who has any psychiatric contact is in trouble? Psychiatry has for too long proselytized that all of us can gain from seeking psychiatric guidance for Meyer to reassign a stigma to seeking such help. (pp. 452–53)

Next they attack the variable of cohabitation, finding that Meyer and Reter do not say what they mean by this term and that the positive and negative ratings are arbitrary; is "living in isolation . . . more adaptive than living with someone whatever his/her sex?" (p. 453). They proceed through other categories, raising questions as to whether Meyer and Reter's conclusions can be legitimately drawn from the uncertain methods used for collecting information and noting that Meyer and Reter's "objective factors are filled with great ambiguities and [we] wonder if reporting emotional data could have been any worse. Meyer and Reter seem to forget the value judgments that underlie their study almost as if assignment of a numerical value rids one of the findings' subjective and qualitative elements and thus raises one's findings to a level of 'pure science'" (p. 455).

Satterfield (1980) has reported on twenty-two patients operated on at the University of Minnesota. Follow-up revealed "a significant improvement in psychological functioning."

By far the most thorough review of follow-up studies I know is that by Lothstein (1982). His opinion is the same as mine:

Those who believe sex reassignment surgery is beneficial for certain patients must acknowledge the lack of hard empirical evidence supporting their views and the lack of even acceptable diagnostic criteria for selecting good candidates for sex reassignment surgery. Those who argue against sex reassignment surgery must account for the reported widespread patient satisfaction with the procedures and evidence of resulting positive life changes. (p. 417)

In spite of the many clinical research studies of transsexualism, very little is actually known about the medical-surgical and social-psychological effects of sex reassignment surgery. Many questions are left unanswered. For example, which, if any, patients derive the most benefit from sex reassignment surgery? What data support the continued use of sex reassignment surgery as a treatment regimen? What is the crucial test for determining the prescription of sex reassignment surgery? (p. 418)

In order to apply the results of . . . follow-up studies to the wider group of postsurgical transsexuals, we must determine whether those who have been studied represent an adequate cross-section of all sex reassignment surgery patients. If not, this sampling bias is a primary methodological problem inherent in all of the published studies on sex reassignment surgery. A review of those studies reveals other serious methodological problems, including a lack of universally accepted criteria for diagnosing gender dysphoria and determining suitable candidates for sex reassignment surgery; lack of an adequate control group; considerable variability among programs in gender identity clinics as well as the quality, training, and experience of clinical staff; failure to include basic data on patients' race and age; frequent use of nonoperationalized criteria for improvement, such as patients' subjective feelings of happiness; use of college grade level systems for evaluating outcome; failure to provide data on the length of time between evaluation, surgery, and follow-up; failure to use uniform diagnostic labels; failure to use standardized clinical instruments to assess patients, even within a single study; limitation of clinical investigation to gross, social-psychological variables; failure to include in-depth psychological analysis; use of hypothetical post hoc analyses to provide missing presurgical data; and use of biased evaluators interpreting outcome data. This list is by no means exhaustive. (p. 423)

In brief, the question is whether the Johns Hopkins study is methodologically too flawed to permit one to draw conclusions.

This controversy leads to broader questions—much more important, I think, than those about "sex change." How do we find what a person is thinking? How do we assign quantities to beliefs? Out of what immeasurable components are the algebraic sum responses "Yes" and "No" composed? When attitudes are as complex, as multilayered, as ambiguous, as ambivalent, as undefined as "happiness" and "unhappiness" and "goodness" and "badness" (because those are what Meyer and Reter, Hunt and Hampson, Fleming, Steinman and Bocknek, and all the rest are really trying to track down), how are we to judge a 4 rating on a scale of 1 to 10? And may not the researchers' morality be even more important in these controversies than this fuzzy business of measuring "happiness" (a.k.a. "adjustment")?[2]

How useful are questionnaires and standardized interviews for issues close to the heart? Which is better and when: data collected by a stranger or near-stranger, one's therapist, a family member? Would an answer be different at a different time of day, or a different day, a different year? In a different setting? Told to a questioner who has a different style of relating to the person questioned?

These rating methods, with their sophisticated (sophistical?) sampling techniques, their controls, their statistical constraints, work as well for fools, hacks, liars, propagandists, cultists, and innocents as they do for hard-core geniuses or even honest workers. When does a larger n not flatten all obstacles?

We are better off remembering that questionnaires and statistics in some circumstances are risky, that there is a price paid when we try to get guarded people to give fast answers to sensitive questions. Anyone who comes to know others, by treating them or by living with them, gets a different sense of their attitudes as the relationship deepens. But researchers usually do not have the time, interest, or—sometimes—ability to allow intimacy and trust to grow. The challenge is to get good data faster and yet not contaminate the results.

I have not forgotten that a case studied in depth also generates dubious data. When being my analyst, I can see good reasons, in some circumstances, for not trusting my first response—or sometimes my fifth—to my own questions. Should we not, then, for the sake of science, check the motives—not just the tables—of all researchers (from analysts to statisticians) who study values-laden attitudes? Can we suspect that our colleagues sometimes start out with the answers? Is not "sex change" a treatment easily contaminated by personal and professional beliefs, commitments, anxieties, defenses? We should not pretend that these issues cannot infiltrate each step in our work.

CONTROVERSY: VOCABULARY, DEFINITIONS, CONCEPTS

Though this is not a chapter on origins of the desire for sex change, most discussions of the treatment issues struggle, for good reason, with problems about etiology and its relation to diagnosis. For instance, if we think that the urge results primarily from a shift in diencephalic function caused by opposite-sex prenatal hormones (Dorner et al. 1975) or reversal of H-Y antigen (Eicher

---

2. Let us not fool ourselves: research on "transsexualism" or "sex change" is as soggy with morality and righteousness as a rum cake is with booze.

et al. 1979; Engel et al. 1980), the patient talking to us stirs us differently than if we think the same patient's condition is heavily influenced by intrapsychic conflict or by aberrant family dynamics.

A concept discussed earlier (chapter 2) that can carry the data related to these sorts of etiologic explanations is "core gender identity." In the vast majority of people, this is clear-cut and easily determined. However, those with sorely disordered gender identity, especially those who want "sex change," complicate, with their facades, disguises, confusions, and complex mixes of masculine and feminine elements, the task of finding that core. And if that fundament has in it a sense of being both male and female—as is found in some hermaphrodites and, in a different way, in primary transsexuals—then our evaluation requires much experience and skill.

But hermaphrodites and primary transsexuals make up only a handful of those who want "sex change." The rest—secondary transsexuals—though they have severe disturbances in masculinity and femininity, strike me as having a pretty intact sense of maleness or femaleness. Their psychopathology is in good part the result of defenses raised to protect that sense of identity. For some of these people, then, destroying their anatomic definition of self assaults their core gender identity and leads to such unhappy sequelae as psychosis, depression, or the need to be once more reassigned, this time to their original sex.

By now you are familiar with my belief that *transsexualism,* a term with a scientific, diagnostic ring, bears no such weight. At best, one might consider this usage to refer to a syndrome, but even that is not accurate, since within the request for "sex change" or the accomplishing of it are myriad behaviors and attitudes. And if a diagnosis is a label for a set of interdependent signs and symptoms (syndrome), underlying dynamics (physiologic and/or psychologic), with common etiology, then "transsexualism" falls as far short as would such designations as "cough," "abdominal pain," "greed," "stamp collecting," or "desire to be a psychiatrist." The individuals who experience any one of these states have fewer commonalities than differences.

In order to resolve uncertainties of diagnosis and the resulting controversies regarding who would benefit from which treatment, the fulsome phrase "gender dysphoria syndrome" was introduced (Fisk 1973; J. K. Meyer 1974). It represents the awareness that though "transsexualism" sounds like a well-secured diagnosis, it is not. The clinical reality, we know, is that the desire to change sex is found in many types of gender-disordered people. Those who prefer "gender dysphoria syndrome" do so because they feel that the desire for "sex change" can only be judged to be a syndrome, a collection of signs and symptoms, not the larger degree of understanding implied by diagnosis.[3]

3. However, the author of the term, when introducing it, said the syndrome is a disease (Fisk 1973).

Despite this advantage, I do not use "gender dysphoria syndrome." First, we are dealing *not* with a syndrome—that is, a complex of signs and symptoms—but rather with a desire (wish, demand) that is embedded in all sorts of different people who suffer all sorts of signs and symptoms. To talk of a gender dysphoria syndrome, then, is like talking of a suicide syndrome, or an incest syndrome, or a wanderlust syndrome.

Second, gender dysphoria syndrome is meant as a reaction against the effort at differential diagnosis. The label serves as a statement that people with disorders of masculinity and femininity make up a continuum, not a series of discrete entities, as is implied by a differential diagnosis. That is true, as it is in so much of psychiatric diagnosing[4] (especially with neuroses and character disorders), but it is also slippery. The concepts "clinical entity" and "continuum" are no more incompatible in gender disorders than in the spectrum of visible light.[5] For me, the advantage of trying to separate out clinical entities from the morass of gender disorders lies especially in our being able to search for etiologies if we do not dissolve the differences in one mix called "gender dysphoria syndrome." By separating out, say, primary from secondary transsexualism and the transvestite route to secondary transsexualism from the homosexual route, we *can* find clusters that differ from one another clinically and in certain etiologic factors.

In brief, then, "gender dysphoria syndrome" ends up with most of the disadvantages that "transsexualism" has when the latter term is used by the general public and the medical profession at large. Both terms say too little because they cover too much. Nonetheless, I find "gender dysphoria syndrome" better than the pseudodiagnosis "transsexualism" in that the wording indicates that it is not masquerading as a diagnosis and therefore cannot contribute to the abuses promoted by the pseudodiagnosis.[6]

So much for this vocabulary exercise on the word *transsexualism*. Let us now take up a few more terms that, without discussion, might leave us confused: *sex change, sex transformation, sex reassignment.*

Though there can be sex reassignment, there cannot yet be—I believe—sex change or sex transformation. Sex reassignment is a social phenomenon to be accomplished by legal means and by convincing others to accept one's changed role (new name, clothes, job, voice, and so on). In brief, the term

---

4. "In DSM-III there is no assumption that each mental disorder is a discrete entity with sharp boundaries (discontinuity) between it and other mental disorders" (*Diagnostic and Statistical Manual of Mental Disorders,* 3d ed. [Washington, D.C: American Psychiatric Association, 1980], p. 6).

5. The clinical situation, I know, is not quite as simple as the metaphor suggests, but I let the metaphor stand rather than inflict on the reader the lengthy description of dozens of cases with which I could support the argument.

6. The most glaring of these abuses is perpetrated by the patient who, wanting to change sex, gives his desire the diagnostic label and, thereby legitimized, expects the treatment to follow. By awarding himself a diagnosis, he converts an impulse into a disease.

does not imply that one has changed sex, for that would require chromosomal and anatomic reversal, but only that an assignment—and therefore a role—has changed. Guppies can change sex; humans cannot. Cosmetic surgery and manipulating secondary sex characteristics with hormones or electrolysis create biologic facsimiles only (Kubie and Mackie 1968).

These meanings are not arbitrary rulings but, rather, touch on fundamental treatment issues. For instance, those who state that sex is truly changed do so in order to legitimize the treatment and thereby make it more available. On the other hand, those transsexuals—primary or secondary—whom I have followed for years all know it is impossible to change sex by ingesting hormones and altering the appearance of genitals; in saying this, they are communicating the despair that came from their knowledge. You must understand that they believe that "sex change," as helpful as it may have been, could not give them what they most wanted: a true change of their sex (Stoller 1975a, chap. 20).

WHO DECIDES WHEN "SEX CHANGE" IS INDICATED?

Like any other medical treatment, "sex change" should have reliably established indications so that patients are not harmed and are also helped. That would seem an absurd statement for this day and age, it being so obvious. And yet, though the treatment has been visible, desired, and increasingly accepted since 1953, the arguments about its suitability persist, intensified. Here is a treatment situation in which powerful hormones are used without restriction; they not only change body form and destroy reproductive capacity but have unknown effects in each sex with prolonged use. Surgical procedures are also easily dispensed (not freely—they are very expensive), though they destroy reproduction and, being of significant technical difficulty, inherently have operative and anaesthetic morbidity, if not mortality.

And all this for unclear indications, since the criteria for suitability have never been established. In the 1950s, when I first made contact with such patients, there seemed no great problem in this regard; if the surgeons felt that someone was suitable, they operated, as often as not independent of psychiatric evaluation. In the 1960s I became increasingly upset about this medical free-wheeling and the fact that no one heavily involved in working with these patients expressed concern. (There were, of course, those with little direct experience who lectured us on the origins, dynamics, and clinical picture, and on the indications for and morality of treatment—for example, Ostow 1953; Socarides 1960; Volkan 1979; Kubie and Mackie 1968). By the 1970s, no follow-ups had appeared other than a few sketchy and anecdotal reviews or meager, uncontrolled series, reports that would be unacceptable elsewhere in medicine. Most of all, there was still no debate among those treating the patients about the wisdom of the procedures. (I tried to get these experts' attention [Stoller 1969, 1973b, 1978] but have seen no published response.

Even Kubie and Mackie's tongue-lashing, filled with good sense, passion, and prejudice, created no stir, perhaps because they were not working with transsexuals.) Had I not observed this disreputable business, it would surely seem bizarre now.

What was going on? Let me, in answering, turn to (on) the groups responsible. In order of increasing blame, they are the public, the patients, the uninvolved medical community, the nonpsychiatric physicians who are applying their treatments, the media, and finally the mental health professionals, with psychologists and psychiatrists in first place.

The public. The public—in this case meaning just about everyone—has always been intrigued by this primally disquieting subject. Here sits an enthusiastic audience for the drama of sex change.

The patients. Once upon a time, there were, of course, no transsexuals. We had not invented the disorder or the solution, and so there was no problem. I know of only a handful of reports before our present era on males or females with so powerful a transsexual wish that they reassigned themselves to the opposite sex (Bullough 1975); undoubtedly there were many more, silent, hopeless. Less implacably driven people—homosexual, transvestic, or whatever—lived more or less humbly with whatever compromises they could manage. But now there seems a cure for this unhappiness, and with the propaganda published in and out of medical circles, anyone with a troubled gender identity hopes to be made whole quickly and efficiently. Encouraged by the lack of criteria for diagnosis or indications for treatment, and not told otherwise by the experts, these people diagnose themselves as transsexuals and, encouraged by what they have read and heard, recommend themselves for hormones and surgery. Their only task, they believe, is to force wide the gates to the treatment to which they feel entitled.

The uninvolved medical profession. The two major medical aspects of "sex change"—hormones and surgery—are powerful manipulations of anatomy and physiology, with short-term consequences that have never been studied by the standards accepted elsewhere in medicine and with unknown long-term consequences. Yet the physicians not personally involved in the treatment have raised no questions, shown no concern in their professional organizations, literature, or schools. There must be few other circumstances in the history of modern medicine comparable to this.

Nonpsychiatric physicians involved in treatment. Endocrinologists, surgeons, and others—specialists or not—who would create change of sex divest themselves of responsibility for their treatments (beyond the immediate responsibilities that always come with, say, giving injections, anaesthesia, or surgery). They note that they are only the technical arm—the machinery, as it were—and that the decision for them to act is made by the psychiatrist. (Let us ignore here the individuals or jurisdictions where no demand is made for psychiatric approval or the situation we know sometimes occurs: psychiatrists who rubber stamp their approvals.) The contribution of this group to the present mess—controversy is too nice a word—is their abdication of good sense when they are beyond the reach of their prescription pads or operating rooms. Uncharacteristically content to be blind servants, admitting lack of interest in the psychiatric aspects of this issue, and uninterested in reporting on immediate and long-term complications, they have failed our profession and society at large. But the blame is not mainly theirs.

The media. Certain journalists, TV gossips, moviemakers. and publishers have linked the patients' and the doctors' exhibitionism to the public's pleasure in freak shows in a venture profitable to all the participants. In this trade, where everyone is satisfied for a price, the media are the pushers.

Mental health professionals. Here are found those most responsible for this shameful episode in the history of medical practice. These people, not really surprisingly, have been as susceptible to the primeval desires and anxieties at the bottom of the interest in "sex change" as everyone else. And they have been happy to feed the curiosity of the less informed. Poor research, poor practice, poor data, and poor ideas have gone hand in hand with high visibility in pandering to and feeding the misperceptions of public and patients.

It need not have been this way had the medical profession acted with integrity. It is obvious that "sex change" is an exciting subject, and no one is surprised that it has been popular. But our profession could have short-circuited the reactions that led to today's obvious controversies. The controversies were there from the start. It is medicine's fault that they were ignored all these years. Instead, we have done poorly by the public, our patients, and ourselves. We failed in two ways. First, we should have insisted that the treatment be kept experimental, in that way restricting its use and development to responsible investigators. Better quality work could have been done; we know from the good examples set by several university clinics. Second, had this cautious approach been valued, the public and patients could have been educated to know that these treatments were not freely available, were uncertain in their effects, had their physical and emotional dangers—in other words, were controversial from the start.

Who can blame the patients for their high hopes before "sex change"? They are deeply troubled people. When social disgrace is added to intrapsychically induced conflict, it takes no great intuition to sense these patients' suffering and how happy they are on learning that there is supposedly a cure for their suffering. If they can wrap all their troubles into one bundle called transsexualism, then happiness forevermore awaits them after a morning in the operating room.

From public, to patients, to medicine at large, to the endocrinologists and surgeons, to the media, everyone acted mostly from self-interest, with minimal ethical friction. But what about the mental health professionals—psychologists, social workers, and especially psychiatrists?

On the other hand, there are those—physicians and others—who feel that hormones and surgery should never be used. How well have these advisers performed? From where came their convictions?

Their argument is based on the sensible position that the surest treatment is that which aims to modify causes of disorder. The desire to change sex originates, they feel, in profound conflicts and is the manifestation of defensive maneuvers invented to ease the pain of these conflicts. Therefore, treatment should consist first in discovering the conflicts and their dynamics and, those insights captured, in freeing the patient to find better solutions. From this point of view, to condone the use of hormones and surgery and to encourage the patient to live as if a member of the opposite sex are to allow the patient to remain maximally and permanently ill. Just as you would not, as a matter of treatment, agree with a grandiose paranoid that he really is Napoleon, so you should not agree with the patient who insists that he or she is in the wrong body. (That a patient even makes such a claim is, in this argument, prima facie evidence of delusion; and delusion is psychosis; and psychosis is to be rooted out.)

Even if we grant that this reasoning is correct (and I do not believe it always is), we are left with an empirical question: why are there no reports of the successful psychoanalysis of a patient who wanted ''sex change''? Why are there not even any reports that reveal, with data gathered from an analysis, the dynamics—not to say the causes—of this desire for ''sex change''? What is the purpose of demanding that analysis—a treatment unproven for profound gender disorder, terribly complex, and expensive—be the only one allowed?

We should not, however, confuse this position with the one saying that, with a careful psychiatric evaluation and psychotherapy, many of those seeking sex change could discover that what they want is not provided by hormones and surgery. Lothstein and Levine (1981) have given us the best review there is of the literature on the problems and uses of psychotherapy in helping patients with strong transsexual urges. Beyond that, Lothstein, in a series of papers (1977a, 1977b, 1978, 1979a, 1979b, 1979c, 1980), has written more and with more thought than anyone else on the indications for and types of psychotherapy most suited for particular clinical issues. His work confirms the impression a few of us had expressed: many patients who insist they need ''sex change'' are really far from sure, even including some who have passed successfully as members of the opposite sex. Though gender disorder rarely remits with psychotherapy, some patients find themselves and in doing so become aware that ''sex change'' will not suit their gender identity.

I still do not know to what extent hormones and surgery are worth using in those patients who, shortly after or years after treatment, say they are glad to have undergone "sex change" even though they know they could not truly change their sex. For me, none of the reports, before or since that of Meyer and Reter, settles the issue. Stubbornly, I am still more impressed by the few patients I have followed for years than by the larger numbers of patients colleagues report on by means of standardized ratings.[7] None of those I have followed feels that he has used his life well, though all are happy that they had a "sex change" and all say they prefer their present problems and miseries to what existed before treatment (Stoller 1975a). But we physicians cannot forget that the cost of this equivocal happiness may be high: in dollars, medical and surgical complications, professionals' time, and low yield to society at large. And because we have done such an abysmal job of follow-up, we cannot measure the size of that cost or the counterbalancing value of patients' relief in living in their new sex. We can only give our private, morality-laden, ethics-laden opinions.

Are these controversies due to investigators' having different data? Yes. Different methods of collecting data? Yes. Different interpretations of the same or comparable data? Yes. When data depend on follow-ups, are positions weakened because patients are flagrantly unreliable? Yes. But these factors do not fully explain the controversies. The reasons are more human, more awful. Though, as you have seen, I have not presented a compelling argument—that would require clean and adequate amounts of data—I believe that almost all those involved in research on "sex change," no matter which sides of which controversies they take, have reported data that are suspect and conclusions that are not yet supported by facts: methodology and a rhetoric of objectivity are molded to fit the conclusions sought. (Is that not true for most hot controversies?)

This happened, I think, because, beneath the visible controversies on research and treatment are deep old moral issues. Hook us up to a plethysmograph and watch the dials spin when we hear: "homosexual," "bisexual," "heterosexual," "fetishist," "promiscuity," "masturbation," "sexual intercourse," "penis," "vagina," "breasts," even "hair." Until we acknowledge the moral issues researchers on sex carry to their laboratories and clinics, it will be mighty hard to trust the data. But is that not the case in much of the psychiatrist's body of knowledge, far beyond these problems of sexuality? Are we not all aware of the unending risk that private morality corrupts public objectivity? Here are items from our working vocabulary, a language shot through with moral judgments: "ego strengths," "psychopathy," "perversion," "latent psychosis," "narcissism," "masochism," "compulsion," "alcoholism," "reaction formation," "identification with the aggressor," "primitive," "schizoid," "poor judgment," "infantile," "anal erotic," "counterphobic," "resistance," "denial,"

---

7. This is not to say that I do not respect a more scientific methodology. I mean only that, so far, the data being fed into the computer are far less reliable than the machine's capacity to calculate.

"negative transference," "low frustration tolerance," "therapeutic alliance," "hysterical," "passive," "aggressive," "neurotic." How about even "doctor" or "patient"? Ours is a "scientific" lexicon that is easily misused in order to hide a therapist's private and shamefaced evaluation of a patient. (We hardly dare say—even to ourselves—"brave" or "cowardly," "selfish" or "generous," "cooperative" or "manipulative," "warm" or "cold," "secretive" or "open," "worthwhile" or "a scoundrel," "dirty" or "clean," "moral" or "immoral," "cruel" or "kind," "good" or "bad.") Everyone knows all this.

We like some patients and dislike others (and often like and dislike the same patient) and translate those convictions, sometimes with good cause, into "treatable" or "untreatable," "good prognosis" or "guarded." Patients who display some aspect of our ego ideal, such as courage, honesty, capacity to love, will be forgiven a lot of pathology; those who incite us must bear our wrath, though we may be too well-mannered, insensitive, or unconscious to express it openly. Morality may be the stiffest countertransference of all.

COMPLICATIONS

What goes wrong in "sex change" treatments? No more sickening remark could be made in this age of modern medicine than that, for the mishaps on the following list, there are no statistics about frequency, severity, or mortality: the usual morbidities and mortalities associated with anaesthesia and extensive surgery (for example, hemorrhage, anuria, cardiac arrest, embolus), perforation of viscera, failure of the grafted phallus to take in females, scarring of the artificial vagina in males with loss of some or all patency, chronic cystitis, strange-looking genitals, abnormal urethra with resulting abnormal urinary stream, sloughing of skin grafts, chronic infections (of vaginas or postmastectomy), paranoid psychosis, psychotic depression, chronic though non-psychotic depression, suicide, hopelessness, regret at the "sex change," lawsuits.

What are the long-term effects, if any, of chronic opposite-sex hormone intake? Does cancer ever result? How many female patients now have normally functioning male genitals? How many males have received a normal-looking vulva or a vagina that retained its full size without scarring down? How many patients need further surgery to correct the effects of complications? I know of no acceptable report on complications, as if they were beneath the dignity of the treating physicians to study, even in order to report—if it were true—that they are insignificant.

CONCLUSIONS

After scattering about in this chapter my opinions and biases, implications and pronouncements, I should now draw them together.

1. Little good has come from the social experiment of "sex change." We do not know how many patients have severe gender problems; how many have been treated; how many were helped and in what ways; how many are less well off and in what ways; what the complications are and how many patients suffer them; what the names and forms of the disorders are that bring patients for treatment; what the etiologies, dynamics, and clinical manifestations of these conditions are; which treatments are the best suited for which patients; what research should be done and how it should be carried out; what criteria we can use to judge reports written on the subject.

I wonder, as I write: can the situation really be this bad? Without question, colleagues who have been more enthusiastic are as aware of the ethical issues and feel themselves to be as committed to ethical practice as those of us who are worried. There seem to have been no disastrous consequences for most patients. Most of the participants—patients and doctors—were responsible, informed, and willing partners, and most are more comfortable than less with the results. Perhaps we have been witness to nothing worse than a freak phenomenon, a lunatic fad that may now be burning itself out. It is possible that gender identity clinics—what a euphemism!—will be closing down soon, the Pygmalions drifting off, the patients giving up their hope of the miraculous cure. If so, we shall probably be left with nothing in our armamentarium more glamorous than those difficult, uncertain, and all too modest techniques known as "management" and "psychotherapy," fortified, perhaps, by new developments in diagnosing and treating children and by effective and humane behavior modification techniques.

2. I was, I believe, the first of those who had worked in depth with "sex change" patients not to share the enthusiasm that had developed by the late 1960s in regard to using hormones and surgery for treatment. My position now is what it was then: most people requesting the change will not benefit much from it. They are better served by careful evaluation, psychotherapy, and/or behavior therapy. On the other hand, the years have not yet revealed treatments that, for a small number of patients, do as well as does "sex change." My impression is still that the most feminine of males and most masculine of females do better with "sex change" than without (Stoller 1968a). Were surgery no longer available, primary transsexuals would be trapped, but most secondary transsexuals—by far the larger group seeking "sex change"— would be at least no worse off, free to find their identities and not literally cut off from themeselves.

3. But impressions are not worth much if not augmented by strong data. In these years, I have also complained (and—let me add in bleak righteousness— with few others joining in) that we did not have enough data to judge competently which patients would do better with which treatment. Time has shown not only that we still lack these data but that reliable methods for collecting the information have not yet been applied. No wonder we are not convinced when

colleagues, even on the basis of formal research, conclude pro or con about any aspect of "sex change."

4. Partly because of these problems of doing follow-up, but for other reasons still unclear, new treatment techniques are introduced, enthusiastically reported, but then do not take hold—for example, behavior modification for adults (Barlow et al. 1973) and children (Rekers 1977) and psychotherapy for children (Greenson 1966).

5. My suggestion, starting years ago, that hormones and surgery be considered experimental and provided only in university research settings has since been endorsed by one or two colleagues but almost never implemented (except in Australia). Everyone has paid a price for that.

6. There has been some interest (for example, Fisk 1973) in my idea that a differential diagnosis of severe gender disorders be developed to improve both our clinical work and our attempts to understand better the nature of gender identity. That effort, however, is blurred when we go for the wastebasket terms *transsexualism* or *gender dysphoria syndrome*.

7. For all the scientific frosting in publications on "sex change" (updating techniques of hormonal and surgical treatments, collecting information on social variables, concern about sampling methods, statistical examination of pre- and posttreatment results), I do not find my colleagues' data to be more reliable than my impressionistic ones. In fact, the failure to study patients in depth by means of years-long contact (as probably can be done only in an extended psychotherapy) often leaves me quite uncertain about the real nature of the clinical statements compacted into the tables of numbers that reinforce most studies.

8. Years ago I felt that whatever we did regarding "sex change" was wrong but that we might, with care, be able to do less wrong. I fear that the same is still true today; we have not moved the subject very far. After almost thirty years, the case for "sex change" is still unproven: both the treatments and the patients (of both sexes) have been, at most, near misses.

10
TWO FEMINIZED MALE AMERICAN INDIANS

For years reports have appeared, especially from anthropologists, on cultures that permit males to choose or be chosen to live in women's roles (see Green 1969, pp. 13–22; Forgey 1975). Among the best known are the *berdache,* who represented the "institutionalized homosexuality" of American Plains Indians, or the *alyha,* who were Mohave. (To save words, *berdache* will be the generic used here.) While reading of these people, I wondered what they would look like if seen through the eyes of one in our culture who has observed transsexuals, transvestites, homosexuals, and other males with cross-gender behavior. These reports present data one cannot judge in regard to questions I like to raise when studying patients with gender disorders.

This chapter is a report on two Indian males I interviewed, who wished to change sex. What follows is rudimentary; a member of a racial minority, poor, and deviant in his own culture, may not give the most crisp, direct, and trustworthy story to a stranger who is a white university doctor. However, this report may alert others to find out whether these impressions can be confirmed.

CASE 1

The patient was seen alone, and when I had used up that situation, his mother was interviewed.

The patient is in his thirties, a full-blooded Indian, single, currently living on the reservation where he was born the third of six siblings. His tribe is geographically and linguistically close to the Mohave, the tribe best studied— by Devereux (1937)—for cross-gender behavior. His father was over sixty at the time of his birth, his mother in her thirties. Both living, they are full-blooded members of this tribe, which has inhabited the same area for unknown generations.

When born, the patient was an anatomically normal-appearing male; there was no question to which sex he was to be assigned and there were no equivocal attitudes about the assignment for the first two years. (Subsequent development to the present is reported to reveal no biologic intersexual problems; I did not do a physical examination or any laboratory studies.)

He says, and his mother confirms, that around age two, as occasionally happens in this tribe, he was first given his definitive name. Up to then, he did not have a precise Indian or Anglo designation, but at that point it was considered the right of an uncle of the mother to name the child. The rule was for his uncle to make a choice he felt suited the appearance (behavior or personality, I am not sure quite how this is done) of the little boy. The chosen name was unambiguously a girl's. The patient's mother says precisely—and unvaryingly in response to repeated reworded questions—that she did not see any femininity in the child up to this time, nor did her husband or other members of the tribe.

The patient's memory starts several years later but is unbroken to the present as indicating no interest in being a male, in taking over aspects of males' roles, or in daydreaming of pleasurable masculine experiences. He says that he played spontaneously only with girls and in games only girls played, and that though, as he grew older—especially on being sent to Indian school—he was coerced to participate with boys in boys' games, he did this unwillingly and without skill.

Since his first several years of life, during which time his mother says that he was indistinguishable from other boys (that is, she had no suspicion he would become unmanly), he has had no episodes of masculine behavior and has never taken on a short-lived or long-term masculine role. His mother says that neither she nor anyone else saw or reported unusual gender behavior in him until around nine or ten, at which time she noted his dislike for boys' games and his preference for being with girls. Her report is vague at this point in the questioning; the years given varied a bit each time I asked, but she answered clearly that in early childhood no gender disorder was apparent.

The patient says that he feels he was interested in girls' roles as early as age five or six, the time of his first memories. On going to Indian school, around seven or eight, he found that older masculine boys were attracted to him and to several other boys like himself from a related but different tribe. Before puberty, he was participating in homosexual experiences. He has always taken what he told himself was the feminine role and would get erections and ejaculate, enjoying the erotic sensations. It was, however, his rule, as is true with primary transsexuals I have known, that his penis not be touched (Devereux 1937, p. 511). He denies erotic experience with any female. He denies ever being sexually excited by women's clothes. He has recently been going exclusively with a man; they wish to marry if he gets a "sex change." He has not heard of a tribal tradition in which certain males are either chosen or permitted to choose to live as females. He does not know of anyone but himself who ever wished this, though there is a boy of eight or nine who he feels seems like himself. However, he has known effeminate males from other tribes since he first went to school.

Both the man and his mother describe his comfortable acceptance in the tribe; he has never been humiliated by others, nor have restrictions been placed on any of his behaviors that might indicate womanliness. In fact, he is now the best basket weaver and dressmaker in the tribe, creating the finest and most accurately traditional products. When museums want examples of the tribe's works in these crafts, they come to him. He was taught these skills by his mother and is accepted by everyone as more adept than any of the women.[1] Both he and his mother say there is no tribal theory, tradition, or myth that covers his gender impulses or status.

To me, his appearance is neuter, not feminine, effeminate, or masculine. He is tall and thin, with long, straight, black hair, which he says is no longer than that of the men in the tribe but which flows freely over his shoulders, the custom only of the women. He is dressed in a purple blouse, black and white checked pants (as today could be seen in the Southwest on men or women, Indian or not), and leather sandals; several turquoise and silver rings adorn his fingers. His eyes are lightly made up with a darkening substance. If he produced in others the impression he did in me, when he passes in the street they will not know if they are looking at a man or a woman, unlike the very feminine males I think of as primary transsexuals, who will look unremarkably like women.

His voice is artificially raised, about an octave, and does not have the typical sultry, husky, transsexual sound but rather is like that of a man imitating a woman's voice. He has a slight lisp, but not the caricatured vocalizing one may hear in effeminate homosexuals. He walks and sits in an erect and firm manner that reveals no sense of masculinity or femininity. As he talks, he gestures with his hands in such a way that one feels him consciously trying to create an effect of gracefulness. However, the gracefulness does not come from within but rather seems veneered onto a body too large, muscular, bony, and strong. The most feminine movement he made was a gentle giggle whereat he covered his mouth with his fingertips when expressing mild embarrassment or coyness.

---

1. "Many berdaches achieved considerable renown for their skill in women's arts and, in fact, excelled the women in these tasks. It would appear, therefore, that many men who adopted the berdache role—thereby abandoning male pursuits—did not simultaneously abandon the male goal involving the intense desire for social prestige. Rather, the means by which prestige might be attained were simply re-channeled to the pursuits of women. Although the Indians themselves explained the berdache's expertise in the female arts as due to 'supernatural assistance,' it is suggested here that their skill was due to an intense motivation to gain prestige in competition. The berdache role, therefore, fulfilled the intended and recognized personal (integrative) function of providing the individual with the chance to obtain prestige" (Forgey 1975, p. 10).

This struck me as a ritualized movement, which I had before seen only in Japanese women expressing shyness. I later read (Devereux 1937) that male homosexual Mohave Indians do this.

The patient was lively, alert, and continuously in good contact with me. I could sense his affects, which were appropriate, not histrionic, not guarded, and played freely within him and on out into communication with me. The sustaining mood throughout the interview was good humor, jokes, and teasing to test me. But, when expressing desire for sex change, his humorousness moved to directness and concern. He was not uncomfortable talking of his sexuality, neither about erotic behavior nor about issues of masculinity and femininity. There were no signs of psychosis or borderline state. There were no grossly neurotic behaviors, nor was there the impression of a person afflicted with chronic anxiety, depression, or their transformations.

An important clue for me in judging gender identity is the masculine or feminine pronoun I find myself using with a person. Regardless of anatomic state, I can unthinkingly say "she" only when a person behaves within the range of women I have known, and the same with "he" and men. But at times one sees those for whom neither masculine nor feminine pronouns are quite correct and others who allege that their gender identity is of one sort but the pronouns in my mouth belie that claim. This patient falls in the latter range; I could not unthinkingly say "she," and while "he" gives me pause it is the easier pronoun to use.

Inquiry to the USPHS Physicians' Assistant who lives on the reservation brought the following information:

Concerning the customs and traditions of the X tribe, on questioning some of the older members of the Tribe and the health workers here in the clinic, they do not seem to be aware of any hard and fast custom of waiting two years to name a child. Although some of the older members did state that some families waited till the children were walking to give them a name, I could find no true basis for this except for the fact that children are named much later and more casually than one would find in a caucasian community.

In reference to the writings of Devereux on the Alyha, I can only state that within the Tribe here, D seems to be accepted without ridicule, and it would seem that most of the local populace have much the same feeling toward D as you registered at your interview, that of a neuter. As far as I can find, there is no beau as such among the local men although many of the younger men accuse each other of being his/her fellow. There appears to be a good amount of acceptance among the women at social gatherings.

CASE 2

This second case is also that of an apparently anatomically normal male who wished to change sex in order to live permanently as a woman. (Again, I did no physical examination or laboratory tests.) The patient, more feminine in demeanor than the first, is a midwestern Indian male of thirty. He is, however,

Indian in a different way from the first. Though born on a reservation, living on or at its border until an adult, categorized by outer society as Indian, educated at Indian schools, and accepting himself as Indian, his heredity is only half Indian. His group is a subtribe, the members of which descend from the marriage of a French settler and an Indian woman over a century ago. They all consider themselves half Indian and half white as a result of this union, and since all claim this background, they consider themselves homogeneous. One can say, therefore, that their identity is Indian but includes the sense of having a generations-old half-white inheritance.

Neither the patient nor his mother or sister, who also were interviewed (each alone), is aware of a tribal tradition that institutionalizes cross-gender behavior.

The patient is a twin, considered by everyone to be identical to his brother (no blood typing was done to confirm this). No one could tell the two apart throughout childhood and adolescence if they were nude and in repose. When dressed or moving, however, the signals of masculinity in the one and femininity in the other easily identified each. They were the ninth and tenth children of a series of fourteen. The family divides itself into two, the first eight forming one unit, the last six another, with each group feeling distinctly different from the other and the members of each feeling filial impulses only within their own group. No siblings are reported to have gender disorders. All fourteen had the same mother and father, though the parents were divorced when the patient was five or six years old. The sister interviewed is the next sibling born after the twins; she is a year younger.

The patient was the second born of the twins and at birth was a bit smaller in size. Mother says:

When he was born, B [patient] had a little stomach trouble, more than the other twin, and I brought him to the doctor because I was so worried. They all said that with twins, one isn't as strong as the other and you lose one. Then I was worried about him, and I did bring him to the doctor. And he said he had a lot of gas in the stomach, and that was all. But he was a little slower than the other, not in mind but with walking and eating. He took more time to eat than the other one. In fact we still laugh about that. We say that the other twin, he would take his bottle and finish it real quick. The first thing you know I would turn around and A [the older] would get done with his eating and crawl over and take his brother's bottle. And A walked sooner than B. A was always more like what I would say, all boy. He liked boys. And this one, B, didn't like to ride. We tried to make him ride. And the other one was just determined to ride if the horse didn't want to go.

Both, as they grew, were healthy and strong; the patient, though unmasculine, when provoked could fight as vigorously and angrily as his masculine twin.[2] But this was rare and the only exception reported to an otherwise

2. Devereux (1937) reports an Indian saying, "If you tease an Alyha, who has the strength of a man, he will run after you and beat you up" (p. 510). One does not hear that of primary transsexuals.

consistently quiet, gentle manner that reflected the patient's sense of being feminine.

He says this feeling goes back as far as he can remember, and his sister confirms it to the beginnings of her memory (age three to four). Their mother, however, does not recall that he was unusual in this regard until perhaps age nine. Though vague about details relating to his femininity, she answers direct questions regarding behavior in a way that reveals that she saw differences but did not read them as being either masculine or feminine. Example: Sister says, ''When we were little, Mother would say, 'Why don't you go out and play with the other kids? Why can't you be more like your brother? Why don't you go and play baseball or ride the horses? [This latter was especially a marker of proper masculinity.] Don't cry so much.' ''

B's earliest memories are of playing with this younger sister; she corroborates the details of his story. They each say that by the time the second ''family'' was created, their mother was too occupied to spend much time with them, and since the marital relationship was deteriorating and in its last years, she often left the children alone. Their father, a quiet, less forceful person than their mother, was present in the household, though working during the day. He was not absent physically, but, as the years passed, he became increasingly alcoholic and so, even when home, was often not emotionally available.

Neither sister nor patient recalls a time before they were constantly together, playing games. Left alone for much of the day by their older siblings and their parents, they amused themselves playing with dolls and in unending versions of ''house.'' Both dressed in girls' clothes; a game was considered begun only when he put on his sister's clothes. This was never done for reasons of sexual excitement; he has never become aroused by clothes. Invariably, the two took women's roles, using the other twin and other available boys for the male roles. None of the participating children ever questioned this; the patient's dressing in girls' clothes was not part of an experience aimed at humiliating him, and he never felt humiliated. Contrast this with the frequent history fetishistic cross-dressers give of having been put into girls' clothes the first time for punishment or humiliation. Brother and sister both say that this play went on for hours every day for years and was their happiest time. I can get no evidence that these games were prompted by hostility on the sister's part. Rather, both found this play most congenial, and more than that, it prevented them from suffering the loneliness that would have otherwise occurred in a family in which the older siblings were not around and the father and mother were rarely home.

Though these activities were disrupted when the twins were sent off to school at age five or six, this un-self-conscious, nonerotic play, as if both were girls, began again whenever the patient and his sister rejoined each other; it continued into adolescence. In time, it expanded to include other girls, and when the games were those in which boys were excluded the patient was still included. So he and his sister, from earliest childhood to the present, have shared a comfortable, nonhostile, nontraumatic, nonconflictual interest in feminine matters, wherein the patient was accepted as his sister's feminine companion. In this Indian subculture, there apparently is no body of role behavior aimed at humiliating boys who are feminine or men who prefer men sexually. And so this boy's peers were not trained to make fun of him and did not use him as a scapegoat. Instead, they accepted him as a boy who felt like a girl. When he went away to Indian school, he still was not pressured to hate his feminine behavior.

In none of this was there even a suggestion that he was not a male; his sex assignment was unequivocal and maintained unquestioned throughout his life. He never felt that he was female, only that he was comfortable in the role of a girl. Since this feeling has persisted to the present, he would like his sex changed so that his body will conform to the only role in which he is comfortable.[3]

As with the first case, I found no evidence of neurotic or psychotic symptomatology. The patient was direct and in good contact at all times: I felt that I was talking to a real person, not to someone who was hidden behind a defensive character structure or floating beyond my reach, as one may experience with schizoid people.

He was soft, gentle—feminine—without mimicry; had he been dressed as a woman, the comfortable pronoun would have been "she." He chose not to appear thus (though until recently he lived intermittently as a woman for a few years) because, he said, he wanted to wait until he could do so legitimately.

DISCUSSION

Considering that the data are thin, I shall add only a few comments.

First, these subjects point up observations long since noted on the deterioration in American Indians of techniques for ritualizing cross-gender behavior. No longer is a place provided for the role—more, the identity—of a male-woman, the dimensions of which are fixed by customs, rules, tradeoffs, or responsibilities. The tribes have forgotten. Instead, this role appears only as a ghost. At least this is all that remains in Case 1, who is considered nothing more than a harmless amusement, allowed to sit around in women's clothes, to weave, and to sleep with men. No one thinks that he is under the influence of the spirits; he brings no magic, nor is he its recipient. He is fully secularized, thought of without drama as a gay man who wants to act like a woman. Case 2 simply dropped out of his tribe in his late teens, but before doing so he was not

3. Green and I (1971) have reported earlier on two sets of identical twins discrepant for gender behavior, where the families responded differentially to the twins and may have encouraged cross-gender behavior in only one of the children. See also Green (1985).

harassed for being feminine; no one seems to have felt threatened. Though the tribes have lost the ritual that made cross-gender behavior not only meaningful but also useful, they do not yet fill the gap, as we do, with shaming techniques; the Anglo culture seems to need these techniques for protection.

The deterioration of the berdache role is hardly news. Devereux reported it in 1937; in 1900 it was already apparent to Stevenson:

There have been but five such persons in Zuni since the writer's acquaintance with these people; and until about ten years ago there had been but two. (p. 37)

Homosexuality among the Mohave has been reported by the earliest travelers in that region. Although there is little or no objection to homosexuality among the Mohave at present there is no avowed homosexual living on the reservation. . . . Nevertheless gossip will have it that certain persons indulge in secret homosexuality. (p. 498)

It may not be unnecessary to recall here that male homosexuals were allowed among many American Indian tribes to assume officially the status of women. Data are very incomplete however, and seldom include actual case histories. (p. 520)

Devereux not only was unable to find any such people during his study of the Mohave, but in reporting two case histories, could collect data only from an informant who had known these people years before.

Opler (1967) writes:

The point about these societies and other nonliterate hunting and gathering societies is that homosexuality is generally rare and, in some instances, virtually nonexistent. In the first tribes this author ever studied under field conditions, the Mescalero and Chiricahua Apache, this rarity stands in marked contrast to modern urban American or English culture. The standard work on Chiricahua, *An Apache Life-Way,* by Morris E. Opler, notes that homosexuality is forbidden among them and considered to be a form of witchcraft. Informants had heard about boys, but not adult men, experimenting homosexually. One berdache, or transvestite, who engaged in women's pursuits (but apparently not in homosexuality) was reported to have died before 1880. A few Lesbians dated back to days of detention at Fort Sill in Oklahoma. Some women had masculine interests. But other than these scattered and historical instances, in which, incidentally, no organic findings were available, homosexuality was notable for its rarity. Later, in fieldwork among Ute Indians of Colorado, this author's check on such topics yielded amusement, disbelief, and counter-questioning on American urban culture.

The reactions of nonliterate peoples, on the simplistic hunting and gathering levels of economic development, help to answer the question whether rates of homosexual behavior vary among different societies. Driver, in *Indians of North America,* discusses typical examples of Plains Indian berdaches, or male transvestites. He notes that relations with women were symbols of male prestige in these cultures and that the general social dominance of men over women was probably stronger here than in any area north of Mexico, except the Northwest Coast. In this setting, some men with strong aversions to the ultra-masculine role donned women's clothing, did women's work, and sometimes (apparently a minority) lived homosexually in actual fact.

Writers on South American Indians offer equally sparse examples. Steward and Faron, in *Native Peoples of South America,* mention examples only for the Calamari, among whom there was a special class of male inverts, as well as one of women prostitutes, who went from village to village selling sexual services, and for the Nata townsmen, among whom there was a class of homosexual male slaves who did women's work. (pp. 252–53)

The second point needs only brief comment. How might the berdache be related to gender patients seen nowadays in Anglo environments? And, of special interest to me, are there early-life, interpersonal—especially intra-familial—influences that contribute to the behavior? If one remembers the data's limitations, a few remarks are possible.

The childhood influences, different in these two cases, sound nonetheless like some we have heard of before. On the one hand the fathers were too removed from their families to serve as models for masculinity, to interfere with feminizing influences emanating from others, or to insist on influencing their sons' behavior. On the other hand, there are people who helped shape feminine behavior in both boys—an uncle who gave a boy an exclusively girl's name and a sister who encouraged a boy to play as a girl. To what extent and on what already developed childhood personality these influences fell we do not know, but they suggest that unusual forces were brought to bear in early childhood that make it less surprising that these boys grew up feminine. (We cannot know about infantile precursors—traumas or gratifications in the mother-infant interplay or primitive fantasies and intrapsychic defenses built in the infant's mind.)

Third, it is hard to judge from the literature what the nature of cross-gender behavior was in American Indians. Did some get sexually excited by women's clothes? How many were anatomically or physiologically intersexed? How many were feminine from earliest life, and in how many did cross-gender behavior appear before age five, or ten, or fifteen, or later? How many were naturally feminine? How many were neuter in demeanor? How many were mimicking women with veiled hostility? Did any tribes condemn such behavior? From the literature and from these two patients with their different clinical pictures and background, I get the impression that Indian cultures did not produce a condition—berdache—different from that mixed bag: "gender dysphoria syndrome."

Fourth, how common was such behavior? Though the subject has caught the attention of anthropologists and psychiatrists, this may be more for its oddity than frequency. Reviewing the anthropologic literature, one cannot judge how many people like this existed at any time. My impression is that this behavior was rare, so much so that whenever an anthropologist heard of such a person, a report was filed. The whole subject is mushy. And now it is too late to know. Perhaps customs like berdache still exist intact somewhere. If so, let us hope that anthropologists studying such groups will answer our questions.

A last comment and an opinion. Before their conquest, American Indians liked their men to be men and their women to be women; each knew his or her place and the behaviors that marked that place. And though Indian males could be as machismatic as any males anywhere, it seems that they nonetheless could deal benignly with those who were turned on sexually by members of their own sex or by those who wished to live as members of the opposite sex. One was not ostracized for these propensities,[4] and no one was forced into treatment. The culture was not threatened: not the ability to raise food or make war, to raise children or pass on the cultural heritage, not the structure of the family or of the religion. The Indians were not harmed by this attitude; we would not be either.

4. Nor completely accepted, though less likely to be teased if open about it. "As a rule, official homosexuals were not teased. The Mohave believe in temperamental compulsions and consider that 'they cannot help it.' The brunt of the inevitable joking was borne by their spouses who had no such excuse" (Devereux 1937, p. 518).

11

THE DEVELOPMENT OF MASCULINITY: A CROSS-CULTURAL CONTRIBUTION

Professor Gilbert H. Herdt co-authored this chapter, which is built from his ethnography.

A new theory of the development of masculinity and femininity, the product of a number of workers, has been recently proposed (reviewed in Stoller 1975a, 1976). If confirmed, it would challenge Freud's belief that the superior biologic and psychologic sex is the male by putting females and femininity in a more primary role.

The argument that femininity is not experienced by either males or females as fundamentally inferior to masculinity is anchored in the findings that underlie the concept of core gender identity, one's sense of being either a male or a female. As I described earlier, this begins to emerge in the first year or so of life as part of the subjectivity connoted by such terms as *self* and *identity*. Freud said that masculinity was the natural, original mode of gender identity in both sexes. He believed that it resulted especially from the boy's heterosexual, and the girl's homosexual, first object relationship with mother—together with the inherent superiority of having a penis. The new theory, however, says that the first form of gender identity (preceding object relationship) is one of being merged with—of not distinguishing one's anatomic and psychic boundaries from—mother. This preverbal "identification"[1] can comfortably augment the creation of femininity in a girl, but in a boy it becomes an obstacle to be surmounted if he is to grow into a separate, masculine person. These processes favoring femininity place the boy's, not the girl's, core gender identity at risk.

The rule that androgens must be added to convert the female diathesis to maleness has survived all experimental challenge. Yet the case for our hypothesis—that the mother-infant relationship throws a greater burden on the earliest gender identity development of boys than of girls—still needs more tests. Such tests have come from the analyses of adults and children; evaluations and

1. The quotes mark our sense of no longer quite understanding what, especially in infants, makes up the process called identification.

nonanalytic treatment of large numbers of adults and children, with or without gender disorders; observations of nonaberrant children not in treatment and of their families; and naturalistic observations of the mother-infant symbiosis in male and female babies. Even the study of sexual excitement—perverse or normative—brings more data and clues (Stoller 1975b, 1979).

And beyond these opportunities lies the long admired but rarely used test that provokes this chapter: the study of gender identity in other cultures.

HYPOTHESES ABOUT THE ORIGINS OF MASCULINITY

To focus the reader on this chapter's argument, we repeat some earlier propositions. We do not believe these cover all the factors that lead to masculinity but rather that these are three that threaten the development of masculinity in its earliest stages.

1. If we put aside biologic factors, such as CNS/hormonal influences (for the sake of isolating the argument, not because these factors can be ignored), the longer, the more intimately, the more mutually pleasurable is a mother–infant son symbiosis, the greater the likelihood that the boy will become feminine; and that effect will persist if the boy's father does not qualitatively and quantitatively interrupt the merging. The less the family constellation is present, the less femininity occurs.

2. Following the first postnatal weeks, in which we need not postulate any behavior or mental elements that can be considered gender-colored (not forgetting that male brains differ from female brains), the earliest stage is not one of masculinity but of protofemininity, a condition induced through the merging that occurs in the mother-infant symbiosis.

3. For masculinity to develop, each infant boy must erect intrapsychic barriers that ward off the desire to maintain the blissful sense of being one with mother. As he develops—the combined results of unfolding biologic functions and learned skills and of the pleasure in mastery—the boy acquires powerful supports in the struggle against his own impulses to merge with mother. Conversely, to the extent that merging is intensified by having been encouraged too much, the sense of being like her—identified with her— interferes with his masculinization.[2] The boy who does not value masculinity—in whom it has not been encouraged—will have little reason to resist his sense of femininity and of being at one with his mother's femaleness. We presume (Freud's "complemental series") that there are biologic forces at work that may make it more compelling for some boys to escape this symbiosis

---

2. We only indicate here, but shall not discuss, that a frustrating, erratic experience of merging with a tantalizing mother can, with its mix of increased need for merging and anger, also interfere with masculinization. The result in this instance is not femininity but its caricature: effeminacy.

and move beyond the protofeminine stage, whereas in others a milder (male) biologic push is insufficient to overcome the pull of earliest protofemininity.

If, as most often occurs, the first year or so of life allows a sufficient desire for masculinity to be laced into the protofeminine impulses, and if that first desire for masculinity is encouraged, then the boy will try not only to preserve but also to enlarge his masculinity beyond the already constructed core of impulses toward femininity. He therefore creates a protective shield— "symbiosis anxiety"—inside himself, in the form of fantasies that, if successful, endure, that is, become character structure. The behavior that societies define as appropriately masculine is filled with the forms of this defensive maneuver: fear of female anatomy; envy and resulting derision of women; fear of entering their bodies; fear of intimacy (of entering—even more than their bodies—into women's inner selves); fear of manifesting and thereby revealing that one possesses "feminine" attributes, in many cultures categorized in such qualities as tenderness, affection, uninhibited expression of feelings, generosity, caretaking, or the desire to envelop others; fear of female attributes such as roundness, hairlessness, high voice; and fear of being desired by a man. Therefore, be tough, loud, belligerent; abuse and fetishize women; find friendship only with men but also hate homosexuals; talk dirty; disparage women's occupations. The first order of business in being a man is: don't be a woman. (As noted earlier in this book, by no means are we implying that only in boys is separation from mother's body crucial for identity development. We want, rather, to stress, first, that merging with mother in the first months of life promotes protofemininity in both sexes, which in itself need cause no problem in a girl. Second, to the extent that a girl delays her intrapsychic separation from her mother, the effects will not be manifest in an unfeminine appearance but rather in other, less gender-involved signs of aberrance.)

CROSS-CULTURAL FINDINGS: NEW GUINEA

To the above tests, we now add another: an anthropologic study from which we draw fragments to challenge and extend these hypotheses. We shall examine our ethnographic findings to see if, in another culture in which there are generally prolonged and warm mother-son bonds and simultaneously weak father-son relationships (though not of the extreme form seen in the families of very feminine boys), the people are aware that the boys are at risk of becoming feminine. Then, following the argument that this other society can survive only if the men are harshly masculine, we shall look for evidence of "symbiosis anxiety"—barriers raised to prevent feminizing effects from erupting into men's consciousness.

The methodology of the field research should be mentioned at the start of our description.[3] Its original aims included a systematic description of the behavior of ritual initiation and its meaning for the boys who have undergone it. Participant observation allowed the documentation of ritual behavior. Both open-ended and structured interviews were used in collecting extended clinical-type case studies of individual boys and men to understand their ritual experience and the psychodynamic functioning of ritual symbols in their sense of self and character structure.

In this clinical work the problem of what constitutes a normative baseline of psychodynamic and behavioral expressions is, of course, critical. The handling of that psychosocial assessment is similar to Levy's (1973). After months of close work with small numbers of Sambia males, Herdt qualitatively classified—and evaluated—what seemed normative or aberrant statistically and what seemed normal or abnormal psychodynamically, on the basis of Sambia culture adaptation, the individual's biography, the interview contexts of communicative acts, and the "evidential continuity" (Erickson 1958) of the ongoing clinical relationship. Structured interviews were also done, using behavioral scoring procedures, on a larger sample of boys, on small samples of women, and on small numbers of parents whose infants had been observed casually. Observations of children and of mother/infant interactions were made to understand normative developmental patterns and how cultural ideals correspond to those norms. The following account of Sambia gender development summarizes those findings.

The Sambia, an isolated tribal people numbering some 2,300 warrior-hunters and horticulturists, inhabit—as did their ancestors—an extremely rugged, mountainous region of the Eastern Highlands[4] of New Guinea. Sambia society functions primarily to perpetuate the warriorhood of its men, all of whom are expected to become fierce fighters capable of killing.[5] Unlike other warrior cultures known from the ancient or contemporary world, Sambia allow for no alternatives to their masculine gender role model, the phallic warrior. Not even the institutionalized escapist role of the shaman admits to real exceptions (compare, Devereux 1937),[6] and, with only one exception (see chapter 10), adult sexual inversion does not exist. Surrounded on all sides by enemy groups that raided and killed, men are even now trained to be unendingly alert,

---

3. Interested readers may also consult G. H. Herdt (1977, 1981) for more ethnographic background. Fieldwork among the Sambia was conducted by Herdt during 1974–76, 1979, 1981, and 1983.

4. "Highlands" is almost a euphemism: the mountains are in the same altitude range as the Alps.

5. The use of the present tense refers to Sambia society in the 1960s, when warfare still occurred, prior to pacification in 1965. Despite the change, however, and more numerous changes toward Westernization in the late 1970s, the facts here recorded about initiation, masculinity, and gender identity are based on observations in the period 1974–76. Though steel axes have replaced stone ones, all armaments and almost all tools are still made of wood and other native materials.

6. Most shamans are male. All those who are male are warriors, and some were also war leaders (Herdt 1977).

aggressive, and suspicious, lest they or their communities be attacked and destroyed. Possessing a Stone Age technology, Sambia men cannot mitigate, by substituting superior weapons for their own strength, the overriding demand that they be physically and emotionally powerful. They possess only their bodies and bows and arrows or clubs as weapons or as implements of power: no guns, bombs, or gases; no electric signals or subtle gadgets; no doctors or hospitals; little art; and a simple, ungrateful religious system comprised of malevolent spirits and techniques for keeping them at bay.

These men exemplify the many people of New Guinea whose individual and group survival depended on the unadorned, farthest reaches of those behaviors that will protect people undefended by the artifacts of a science-induced technology. Theirs is a living example—though an anachronism—of a particularly harnessed maleness, a primordial masculinity. How is it created? What do Sambia know subliminally that has enabled them to evolve a culture, a family unit, and a form of ritualized male gender identity that reproduces itself and succeeds over generations? And how may they serve us as a "natural experiment" for the study of gender identity? Let us begin with a summary description of Sambia masculinity, their theory of the origins of sex (maleness and femaleness) and gender (masculinity and femininity), and the cultural context of these attributes.

Sambia society—in both scale and numbers—is small by the standards of Highlands groups, and the social world of its tiny hamlets is smaller still. Those realities help account for—are challenges that form—Sambia marriage and the family unit, the mother-child bond, and the rigidly molded femininity and masculinity that identify each female as a prospective wife and each male as vital for communal productivity and military defense.

These hamlets, nestled on high ridges, are fortified, nearly impenetrable stockades. The population of each seldom numbers over a hundred people. Men hunt in nearby forests, and women garden close by. Children are always within earshot. Kinship is patrilineally based, and residence is patrilocal; two or more exogamous clans constitute hamlets, thus allowing intrahamlet marriage. Women imported from other hamlets belong to potentially hostile enemy groups. But whether wives come from inside or outside the hamlet, all marriage, except by abduction, is prearranged (either through infant betrothal or sister exchange). Courtship is unknown, and marriages occur, without much personal choice, between strangers. This condition only exacerbates the sexual polarity that, as in other Melanesian societies, is institutionalized through a secret male cult and a misogynist belief system that disparages women as polluting, depleting inferiors a man distrusts his entire life.[7]

Each married couple and their children cohabit in small, separate round huts, a dozen or so of which make up a hamlet. All ritual initiates (ages seven-

7. Compare, Brown and Buchbinder 1976; Langness 1967, 1974; Meggitt 1964; Read 1954.

twelve) and bachelors (ages thirteen-eighteen) reside in the men's clubhouse centrally located in the village, an institution that serves as the nerve center of the warriorhood and the focus of male ritual activities in the community. Into such small, inward-looking worlds, Sambia children are born and reared.

For the Sambia to prevail in this environment, they must depend on the success of two complex, conflict-laden components. The first is a persisting family unit, the homeostasis of which is sorely strained by the above-noted male-female polarity. The second element is the fierce yet steadfast masculinity of the men. Let us look more closely at these two factors, their interaction, and their effects on the culture and its individual members.

Men believe that women are contaminating because of their inherently dangerous menstrual and vaginal fluids; thus, strict rules govern all contact between the sexes, and especially spouses. Eating, drinking, spitting, talking, sitting, looking, and particularly sexual intercourse—all are scrutinized, ritualized, and inhibited in ways, gross and subtle, that maintain separateness and distance between the sexes. (This generalization deserves emphasis: in three years of living with Sambia, H. never once observed a man and woman purposely touch each other, not even hold hands, either publicly or in the privacy of their homes.) The hamlet itself is a maze of tabooed spaces and traffic signs: paths are either "male" or "female"; many areas are off-limits to one or the other sex; and the interiors of houses are split up into "female" and "male" spaces where women are respectively consigned or forbidden to enter. All this is to reduce the chances that a woman's lethal body, body fluids, or other products, smells, and glances will be absorbed into a man's food, water, possessions, or insides.

Beyond this is the conviction that women deplete men of their strength and eventually even of life itself by robbing—emptying—them, through sexual intercourse, of their male substance, semen. For men, semen is literally the stuff of existence, of vitality, and the sole origin of the anatomy identified as maleness. Yet it is also needed by women to strengthen themselves, so that they can produce breast milk and can create and form babies. Boys cannot become men without a steady supply of exogenous semen, for, men believe, the male body cannot manufacture semen. But women want it too, and their needs and demands are endless (and not the less exciting to men for that reason).

Women pollute and deplete: two strains that threaten masculinity and forever intrude into marriage. Examples: Men are uneasy about what they eat, particularly their wives' food; they fear intimacy; inexplicable illness and failure in hunting can be blamed on one's wife; sexual relationships are often poisoned with suspiciousness, covetousness, and expectations of adultery. And yet, out of this morass of hostility and silence, demands and punishments, squabbles and curses, wife-beating, murder, and female suicides, family units are created. For there are also, between the sexes, need and gratification, respect, sharing, and pleasure in children. And the children are party to—objects, audiences, loved ones, and pawns in—these dramas.

When a woman goes into labor, she retires to the menstrual hut. There she is attended only by women; men are excluded. Mother and infant are thought to be infectious because of the mass of pollutants released there, so men fiercely avoid the area.[8] The woman returns to her house in a week or two, but ritual postpartum taboos strictly forbid a father from seeing his baby for months after. Moreover, the infant is always covered by its mother's bark cape since its father's glances are believed to harm it and dry up the mother's milk.

Postpartum taboos prohibit all sexual activities between the couple until the child is in its second year. The young father must avoid mother and child, first, because either could pollute him simply through the mother's birth contaminants and, second, because sexual arousal from watching breast-feeding might lead him to break the postpartum taboos, bringing sickness or death to the infant and shame to all. (If the father has but one wife, Sambia say he is frustrated and irritable, since wet dreams are his only socially acceptable erotic outlet.)

For two years and more this situation continues, the father gradually seeing more of his child, taking a more active part in its life. With weaning, these arrangements change; until then, father's presence, physical and psychologic, is shadowy. (In contrast to our transsexuals and their fathers, however, this father is considered strong, manly, dangerous, someone—in time—worth emulating.) Sambia tend to think of an infant as an appendage of its mother's body for the first nine months. For instance, fearing grief should the infant die (infant mortality is high), parents rarely name their baby until then, referring to it only in pronouns. The child has constant, ready access to the breast, sometimes into its third year. In skin-to-skin contact, it eats, is carried, and sleeps naked with its mother. There is little concern with toilet training until long after the baby is walking.[9]

Only after weaning do children—girls and boys—sleep separate from their mothers, in a bark blanket, a foot or two away. In time, boys are encouraged by both parents to sleep even farther away from mother, nearer to but still separate from their father, in the "male space" of the house. Despite increasing contact with their fathers, however, boys continue to be mostly with their mothers,

8. Indeed, the associated secret initiatory rites of men emphasize nose-bleeding and other purificatory acts aimed at purging the contaminants all boys and men carry in their bodies, from the time they resided within their mothers' bodies and were delivered therefrom, drenched in the most extreme of pollutants—female blood, secretions, and tissues.

9. The difference, roughly, between this closeness and that of the very feminine boy and his mother is that the latter relationship is never casual but is at every moment intense, because the boy's mother is forever threatened by her lifelong despair and sense of worthlessness.

siblings, and playmates, not their fathers. An abrupt changeover to maternal separation comes only—and precipitously—with the first-stage initiation, which occurs between ages seven and ten.

Men are concerned with the effects of prolonged maternal attachment on children, especially their sons. Stated briefly, men regard attaining adult reproductive competence as far less certain for males than females. Maleness depends on a boy's acquiring semen; only this can produce male physical maturation and erotic-reproductive ability. Femaleness, the primordial state of both boys and girls, rests on the creation and continuing presence of blood, which is believed to stimulate the menarche, the production of menstrual blood, and fertility. Because girls possess a self-activating menstrual-blood organ (*tingu*), their maturation is viewed as an unbroken process leading from birth and maternal bonding into adulthood. For boys, however, two obstacles block male growth. First is pollution by mother's body, the food she prepares, and her overall caretaking, which at first nurtures but then stifles. Second, boys innately lack semen, since the semen organ (*keruku-keruku*) can only store, not manufacture, sperm. This difference, men reason, results in the very visible fact that girls physically outpace boys in their maturation.[10] In other words, femaleness is a natural development leading into feminine adulthood, but maleness is not natural. It is, rather, a personal achievement, a power that boys and men seize only through the initiations of their ritual cult.

In the initiations, then, men try by radical, brutal, and heroic means to cut off, in an instant, mothers' loving embrace of their sons. Ritual must do what parents cannot or will not do: forcibly separate and individuate boys by conscripting them into the secret male cult. Boys are initiated into that fierce warriorhood by means of a very long, difficult set of ritual ordeals that follow from the men's careful preparations and goal to make the boys into men—if need be by forcibly taking the boys from their screaming mothers' embrace. From that instant on, the boys, under threat of severest sanctions, will not talk with, touch, or look at their mothers. (We should note but cannot describe in detail that some boys and some mothers resist initiation down to the wire.) Over the ensuing ten to fifteen years, they undergo five other initiation ceremonies that lead finally to full manhood—marriage and fatherhood.

Ritualized Obligatory Homosexual Fellatio and the Semen Cult

This pattern of initiation as the route to manhood is well known elsewhere in New Guinea (compare, Allen 1967). Where Sambia differ is in the striking form of ritualized homosexual fellatio activities that they believe are necessary to effect the transition from the contaminating pull of femaleness to the brave

---

10. Compare, Malcolm 1966 on this problem more widely in New Guinea.

separateness of maleness and masculinity.[11] Since maleness (as opposed to the mere possession of male genitals) is not natural or innate, and since the male body is felt to lack an endogenous mechanism for creating semen—the basis of masculine development—it follows that men regard constant insemination (which they compare to breast-feeding) as the only means for boys to grow, mature, and attain manly competence. Hence, starting with first-stage initiation, fellatio—to be indulged in as often as possible—is fully institutionalized. (Semen, in this respect, functions analogously to the artificial intake of androgens in a eunuch.) This behavior is a tremendous secret that must be kept, under pain of death, from all children and women.

In the most powerful, frightening, and yet seductive circumstances, during the first-stage initiation, following forcible separation from their mothers, the boys are compelled to engage in fellatio with (take semen from) the bachelors.[12] At puberty and its third-stage initiation, adolescent youths become the dominant fellateds themselves—the suppliers of semen—for a new group of initiates. During this time, all contacts with females are prohibited, and the strongest social pressures are brought to bear on boys so that they will conform to their fellator role. This results in a precise, rigid structure of ritualized masculinity, which, as a regular part of development, enables males to be excited first by (and daydream about) boys as sexual objects (particularly their mouths, which are fetishized) and later by women, whose mouths,[13] vaginas, and bodies are exciting, dangerous, fetishized. Later, with marriage and a family, all homosexual activity is to end. Men thereafter act exclusively as heterosexual adults. But adult heterosexuality, with its interwoven masculinity, will forever carry the stresses introduced by the close mother-son symbiosis, the father's relative absence, and the traumatic initiation rites created to check the threat of femininity introduced by these family dynamics.

We regret but are alert to the inadequacy of our data for revealing the unconscious complexities of meaning and motivation in the Sambia boys' fellatio practices. What we cannot know is the extent to which the Sambia carry into *their* homosexual behavior the same dynamic themes (though undoubtedly in different proportions and mixes) that lead to (unconscious, pre-

11. Ritualized homosexuality has been reported from some twenty New Guinea societies besides Sambia; see, for example, Deacon 1934, pp. 191ff.; Schieffelin 1976, pp. 124–26; Williams 1936, pp. 158ff. (which are partially reviewed in Herdt 1981). Though these represent a small sample (out of hundreds of tribal groups), we believe their significance to be great for gender identity research.

12. A few notes about ritualized homosexuality: it is rigidly structured by incest rules that prevent such contacts with kinsmen; it is generally promiscuous, so boys may engage in it only with youths of hostile enemy groups; boys come to experience it as both exciting and humiliating; boys may act only as fellators, never as the one sucked; and bachelors may never serve as fellators to young boys. To want to suck a prepubescent boy's penis would be perversion—shocking. It would be, in our terms, homosexuality.

13. Initial heterosexual intercourse is also only through fellatio.

conscious, or conscious) homosexual impulses in other cultures: fear of intimacy with females as penisless creatures; fear of females' power; deflection of
hostility away from other males (ultimately from father, brothers); narcissistic
choice of someone like oneself; avoiding the perils of heterosexual incestuous
urges; yearnings for father; identification with women; stealing of masculinity
from other males by taking in their semen; hatred of women; love of father as a
substitute for a missing, hateful, or dangerous mother; mother's disparaging of
father; envy of a brother preferred by a father or mother; revenge against and
triumph over a mother or father who shows obvious preference for a masculine, heterosexual son. (Many of these factors were described years ago by
Nunberg [1938].) We also cannot see into the boys' minds to determine to
what degree their fathers' terrifying threats may be the result of the boys'
oedipal desires for their mothers.

The ritual cult applies an absolute brake on the manifest development of
heterosexuality. Three mechanisms do most of the work: institutionalized
fellatio; female avoidance taboos, especially regarding menstrual pollution;
and fears of semen depletion. But we must stress that when speaking of the
absolute obligatory homosexual relationships between the boys and youths,
we refer only to *overt practices*. Not all heterosexuality is ruled out, of course,
only its overt expression. And though heterosexuality is severely suppressed,
boys are encouraged by their fathers and elders to acquire semen so that they,
too, can achieve marriage and fatherhood. The function of the ritual cult is to
create a powerful, dependable warrior's masculinity, with its very precisely
tuned mode of heterosexuality. And that will have to suffice. If, for survival,
the Sambia need both savage warriors to defend the community and heterosexuality for producing future communities, the first must be highly efficient,
while with the second—heterosexuality—there can be more leeway: the men
must be great warriors but not necessarily loving lovers. This is fortunate, for
the world produces few men who are both savage warriors and loving husbands.

To summarize: the following set of developmental faultlines are external
forces crucial for Sambia adult male character structure: prolonged maternal
attachment and symbiosis; father's low profile in the household; parental
conflict; initiation, through traumatic rituals, into a secret cult that demands
continuous, exclusively homosexual activity until marriage; and severe avoidance of all females (mother most of all) for years in later childhood and
adolescence. Masculinity is achieved only after an immense, frightening,
painful struggle, made especially poignant because the boy must separate
precipitously from his warm and loving mother. And even though the men
teach that the boys *must* be initiated and *must* be separated from women,[14]

---

14. "A common admonition is: 'If you stay always with women, you must expect to become weak
as they are, and you will never become a killer of men' " (Meggitt 1977, pp. 60–61).

many boys try to resist this split, some even saying—until they fear to—that they do not care if they reach manhood or warrior prowess.

Since men believe that maleness is artificial, it makes sense that they fear atrophy of masculinity and maleness: an awful fear resulting from this line of development, for what is artificially constructed can also wither away. First, for years after puberty, one loses his semen continuously to the initiates in order that they can grow their maleness; and second, after the phase of ritual homosexuality, one cannot but continue his semen depletion in the lustful pleasures of heterosexuality. (This is why, following heterosexual intercourse, men regularly and secretly ingest white tree sap ''milk'' in the forest, it being one of the few substitutes for lost semen, whose replenishment by fellatio ends at puberty. Note that this is, curiously, done only after heterosexual intercourse; homosexual insemination is not felt to be as depleting as is later heterosexual, particularly genital, intercourse.)

What a complex developmental experience, then, is heterosexuality for Sambia men. The touch of a woman and—far more so—her secretions inevitably cause illness and even death if not exorcised. And yet women are desired as well. The intensity of the conflict causes some men to tremble, even panic, before and after heterosexual relations. (It seems so exotic to us, unless we recall that similar mechanisms and symptoms are also found in the Western world.)

DISCUSSION

Let us sort out the factors shared by these two contrasting states in males: extreme femininity in primary transsexuals and extreme masculinity in Sambia. And then we must try to explain—in the face of the exclusive and intense homosexual practices of boys and youths, the fear and envy of women by men, and the blatant hostility between the sexes—how Sambia create a society that has worked for generations. Out of what forces emerge these warriors who not only preserve the hamlet, establish family units of persisting heterosexuality, and are committed to fatherhood, but, in addition, offer a tempting masculinity from which their sons can model the identifications necessary to create and protect the next generation?

Before examining the Sambia data further, we review again our hypotheses. *Parental factors:* a prolonged and warm mother-son relationship puts boys at risk of being feminized in early life, the amount of risk determined by biologic factors; the degree to which a mother creates and preserves a state of frustrationless, painless, atraumatic bliss in her son; the number of hours a day and the number of years she does so; how much she supports his feminine behavior once it starts; how, when, and how often the boy's father or father figure interrupts the symbiosis; and how his father serves the boy as a model for masculinity. *Intrapsychic factors:* to the extent that anlagen of masculinity (these can be observed at roughly a year or so of age) develop and are valued by the boy, he must defend that core—which is himself—by resisting the primal pull of impulses to stay merged with mother. He does this through the fear that he will not remain separate from his mother—"symbiosis anxiety." This protective reaction leads to behaviors that become the overriding impetus for masculinity in many men of many cultures: to be a male, one must guard against being (like) a female in one's physical features, movements, emotions, erotism, and so on. This task can become a frantic preoccupation (for example, machismo) in sexually polarized cultures where boys in early life are close to their mothers and have aloof fathers (B. Whiting 1965; J. W. M. Whiting and B. Whiting 1975; J. W. M. Whiting et al. 1958, pp. 359–70).

On reviewing the Sambia material we also find confirmation that too much mother and too little father put a boy's masculinity at risk. As a cultural "experiment," the Sambia provide a more interesting—and more complex—test than individual cases of psychopathology reported to date, for in this instance we are confronted by an institutionalized complex: men, women, children, their cultural practices and beliefs—all interacting to maintain a society. Compared to our earlier clinical "experiments," where the outcome is a more or less aberrant individual, here we face a society of individuals who not only are not aberrant but are normative—and necessary—for the survival of their way of life.

Left unchecked, Sambia would court disaster in the consequences of letting boys remain close to their mothers for so long. (No warring society could survive in the impossible position of developing only feminized men.) But then, by means of ritual initiation, myth, and taboo systems, these people institutionalize a fiercely focused response—extreme symbiosis anxiety—whose outcome eventually extracts boys from their mothers' embrace. From the first initiation on, the men terrorize the boys, instilling fear of females, while at the same time fathers encourage the development of masculinity through exclusive, promiscuous, constant homosexual activities. Our theory must therefore account for the eventual development of heterosexuality. We want to make sense of this complex homeostatic system in which two great imperatives must be assured: first, *preservation* of the tribe—today, every day—by that primal mixture of physical power, skill and cunning in battle, bravery, and altruism (bonds of affection and identification with fellow warriors); and second, *reproduction* of the tribe by creating enough heterosexuality to enable sexual intercourse, enough syntonic bonding between men and women to allow for family units in which children are socialized and protected, and enough care and responsiveness by boys and girls vis-à-vis their warrior fathers to result in a socially workable (though by our standards radical) oedipal resolution—the initiations.

The Sambia data can be understood only if one uses a preoedipal/oedipal framework. (We need *both* frameworks, not one or the other.) Creating and maintaining the Sambia family poses a cross-cultural test for the universality of this fundament of analytic theory—the development of the oedipal situation. We should want to know, then, how boys, despite many obstacles, advance in a masculine line sufficiently to be able to experience oedipal conflict without its overwhelming them and then resolve that conflict well enough to marry and have families.

What are the origins of a boy's heterosexuality? We believe it especially results, as one also finds in our society, from the attitudes and actions of mothers and fathers.[15] When a mother, however loving, also allows, encourages, and insists that her son separate from her body and psyche, the boy will be better able to let go. This process is especially effective when it is fitted to his innate pace of neuromuscular and neuropsychologic development.

The key word in the above is *loving*. There is lovingness that comes from idealized identification. An extreme example is the mother of the very feminine boy who loves[16] her son as the embodiment of the maleness she could not achieve without having grown him from her body, as the recipient of a sense of self-value she never got from her own mother, and as an externalization of her self, now to be loved endlessly by a mother (herself) who will superhumanly try to be the all-good mother. Though we expect a touch of this idealization in all mothering (compare, Winnicott 1956), in nonmalignant mothering we know it will eventually let up spontaneously.

Then there is a very different lovingness, the one that consists in recognizing this loved object to be separate from oneself and possessed of its own independent identity. When this kind of loving predominates, a boy will drink in his mother less, no matter how long he drinks her milk. This is the mother-son relationship—a true object relationship—that Freud recognized as the basis for the positive oedipal situation.

We wish to emphasize that though both the mothers of very feminine boys and Sambia mothers are thrilled to have sons, the former do all they can to discourage rough, penetrating, raucous behavior in their sons. They consciously define these actions not as masculine but as "bad," "distasteful," "uncouth." In contrast, the Sambia mothers encourage any behavior that their culture defines as masculine; they know that survival will depend on that masculinity and that a Sambia woman cannot, in the development of her identity, define herself as a woman until she establishes a family with such a manly man. Though we do not have analytic data on the Sambia mothers, we feel it is obvious that the sum of their intrapsychic processes vis-à-vis their sons is grossly different from that observed in the mothers of very feminine

15. In the absence of data gathered in psychoanalyses, we must weight our descriptions from the viewpoint of parental influences; the boys' intrapsychic dynamics are available for inspection only at a conscious/preconscious level.

16. Needs; admires; treats with altruism; handles with gentleness and care to maximize his pleasure and prevent his suffering physical and psychic pain.

boys. The latter produce a thing, a (nonerotic) fetish of sorts, whereas the Sambia mothers wish to create a potent man. The fantasy systems of the women of the two cultures are therefore quite different—though perhaps they share one unconscious dynamic: "my son is the phallus I could not otherwise have."

There is, of course, far more to the development of masculinity in the Sambia boys and the failure of that development in very feminine boys than what results in and from the close symbiosis. As the years pass, the Sambia boys are encouraged toward masculine behavior and to turn to the men of the hamlet as models. Most decidedly, this cannot be said in the transsexual situation.[17]

Observation of Sambia mothers and their infants/children—by Herdt extensively and Stoller briefly—never revealed behavior we could interpret as an excessively close symbiosis. On becoming mobile, children are free at all times to be in physical contact with their mothers. But as they grow into their second year, a casual quality appears in the relationship: no great effort, beyond protecting them from environmental dangers, is made to keep them close. The breast may remain ever-available, even until around three years, but the children come to handle it more and more as if it were a gadget and less as a synonym for love. Unlike the primary transsexuals' mothers, the Sambia women are often with others who act as caretakers, and they are not passionately concentrated on the intimacy. They carry their babies mostly because it is practical to do so. Still, there *is* that prolonged closeness between mother and son, years beyond what is typical in our society. Nor is the closeness drastically interrupted, as with us, by the start of school which, in our society around age five, forcibly disrupts the symbiosis. That is the age when very feminine boys are often sent for evaluation, not by the boy's parents but by the school or neighbors.

To continue, unlike Sambia women, the mothers of very feminine boys encourage all behavior we define as feminine. But with the Sambia, no one devalues masculine behavior, for only it stands between survival and destruction.

Sambia (men and women) prefer a boy as the first born (Herdt 1981, chaps. 6, 7). But women also practice—illicitly—male infanticide, mostly when there are too many boys already. Women say they like boys better than girls since boys stay in the hamlet after marriage and can support them in old age. But in certain ways, as with us, girls are closer to their mothers and remain close years longer than do sons; daughters are better companions, learn more about garden magic, share secret stories, and gossip with their mothers. Boys

---

17. For further discussion of the role of learning, cueing, and nonconflictual preoedipal identification and their contributions to the development of gender identity, see Blum (1976) and Kleeman (1976).

are expected to act rougher than girls; women tease boys more than girls (who cry more easily than boys); and boys are more spoiled and pampered than girls. Boys are sassier and rowdier than girls, and they are allowed—even expected—to throw temper tantrums as girls are never permitted to do. But, at the same time, there is a different kind of closeness that a boy can have with his mother, a different kind of love, a cuter and coyer kind, with a boy being more demanding of his mother's attentions than his sister and then crying if he does not get what he wants.

Sambia women, then, are proud to have sons: they could never reward in boys behavior that their culture defines as feminine. From her own infancy on, a Sambia woman encounters male-female relationships filled with danger and hostility. (Many women, to repeat, are recruited as wives from hamlets that have warred against the one into which they marry.) A woman's husband, his relatives, or his friends may have killed her people in battle. So, though proud to have sons, she has cause to be uneasy, for she knows that this admired child will grow up to be as phallic and dangerous as his father and the rest of his cruel sex.

The best proof of our hypothesis that Sambia boys are at risk for being feminine lies in the initiations. In these experiences, the men pound in their expectation that, because the boys have been too much with their mothers, masculinity is endangered. This is not our theory but their expressed experience. Men also know intuitively that they must powerfully, rapidly make up for having been distant fathers. In the initiations, therefore, the men are suddenly and overwhelmingly present. From there on, the boys can live only in a male world, isolated, on pain of sickness and death, from females. Cut off from their mothers, the boys are harangued, beaten, radically resocialized, and threatened with terrible physical dangers, including death. The initiations demonstrate overwhelmingly the fathers' power to punish, and whatever incestuous yearnings the boys have for their mothers are shockingly thwarted in the rituals. But in the same ceremonies, the boys are also enticed with the firm promise of growing to be one of the men, of becoming a husband, a father, a warrior, a hero, and even in time an honored ancestor.

Stripped of its tremendous drama, does this not also describe the culminating stage of oedipal conflict for boys in our own, manifestly blander world: one shall forego present desire, the task made bearable by the promise that lies in identifying with adult men?

If our view of the Sambia is correct, then they provide confirmation for both the preoedipal and oedipal aspects of the development of masculinity. For the preoedipal stage, there is the protofemininity formed within mother's embrace, in time—though delayed as compared to our society—to be counteracted by the barriers of symbiosis anxiety. Having thereby separated psychologically from mother, a boy can advance to oedipal matters: to desire to have her, not just to *be* her (Greenson 1968). And, with that accomplishment, he has earned the right to neurosis—oedipal conflict—and to the resolution of that neurosis by means of identification with a desired, feared, admired father. The promise at the center of that identification becomes explicit for the Sambia in the progression of initiations now made known to the boy: in time one is fit for marriage, sets up a separate household, is a father, and reaches full adult status as a warrior, perhaps becoming even a war leader. (That is the highest status one can achieve: Sambia have no chiefs, princes, or poets.)

The question arises whether it is not closer to the facts to see the first-stage initiation as simply a scene in the wider oedipal drama. That is, rather than being the product of the fathers' awareness of the too-gratifying symbiosis that leads toward femininity (a preoedipal matter), initiation serves to remove the boys from rivalry with their fathers for the mothers' affection and intimacy (Whiting et al. 1958). There are clues in our data to help us; they suggest that both oedipal and preoedipal factors are at work. Pointing toward the oedipal inference is our knowledge that women have plenty of rage toward their husbands because the men are unsatisfying companions and lovers.[18] Besides this, the marriages are arranged contracts, often between strangers, and one can see that sons are likely to be preferred in some regards over husbands, who would become jealous. The initiations thus serve notice on the boys that their hopes to possess their mothers, encouraged by a lengthy, comfortable intimacy, must be ended. The fathers—those insurmountable rivals—lay down the law. That above all, as Freud described, forces boys into the conflict whose successful resolution leads to masculinity and heterosexuality.

The second factor making possible a successful resolution of oedipal conflict for boys is the opportunity to identify with their admired fathers, the identification pointing the way to, and more or less promising, future heterosexuality and fatherhood. And for that, too, we find evidence in the initiations. Far more than simply attacking the boys as rivals, the men—as observed throughout the initiations—coax the boys into being just like these fathers: in maleness, in skill, in strength, and in the willingness to die for the hamlet. It only seems a paradox that Sambia men promote heterosexuality and masculinity by means of enforced, exclusive homosexuality. Note that even if these fathers *are* jealous of their sons, that jealousy is not destructive of masculinity, as it often tends to be in the fathers of some effeminate homosexuals and transvestites.

Why then, with this evidence of oedipal conflict, do we argue that this is also a preoedipal issue? Because we believe that the oedipal explanation, though correct, is incomplete. It does not account for the severity and massiveness (in effort, time, planning, and excitement) of the initiations; the extreme emphasis put on the lethal danger of contact with female bodies, menstrual blood, and other female secretions; the infecting pollution that may

---

18. At least in part because of fear of women's bodies, Sambia men do not use foreplay; most men keep intercourse as short as possible, in order to decrease contact with the "polluting" woman.

come from food and objects touched by women; or the expectation that women are tempted to kill and have killed men with their sorcery.[19]

Lidz and Lidz (1977), in their review of ethnographic studies on blood-letting rites[20] in Melanesia, came to conclusions we believe are confirmed by our data:

The fundamental task that must be carried out in all societies is the differentiation of the child from the initial symbiosis with the mother and establishing adequate boundaries between the child and mother; and then in guiding the boy to rescind his initial identification with his mother and gain a firm identity as a male. Whereas the girl must establish boundaries, she does not rescind the initial identification with her mother as a female. Herein lies one of the reasons why Freud's early efforts to describe the girl's oedipal transition as a mirror image of the boy's failed. It also seems to be one reason why in New Guinea it is believed that the girl matures naturally and female puberty ceremonies celebrate the girl's maturation whereas the boy's initiation is required to induce maturation. The boy does not grow into a man spontaneously because he was born from a woman and initially identified with a woman. . . . the boy's developmental task in reversing his basic identification is more difficult and thus requires more reinforcement than does the girl's achievement of a firm gender identity. (p. 28)

The Sambia material, by illustrating how the men detach their sons from their wives (by conscripting the boys into the secret male cult), underlines the Lidzes' support of our hypotheses on the development of masculinity. But we want to update and correct their view that "no evidence [can be found] that the rituals are efforts made by fathers to torment the boys with threats of death or castration unless they give up their libidinal attachments to their mothers, as has so often been maintained" (p. 30). Obviously, dramatic and terrifying surprise attacks on boys in which they are forcibly nose-bled or bled from the penis (Salisbury 1965; Tuzin 1980) are traumatic; Read's (1954) classical description of the Gahuku-Gama made that clear. Sambia nose-bleed and they, and probably others, too, *in rituals*, threaten nose-bleeding later on unless boys become obedient to male authority.[21] Sambia boys, like other Eastern Highlanders (Read 1954; Watson 1960, pp. 127–73), say very precisely that

19. We cannot help but think, therefore, that when, in our psychoanalytic practice, men show aspects of this oedipal stage identification with father, we are then, too, looking back through attempted oedipal resolution to that earlier resolution—separation-individuation—made possible by symbiosis anxiety. We suggest that, in our society as with the Sambia, fathers who want their sons to be successfully masculine and heterosexual are working intuitively, even as late in childhood as at the height of the oedipal conflict, to draw their sons away from mothers' enfeebling, feminizing influences and toward themselves.

20. They call this "male menstruation," a loaded term, alluded to by such ethnographers as Hogbin (1970), Newman (1965), and Salisbury (1965, pp. 50–77). The subject of ritual blood-letting is, as the Lidzes discuss in detail, full of the question of preoedipal versus oedipal factors, and identificatory versus separate-object dynamics, as the center of gender identity.

21. In other words, threats against boys are sanctified and perpetuated by the collective authority of men, in groups, during ritual; unless observers were actually present in the rites, they would miss these threats, and, retrospectively, boys might repress them in idealizing the events later to observers.

they feared being killed during blood-letting. Sambia men, Herdt (1981) observed, use secret threats, both of death and of castration, in first-stage initiation so as to force the boys' absolute avoidance of women (not just avoidance of heterosexuality) and to command the boys' silence about ritual secrets, especially concerning homosexual activities.[22]

DENOUEMENT

The effort to create and maintain this belligerent masculinity in the face of brutal environmental threats is the cement that binds Sambia culture. If external reality became less dangerous, the traditional culture might disintegrate. For instance, if warring ended or if more efficient weapons were introduced, men would no longer have to rely, in hunting and in war, on their own strength, skill, and readiness to fight and kill. And such a shift in power would go a long way toward equalizing men and women.

In fact, the Sambia have not gotten new weapons. They still fight and hunt with the same Stone Age equipment as before. But what did happen was that an external power intervened with modern weapons, forbidding the Sambia from warring among themselves.

Until the 1930s, the huge, impenetrable, mountainous area of New Guinea known as the Highlands was believed to be uninhabited. Westerners were astonished to find, mountain range by range and valley by valley, that large human populations lived there. Frightened by the Highlanders' fierce capacity to war and defend themselves by killing, the Australians mobilized, advancing into increasingly remote areas. Pacification accelerated with the end of the campaigns of World War II, and the open warfare of the tribes was suppressed; only sporadic payback (talion) killings continued.[23]

This also happened to Sambia when the Australian forces penetrated the area and subdued the warriors in the 1960s. The Sambia raison d'être was undermined; the grounding of its warriorhood in a dangerous reality disappeared. We would expect, then, a transmutation of the culture, manifested principally in shifts in the forms and functions of masculinity (and femininity). If this occurs gradually, over centuries, as happened in Western societies, *transmutation* is the appropriate word to describe that process. When it happens in a matter of years, not even decades, however, the familiar form of masculinity no longer serves its old functions; the traditional culture shudders and collapses. As with other Highlanders, this is happening to the Sambia.

These people, whose remote valleys held no temptations, hardly a chal-

22. Jucovy (1976) has shown links among such initiation rites, reinforcement of masculinity, and transvestism in our culture.

23. Civil order still breaks down when the authorities relax. In the summer of 1979, while in the Western Highlands, I observed two large groups openly at war, the government scrambling to suppress the murderous violence. See also Meggitt (1977, pp. 156ff.).

lenge, and certainly no threat to outsiders, have never attracted the attention of the authorities. After an initial skirmish or two and some arrests—a terribly humiliating public experience for a warrior—the people were forcibly resigned to the Australians' guns and money. Thereafter, young men left for the coast to find another, urban life. In these past few years, the institutions and other cultural mechanisms through which Sambia masculinity was created—initiation ceremonies, taboos, a proud warriorhood—began to lose their generative functions. A masculinity that was at its sharpest in battle, that was needed to prevent personal and community destruction, that created and passed on its own kind of heterosexuality to the next generation, started becoming an anachronism. Enemies will probably never again attack. What, then, is the use of initiations focused on creating a warriorhood? The rituals had their terror, their agonizing ordeals, but in suffering them a boy generated great pride. Now, with the end of warring, that has melted away. It seems certain to us that the massing of the men and boys for warriorhood initiation is forever gone.

12

A PRELIMINARY PROGRAM
FOR NATURALISTIC OBSERVATION
OF A PSYCHODYNAMIC ISSUE

I have presented a hypothesis that I believe is being confirmed plus a guess that is beyond confirmation. The hypothesis is that a mother who tries to create a limitless and unending blissful merging between herself and her yearned-for beautiful son will put him at great risk for becoming feminine if his father does not interrupt the process. The guess is that this malignant process is not caused primarily by the boy's defenses against unbearable anxiety—is not at first a neurotic structure in the sense of being a compromise, a defense, a resolution of conflict—but is the result of a developmental arrest that prevented the otherwise expected unfolding of masculinity.

To test the hypothesis, I have proceeded with the following categories of investigation. (These are less recommendations to others than to myself, but they suggest that psychoanalytic issues might be transformed into researchable endeavors.)

1. Styles of data collecting
    a. Whenever possible, collect data by treatment rather than by evaluations or formal research techniques such as questionnaires and standardized tests.[1]
    b. Presume that the relationship with patients will go on indefinitely. This does not, however, mean that *treatment* continues forever.
    c. Always, when possible, see the families of patients—children or adults—in consultation.
    d. When indicated, treat other family members. The guiding rule is always that the indication for treatment is distress, not research.
2. Techniques of data collecting
    a. Consultation—with patient; with families.

---

1. Because treatment, especially analysis, is a long and slow process, today I do not treat anyone not related to this study of gender identity. But even that must be modified, for now having some idea of the dynamics of normative gender identity, I suspect that all people can teach us about this subject.

    b. Case management (advice, referral, follow-up).

    c. Psychotherapy.

    d. Analysis of people with gender disorders.

    e. Analysis of parents of people with gender disorders and simultaneous treatment of the aberrant person (usually a child).

    f. Confirmation by seeing larger numbers of cases and families.

    g. Confirmation by having colleagues connected with the research see patients and families.

    h. Confirmation by reports from those not connected with the research; especially useful here are reports in the literature, the most valuable, perhaps, being those published before I began reporting my findings and theories.

    i. Cross-cultural studies.

3. Mechanical devices

    a. Snapshots, movies, diaries, letters.

    b. Take my own photographs and movies.

    c. Tape record every encounter—consultation or treatment—unless contraindicated (as in some analyses).

    d. On hours not taped, dictate process notes (eventually to be typed and used in writing reports).

    e. Drawings and written stories from children and adults.

4. Presentations

The responsibility of communicating data induces one to edit and synthesize. In this way one may see new arrangements leading to new hypotheses; one may also force data into unreal arrangements and faulty hypotheses. At any rate, unless one's research is formalized for spoken or written presentation, not only are one's ideas unexamined but they are not subject to the pounding, by author and critics, that all research needs in order to take proper shape.

5. "Control" patients

To test the hypothesis and its corollaries, using one or another of the methods listed above, I have seen patients and families in the following categories:

    a. Identical twin males, one of whom is masculine and the other feminine.

    b. Identical twin females, one of whom is masculine and the other feminine.

    c. Families in which more than one son is very feminine.

    d. Adopted male transsexuals.

    e. Intersexuals.

    f. Fetishistic cross-dressers.

    g. Effeminate homosexuals.

    h. Patients requesting sex change who either are masculine-appearing at present or have had periods of masculinity in the past.

i. Psychotics: those who are anguished in their delusional and hallucinatory belief that their bodies are changing sex and also those who wish a "sex change."

j. Female transsexuals.

k. People without gender disorder in themselves or their family.

So far, in each of these categories—*keeping in mind that the numbers of cases seen are far too few*—the hypothesis and its corollaries have been confirmed. In *no* cases except those of primary transsexualism (remember: biologically normal, the most feminine of males, with no episodes of masculinity, and starting from the earliest appearance of any gender behavior) were the family dynamics found. Nonetheless, the more femininity—past and present—in those who are not primary transsexuals, the more elements of the transsexual family dynamics were found.

In addition to conducting follow-ups of as many patients in as many of the above categories as possible, I studied three families in which were boys with cross-gender behavior, none of whom was a primary transsexual. In each, I worked via analysis or analytically oriented psychotherapy with the mother; the boy was in treatment at the same time, but the father was not willing to commit himself to anything beyond the evaluation. In one case, the boy was a very feminine child but with masculine attributes mixed in (chapter 6), the second was a two-and-a-half-year-old whose mother's pantyhose excited him sexually (chapter 7), and the third was a teen-age fetishistic cross-dresser (chapter 8).

As you saw, the feminine boy came from family dynamics in many ways similar to those described for male transsexuals (for example, a close symbiosis, the infant beautiful, the mother's sense of worth damaged by a distant, empty mother), but his father, though passive and distant, spent a lot of time with his son. Father saw no significance in his son's dressing in women's clothes and wearing makeup, having done the same in his own childhood. The other two boys were both masculine except that their behavior was punctuated by fetishism. In neither case were the family dynamics present as in very feminine boys.

Two exceptions to the hypothesis have shown up, making the issue more interesting. The first was a boy, as feminine as the most feminine, with no discernible biologic defect, whose femininity, starting when he was a little over a year of age, was unbroken by masculinity to the time when, at age five, he was seen in evaluation. None of the described family dynamics was ever found. The only way this boy differed from the other very feminine boys studied was that the behavior disappeared in a few months with only the most superficial treatment: advising the parents to discourage the behavior (Stoller 1975a).

The second case, representing a class deserving more study, was also that of a very feminine boy. Though his father was distant and inconsequential throughout the child's infancy and childhood, his mother was different from the other mothers. She set out, quite consciously, to feminize the boy and so did everything possible—such as dressing him continuously in girls' clothes and styling his hair in the manner of feminine girls in that culture—so that, though never denying he was a male, she enjoyed his appearing female (Stoller 1975a).

Unfortunately, the price the analyst pays for being able to develop powerful, minute data—far beyond the reach of simple questioning, questionnaires, or statistical massing of other superficial observations—is that each analysis takes years. I cannot cover all the possibilities even once in a lifetime, much less confirm the first observations with adequate numbers of cases. Still, as analysts know, in the transference the old patterns of infancy and childhood are relived. We do not just take a history; we directly observe the past still present. One must, however, be cautious. In the analysis, we do not see once more what was done to the child. Rather, we learn what the child, now adult, thought was done and what responses were then created. For that reason, I need also to analyze parents to get their version, including their fantasies, conscious and unconscious, and to observe parents and children reacting together.

As others have found, a study of extreme cases can teach us about mechanisms of similar nature but lesser degree. In short, we begin to make sense of ordinary behavior. Example: if an excessively close and blissful symbiosis leads to femininity and if a less intimate symbiosis is followed by less femininity, does the ordinary mother-infant symbiosis also put boys a bit at risk for femininity? The answer may be yes. At least, one can state a hypothesis that will allow this hunch to be tested. Perhaps, with these findings on very feminine boys, we have a clue to the unsureness many men express about their masculinity (Stoller 1975b). So we are on the way to a better understanding of the dynamics of hostility between men and men and between men and women. Not that understanding will be of use. It isn't as gratifying as hatred.

Let me here, just before the end, take a swipe at those of my colleagues who believe psychoanalysis is a science, "our science", as they endlessly repeat.

In defining *science,* the dictionary (*Webster's*, 1961) gives as examples reading, writing, ciphering, theology, sport, the science of evading work, cards, fencing, boxing, aesthetics, and so on. Is that acceptable to psychoanalysts? Different, however, from what it says about science, the dictionary defines *scientific method*, this time rigorously enough to exclude from the scientific method most sciences it lists. "Scientific method: the principles and procedures used in the systematic pursuit of intersubjectively accessible

knowledge and involving as necessary conditions the recognition and formulation of a problem, the collection of data through observation and if possible
experiment, the formulation of hypotheses, and the testing and confirmation of
the hypotheses formulated.'' So, if we want to call psychoanalysis a science,
we can. But, if we subscribe to the dictionary's definition, we must admit that
psychoanalysis does not conform to the scientific method; until we have
intersubjectively accessible knowledge, we have, as with religions, no ways
other than acclamation or denunciation to confirm hypotheses.

Still, what counts is not the labeling but the commitments and capabilities of
the labeled discipline. For me, *science* stands for a state of trust, as implied in
objectivity: not interpersonal trust so much as trust that a description of an
alleged fact (event, object, state, dynamic) is an accurate description. The key
word is *accurate*. Science is not defined by its certitude, its area of study, or its
findings but by its method (a reflection of seriousness of intent): measurability
and replicability.

By far the greatest amount of the data of ''our science'' is drawn from
analytic treatment. But we cannot present even the most minute fragment of
that experience to a third party. There are several reasons. Another person's
inner life cannot be observed but only inferred. The patient's privacy must be
preserved. If we want to be more than anecdotal, a summary would not do. A
written transcript of the words spoken does not, either. (In the transcripts you
read in earlier chapters, you have only your impression from my edited version
of conversations you never observed.) Nor would a tape recording, though it
would get the sounds—words, pauses, inflections—more accurately. An
audio-visual record would fail us, too, even if in color; any small detail, such
as moving the camera, changes observation. Much of the data—feelings,
fantasies, memories: the unending flood of inner experience that, beyond
dimensions and words, fills the participants—cannot, we know, be caught by
recording. And then, if this were science and the third parties could be introduced to the data, we would have to account as much for the new obsrver's
psychic life as the participants'. So when we read that ''it is clear that . . . ,''
we should be sure to recognize we are not clear.

Everyone knows that the patient's version of a clinical hour—or a clinical
moment—is different from the analyst's; and that the analyst's notes at the end
of the hour are different from what is experienced in the hour; and that if we
look at our notes later, our interpretation is still different (even to the extent,
sometimes, of our not having the faintest idea to what the notes refer); and that
when we incorporate the clinical moment into a published report, the product
is even farther removed from (that effervescence we call) reality. Everyone
knows that a different analyst, at that clinical moment, would have been
different from the analyst who was there; and that the analyst who was there
would have done something different had the same clinical moment come a
moment later.

No analyst knows what another analyst does in his practice. If nothing in the analysis is measurable (in the usual meaning of "to measure"), if it cannot be reproduced, if other observers cannot participate in the "experiment," if the experience cannot be repeated, and if working models of a clinical moment cannot be constructed, is psychoanalysis a science? Only if the definition of science is broadened far enough that any effort to know (*scire,* to know) is a science.

Different analysts have different clinical ability; the same analyst has different skill from moment to moment as the day passes and as the years pass; the same analyst works better with one person than with another. One analyst with great clinical skill has little ability in communicating to others what he observes; another is a brilliant and poetic writer but there is little connection between what he observes and what he reports. Think how differently we evaluate the writings of a friend as compared to a stranger or how reputation moves our judgment. But these factors, so well known, are supposedly held constant in the building of psychoanalytic theory from "the data." When I read someone's paper, how can I tell how true is the description? Where is the evidence that my opinion is more accurate than his/hers or yours?

We analysts have an unbearable problem we must bear: we cannot deal objectively with our data. We can only absorb, digest, and transform them as an artist does; Freud knew what he was doing when he made his clinical reports read like fiction. (They *are* fiction.) How then are we to reproduce our data; how are we to say which clusters of clues are the ones to which we attend—or should attend? What one analyst hears as tragedy is opera to another: I have treated—this experience is familiar to analysts—patients who convinced a previous therapist that their associations were rich with archaic truths but that sounded to me like the baloney a patient provides an analyst hungry for rich, archaic truths. Interpretations are speculations.

Let Freud's statement that he never in his practice abused suggestion[2] exemplify the endless times when we must accept a declaration because, as different from genuine science, the data are not available. Instead of observations, there is a fight in which one side argues that, for instance, Freud can be taken at his word because he is Freud while the other argues that he cannot. But all the reasons mobilized cannot tell us what happened in his office. I am insisting only that our nervous complacency in declaring we do science helps us avoid doing better work. (And, perhaps, other kinds of discovery we might do if our morale were not low because we energetically deny the weakness of our our-science.) Psychoanalysis is investigation, sometimes research. Not all fruitful investigation requires scientific method.

Let us stop defending "our science." I think we are posturing with our new

2. Presence, fame, letting oneself be called "the Professor" may not influence—may not abuse—patients?

jargon that dehumanizes its subject, with our redefining "science" until it is vague enough to include our work, with our heavy and dull style of presentation that is supposed to indicate objectivity, with our denying the subjectivity out of which we create both our data and our theory, with our metaphors that, filled with imagery of biology and the harder sciences, subtly shift so as to lose their metaphoric quality, and with our using the vocabulary of quantities to refer to the unquantified and the unquantifiable.

REFERENCES

Abelin, E. L. 1971. The Role of the Father in the Separation-Individuation Process. In J. B. McDevitt and C. F. Settlage, eds., *Separation-Individuation*. New York: International Universities Press.

———. 1975. Some Further Observations and Comments on the Earliest Role of the Father. *Internat. J. Psycho-anal.* 56:293–302.

Abraham, F. 1931. Genitalumwandlung an Zwei Maennlichen Transvestiten. *Z. Sexualwissenschaft* 18:223–26.

Akesode, F. A., W. J. Meyer, and C. J. Migeon. 1977. Male Pseudo-hermaphroditism with Gynaecomastia due to Testicular 17-ketosteroid Reductase Deficiency. *Clin. Endocrin.* 7:443–52.

Allen, M. R. 1967. *Male Cults and Secret Initiation in Melanesia*. Melbourne: Melbourne University Press.

Bak, R. C. 1953. Fetishism. *J. Amer. Psychoanal. Assn.* 1:285–98.

———. 1974. Distortions of the Concept of Fetishism. *Psychoanal. Study Child* 29:191–214.

Barlow, D. H., E. J. Reynolds, and W. S. Agras. 1973. Gender Identity Change in a Transsexual. *Arch. Gen. Psychiat.* 28:569–79.

Blum, H. P. 1976. Masochism, the Ego Ideal, and the Psychology of Women. *J. Amer. Psychoanal. Assn.* 24 (Supplement): 157–91.

———. 1981. The Maternal Ego Ideal and the Regulation of Maternal Qualities. In S. I. Greenspan and G. H. Pollock, eds., *The Course of Life*, Vol. 3, *Adulthood and the Aging Process*. Maryland: U.S. Department of Health and Human Services, pp. 91–113.

Blumer, D. 1969. Transsexualism, Sexual Dysfunction, and Temporal Lobe Disorder. In R. Green and J. Money, eds., *Transsexualism and Sex Reassignment*. Baltimore: Johns Hopkins University Press, pp. 213–19.

Brown, P., and G. Buchbinder. 1976. Introduction. In P. Brown and G. Buchbinder, eds., *Man and Woman in the New Guinea Highlands*. Washington, D.C.: American Anthropological Association, pp. 1–12.

Bullough, V. L. 1975. Transsexualism in History. *Arch. Sex. Behav.* 4:561–71.

Deacon, A. B. 1934. *Malekula: A Vanishing People in the New Hebrides*. London: Routledge.

Devereux, G. 1937. Institutionalized Homosexuality of the Mohave Indians. *Hum. Biol.* 9:502–27.

Dickes, R. 1963. Fetishistic Behavior. *J. Amer. Psychoanal. Assn.* 11:303-30.

Dörner, G., W. Rohde, F. Stahl, L. Krell, and W-G. Masius. 1975. A Neuroendocrine Predisposition for Homosexuality in Men. *Arch. Sex. Behav.* 4:1–8.

Eber, M. 1982. Primary Transsexualism. *Bull. Menn. Clin.* 46:168–82.

Eicher, W., M. Spoljar, H. Cleve, J-D. Murken, K. Richter, and S. Stengel-Rutkowski. 1979. H-Y Antigen in Trans-sexuality. *Lancet* 2:1137–38.

Engel, W., F. Pfäfflin, and C. Wiedeking. 1980. H-Y Antigen in Transsexuality, and How to Explain Testis Differentiation in H-Y Antigen-negative Males and Ovary Differentiation in H-Y Antigen-positive Females. *Hum. Genet.* 55:315–19.

Epstein, A. W. 1960. Fetishism: A Study of Its Psychopathology and Particular Reference to a Proposed Disorder in Brain Mechanisms as an Etiological Factor. *JNMD* 130:107–19.

Erikson, E. 1958. The Nature of Clinical Evidence. *Daedalus* 87:65–87.

Ferenczi, S. 1930. The Principle of Relaxation and Neocatharsis. *Internat. J. Psycho-anal.* 11:428–43.

Fisk, N. 1973. Gender Dysphoria Syndrome (The How, What, and Why of a Disease). In D. R. Laub and P. Gandy, eds., *Proceedings of the Second Interdisciplinary Symposium on Gender Dysphoria Syndrome.* Stanford, Calif.: Stanford University Medical Center.

Fleming, M., C. Steinman, and G. Bocknek. 1980. Methodological Problems in Assessing Sex-reassignment Surgery: A Reply to Meyer and Reter. *Arch. Sex. Behav.* 9:451–56.

Forgey, D. G., 1975. The Institution of Berdache among the North American Plain Indians. *J. Sex. Res.* 11:1–15.

Freud, A. 1965. *Normality and Pathology in Childhood.* New York: International Universities Press.

Freud, S. (1905) 1953. Three Essays on the Theory of Sexuality. *Standard Edition* (hereafter *S.E.*) 7:135–243. London: Hogarth.

———. (1909) 1955. Analysis of a Phobia in a Five-Year-Old Boy. *S.E.* 10:5–149.

———. (1919) 1927. A Child Is Being Beaten. *S.E.* 17:179–204. London: Hogarth.

———. (1927) 1961. Fetishism. *S.E.* 21:152–57. London: Hogarth.

———. (1933) 1964. Femininity. *S.E.* 22:112–25. London: Hogarth.

———. (1937) 1964. Analysis Terminable and Interminable. *S.E.* 23:216–53. London: Hogarth.

———. (1940a) 1964. An Outline of Psycho-analysis. *S.E.* 23:144–207. London: Hogarth.

———. (1940b) 1964. Splitting of the Ego in the Process of Defence. *S.E.* 23:275–78.

Friedjung in Wulff, M. 1946. Fetishism and Object Choice in Early Childhood. *Psychoanal. Q.* 15:450–71.

Garma, A. 1956. The Meaning and Genesis of Fetishism. *Internat. J. Psycho-anal.* 37:414–15.

Gill, M. M. 1976. Metapsychology Is Not Psychology. In M. M. Gill and P. S. Holzman, eds., *Psychology versus Metapsychology.* Psychol. Issues 36:71–105.

Gillespie, W. H. 1940. A Contribution to the Study of Fetishism. *Internat. J. Psycho-anal.* 21:401–15.

———. 1952. Notes on the Analysis of Sexual Perversions. *Internat. J. Psycho-anal.* 33:347–402.

Glover, E. 1932. On the Aetiology of Drug-Addiction. *Internat. J. Psycho-anal.* 13:298–328.

———. 1933. The Relation of Perversion-Formation to the Development of Reality-Sense. *Internat. J. Psycho-anal.* 14:486–504, p. 496.

Green, R. 1969. Mythological, Historical, and Cross-Cultural Aspects of Transsexualism. In R. Green and J. Money, eds., *Transsexualism and Sex Reassignment.* Baltimore: Johns Hopkins University Press, pp. 13–22.

———. 1987. *The "Sissy Boy Syndrome" and the Development of Homosexuality.* New Haven: Yale University Press.

Green, R., and R. J. Stoller. 1971. Two Monozygotic (Identical) Twin Pairs Discordant for Gender Identity. *Arch. Sex. Behav.* 1:321–27.

Greenacre, P. 1953. Certain Relationships between Fetishism and the Faulty Development of the Body Image. *Psychoanal. Study Child* 8:79–98.

———. 1955. Further Considerations regarding Fetishism. *Psychoanal. Study Child* 10:187–94.

———. 1960. Further Notes on Fetishism. *Psychoanal. Study Child* 15:191–207.

———. 1968. Perversions: General Considerations regarding their Genetic and Dynamic Background. *Psychoanal. Study Child* 23:47–62.

———. 1969. The Fetish and the Transitional Object. *Psychoanal. Study Child* 24:144–64.

———. 1970. The Transitional Object and the Fetish with Special Reference to the Role of Illusion. *Internat. J. Psycho-anal.* 51:447–56.

Greenson, R. R. 1966. A Transvestite Boy and a Hypothesis. *Internat. J. Psycho-anal.* 47:396–403.

———. 1968. Dis-identifying from Mother. *Internat. J. Psycho-anal.* 49:370–74.

Hamburger, C., G. K. Stürup, and E. Dahl-Iverson. 1953. Transvestism: Hormonal, Psychiatric, and Surgical Treatment. *JAMA* 152:391–96.

Hamilton, J. W. 1978. Preoedipal Factors in a Case of Fetishism. *Bull. Menn. Clin.* 42:439–44.

Herdt, G. H. 1977. The Shaman's "Calling" among the Sambia of New Guinea. *J. de la Societé des Océanistes* 33:153–57.

———. 1981. *Guardians of the Flutes.* New York: McGraw-Hill.

Hogbin, I. 1970. *The Island of Menstruating Men.* Scranton, Pa.: Chandler.

Hopkins, J. 1984. The Probable Role of Trauma in a Case of Foot and Shoe Fetishism: Aspects of the Psychotherapy of a 6-year-old Girl. *Internat. Rev. Psycho-anal.* 11:79–91.

Hunt, D. D., and J. L. Hampson. 1980a. Follow-up of 17 Biologic Male Transsexuals after Sex-Reassignment Surgery. *Am. J. Psychiat.* 137:432–38.

———. 1980b. Transsexuals: A Standardized Psychosocial Rating Format for the Evaluation of Results of Sex Reassignment Surgery. *Arch. Sex. Behav.* 9:255–63.

Hunter, D. 1962. Object-Relation Changes in the Analysis of a Fetishist. *Internat. J. Psycho-anal.* 35:302–12.

Idelsohn in Wulff, M. 1946. Fetishism and Object Choice in Early Childhood. *Psycholanal. Quart.* 15:450–71.

Imperato-McGinley, J., R. E. Peterson, T. Gautier, and E. Sturla. 1979. Androgens and the Evolution of Male-Gender Identity among Male Pseudohermaphrodites with 5α-Reductase Deficiency. *N. Eng. J. Med.* 300:1233–37.

Jost, A. 1972. A New Look at the Mechanisms Controlling Sex Differentiation in Mammals. *Johns Hopkins Med. J.* 130:38–53.

Journal of the American Psychoanalytic Association. 24 (Supplement) 1976.

Jucovy, M. E. 1976. Initiation Fantasies and Transvestism. *J. Amer. Psychoanal. Assn.* 24:525–46.

Katan, M. 1964. Fetishism, Splitting of the Ego, and Denial. *Internat. J. Psycho-anal.* 45:237–45.

Kleeman, J. A. 1971. The Establishment of Core Gender Identity. I and II. *Arch. Sex. Behav.* 1:103–29.

———. 1976. Freud's Views on Early Female Sexuality in the Light of Direct Child Observation. *J. Amer. Psychoanal. Assn.* 24 (Supplement):3–27.

Krafft-Ebing, R. v. (1906) 1932. *Psychopathia Sexualis.* Brooklyn: Physicians and Surgeons Book Co.

Kubie, L. S. 1974. The Desire to Become Both Sexes. *Psychoanal. Quart.* 43:349–426.

Kubie, L. S., and J. B. Mackie. 1968. Critical Issues Raised by Operations for Gender Transmutation. *JNMD* 147:431–43.

Langness, L. L. 1967. Sexual Antagonism in the New Guinea Highlands: A Bena Bena Example. *Oceania* 37:161–77.

———. 1974. Ritual Power and Male Domination in the New Guinea Highlands. *Ethos* 2:189–212.

Levy, R. I. 1973. *The Tahitians.* Chicago: University of Chicago Press.

Lidz, R. W., and T. Lidz. 1977. Male Menstruation: A Ritual Alternative to the Oedipal Transition. *Internat. J. Psycho-anal* 58:17 –31.

Limentani, A. 1979. The Significance of Transsexualism in Relation to Some Basic Psychoanalytic Concepts. *Internat. Rev. Psycho-anal.* 6:139–53.

Loeb, L., and M. Shane. 1982. The Resolution of a Transsexual Wish in a Five-Year-Old Boy. *J. Amer. Psychoanal. Assn.* 30:419–34.

Loewald, H. W. 1951. Ego and Reality. *Internat. J. Psycho-Anal* 32:10–18.

Lorand, A. S. 1930. Fetishism in Statu Nascendi. *Internat. J. Psycho-anal.* 11:419–27.

Lothstein, L. M. 1977a. Countertransference Reactions to Gender Dysphoric Patients: Implications for Psychotherapy. *Psychotherapy: Theory, Research and Practice* 14:21–31.

———. 1977b. Psychotherapy with Patients with Gender Dysphoria Syndromes. *Bull. Menn. Clin.* 41:563–82.

———. 1978. The Psychological Management and Treatment of Hospitalized Transsexuals. *JNMD* 166:255–62.

———. 1979a. The Aging Gender Dysphoric (Transsexual) Patient. *Arch. Sex. Behav.* 8:431–44.

———. 1979b. Psychodynamics and Sociodynamics of Gender-Dysphoric States. *Am. J. Psychother.* 33:214–38.

———. 1979c. Group Therapy with Gender-Dysphoric Patients. *Am. J. Psychother.* 33:67–81.

———. 1980. The Adolescent Gender Dysphoric Patient: An Approach to Treatment and Management. *J. Ped. Psychol.* 5:93–109.

———. 1982. Sex Reassignment Surgery: Historical, Bioethical and Theoretical Issues. *Am. J. Psychiat.* 139:417–26.

Lothstein, L. M., and S. B. Levine. 1981. Expressive Psychotherapy with Gender Dysphoric Patients. *Arch. Gen. Psychiat.* 38:924–29.

MacLusky, N. J., and F. Naftolin. 1981. Sexual Differentiation of the Central Nervous System. *Science* 211:1294–1303.

Mahler, M. S. 1968. *On Human Symbiosis and the Vicissitudes of Individuation.* New York: International Universities Press.

Malcolm, L. A. 1966. The Age of Puberty in the Bundi Peoples. *Papua New Guinea Med. J.* 9:16–20.

Medawar, P. B. 1963. Is the Scientific Paper a Fraud? *Listener,* September 12, pp. 377–78.

Meggitt, M. J. 1964. Male-female Relationships in the Highlands of Australian New Guinea. *Amer. Anthrop.* 66 (Part 2): 204–224.

———. 1977. *Blood Is Their Argument.* Palo Alto: Mayfield.

Meyer, J. K. 1974. Clinical Variants among Applicants for Sex Reassignment. *Arch. Sex. Behav.* 3:527–58.

Meyer, J. K., and D. J. Reter. 1979. Sex Reassignment. *Arch. Gen. Psychiat.* 36:1010–15.

Mittelmann, B. 1955. Motor Patterns and Genital Behavior: Fetishism. *Psychoanal. Study Child* 10:241–63.

Money, J. 1955. Hermaphroditism, Gender, and Precocity in Hyperadrenocorticism: Psychologic Findings. *Bull. Johns Hopkins Hosp.* 96:253–64.

Money, J., and A. A. Ehrhardt. 1972. *Man & Woman Boy & Girl.* Baltimore: Johns Hopkins University Press.

Money, J., J. G. Hampson, and J. L. Hampson. 1955a. An Examination of Some Basic Sexual Concepts: The Evidence of Human Hermaphroditism. *Bull. Johns Hopkins Hosp.* 97:301–19.

———. 1955b. Hermaphroditism: Recommendations Concerning Assignment of Sex, Change of Sex, and Psychologic Management. *Bull. Johns Hopkins Hosp.* 97:284–300.

———. 1957. Imprinting and the Establishment of Gender Role. *Arch. Neurol. Psychiat.* 77:333–36.

Newman, P. 1965. *Knowing the Gururumba.* New York: Holt, Rinehart & Winston, 1965.

Nunberg, H. 1938. Homosexuality, Magic and Aggression. *Internat. J. Psycho-anal.* 19:1–16.

Ohno, S. 1978. The Role of H-Y Antigen in Primary Sex Determination. JAMA 239:217–20.

Opler, M. K. 1967. *Culture and Social Psychiatry.* New York: Atherton.

Ostow, M. 1953. Letter to the Editor. *JAMA* 152:1553.

Payne, S. M. 1939. Some Observations on the Ego Development of the Fetishist. *Internat. J. Psycho-anal.* 20:161–70.

Peabody, G. A., A. T. Rowe, and J. H. Wall. 1953. Fetishism and Transvestitism. *JNMD* 118:339–50.

Read, K. E. 1954. Cultures of the Central Highlands. *Southwest J. Anthrop.* 10:1–43.

Reinhardt, R. F. 1970. The Outstanding Jet Pilot. Amer. J. Psychiat. 127:732–36.

Rekers, G. A. 1977. Assessment and Treatment of Childhood Gender Problems. In B. B. Lakey and A. E. Kazdin, eds., *Advances in Child Clinical Psychology,* Vol. 1. New York: Plenum, Chap. 6.

Renik, O., P. Spielman, and J. Afterman. 1978. Bamboo Phobia in an Eighteen-Month-Old Boy. *J. Amer. Psychoanal. Assn.* 26:255–82.

Roiphe, H., and E. Galenson. 1973. The Infantile Fetish. *Psychoanal. Study Child* 28:147–66.

———. 1975. Some Observations on Transitional Object and Infantile Fetish. *Psychoanal. Quart.* 44:206–31.

Saez, J. M., E. de Peretti, A. M. Morera, and J. Bertrand. 1971. Familial Male Pseudohermaphroditism and Gynecomastia due to a Testicular 17-Ketosteroid Reductase Defect. I. Studies *in vivo. J. Clin. Endocrin Metab.* 32:604–10.

Salisbury, R. F. 1965. The Siane of the Eastern Highlands. In P. Lawrence and M. Meggitt, eds., *Gods, Ghosts and Men in Melanesia.* Melbourne: Melbourne University Press, pp. 50–77.

Satterfield, S. 1980. Outcome of Transsexual Surgery. Paper read at American Psychiatric Association Annual Meeting, San Francisco.

Scharfman, M. A. 1976. Perverse Development in a Young Boy. *J. Amer. Psychoanal. Assn.* 24:499–524.

Schieffelin, E. L. 1976. *The Sorrow of the Lonely and the Burning of the Dancers.* New York: St. Martins Press.

Schwabe, A. D., D. H. Solomon, R. J. Stoller, and J. P. Burnham. 1962. Pubertal Feminization in a Genetic Male with Testicular Atrophy and Normal Urinary Gonadotropin. *J. Clin. Endocrin. Metab.* 22:839–45.

Silverman, M. A. 1981. Cognitive Development and Female Psychology. *J. Amer. Psychoanal. Assn.* 29:581–605.

Socarides, C. W. 1960. The Development of a Fetishistic Perversion: The Contribution of Preoedipal Phase Conflict. *J. Amer. Psychoanal. Assn.* 8:281–311.

Sperling, M. 1963. Fetishism in Children, *Psychoanal. Quart.* 32: 374–92.

Sterba, E. 1941. An Important Factor in Eating Disturbances of Childhood. *Psychoanal. Quart.* 10:365–72.

Stern, D. 1983. Some Implications of Infancy Research for Clinical Theory and Practice. *Dialogue* 6:9–17.

Stevenson, M. C. 1901–02. The Zuni Indians—Destruction of the Kianakwe. Washington, D.C.: U.S. Bureau of American Ethnology Annual Report.

Stoller, R. J. 1964. A Contribution to the Study of Gender Identity. *Internat. J. Psychoanal.* 45:220–26.

———. 1968a. *Sex and Gender,* Vol. 1. New York: Science House.

———. 1968b. A Further Contribution to the Study of Gender Identity. *Internat. J. Psycho-anal.* 49:364–68.

———. 1969. Editorial—A Biased View of "Sex Transformation" Operations. *JNMD* 149:312–17.

———. 1973a. *Splitting.* New York: Quadrangle.

———. 1973b. Male Transsexualism: Uneasiness. *Am. J. Psychiat.* 130:536–39.

———. 1975a. *Sex and Gender,* Vol. 2. London: Hogarth.

———. 1975b. *Perversion.* New York: Pantheon.

———. 1976. Primary Femininity. *J. Amer. Psychoanal. Assn.* 24 (Supplement):59–78.

———. 1978. The Indications Are Unclear. In J. P. Brady and H. K. H. Brodie, eds., *Controversy in Psychiatry.* Philadelphia: W. B. Saunders Co., pp. 846–55.

———. 1979. *Sexual Excitement.* New York: Pantheon.

———. 1985. *Observing the Erotic Imagination*. New Haven: Yale University Press.

Stoller, R. J., and A. C. Rosen. 1959. The Intersexed Patient. *Calif. Med.* 91:261–65.

Szasz, T. 1979. Book review of *The Transsexual Empire*, by J. G. Raymond. *New York Times Book Review*, June 10.

Tuzin, D. F. 1980. *The Voice of the Tambaran: Truth and Illusion in Ilahita Arapesh Religion*. Berkeley: University of Calif. Press.

Volkan, V. D. 1979. Transsexualism: As Examined from the Viewpoint of Internalized Object Relations. In T. B. Karasu and C. W. Socarides, eds., *On Sexuality*. New York: International Universities Press.

Watson, J. B. 1960. A New Guinea "Opening Man." In J. B. Casagrande, ed., *In the Company of Man*. New York: Harper & Row.

Weissman, P. 1957. Some Aspects of Sexual Activity in a Fetishist. *Psychoanal. Quart.* 26:449–507.

Whiting, B. 1965. Sex Identity Conflict and Physical Violence: A Comparative Study. *Amer. Anthrop.* 67 (Part 2):123–40.

Whiting, J. W. M., R. Kluckhohn, and A. Anthony. 1958. The Function of Male Initiation Ceremonies at Puberty. In E. E. Maccoby, T. M. Newcomb, and E. L. Hartley, eds., *Readings in Social Psychology*. New York: Holt.

Whiting, J. W. M., and B. Whiting. 1975. Aloofness and Intimacy of Husbands and Wives: A Cross-Cultural Study. *Ethos* 3:183–207.

Williams, F. E. 1936. *Papuans of the Trans-Fly*. Oxford: Clarendon Press.

Winnicott, D. W. 1953. Transitional Objects and Transitional Phenomena. *Internat. J. Psycho-anal.* 34:89–97.

———. (1956) 1958. Primary Maternal Preoccupation. In *Collected Papers*. London: Tavistock, pp. 300–05.

Wolf, E. 1976. Ambience and Abstinence. *Annual Psychoanal.* 4:101–15.

Worden, F. G., and J. T. Marsh 1955. Psychological Factors in Men Seeking Sex Transformation. *JAMA* 157:1291–98.

Wulff, M. 1946. Fetishism and Object Choice in Early Childhood. *Psychoanal. Quart.* 15:450–71.

Yalom, I. D., R. Green, and N. Fish. 1973. Prenatal Exposure to Female Hormones. *Arch. Gen. Psychiat.* 28:554–61.

Zavitzianos, G. 1982. The Perversion of Fetishism in Women. *Psychoanal. Quart.* 51:405–25.

Zilboorg, G. 1944. Masculine and Feminine. *Psychiatry.* 7:257–96.

Zuger, B. 1984. Early Effeminate Behavior in Boys. *JNMD* 172:90–97.

INDEX

Abandonment, childhood, fear of, 119–20, 129, 146

Abelin, E. L., 44, 59

Abortion, 23, 109

Abraham, F., 152

Adoption, 96, 99, 108–11, 115, 129, 130

Alcoholism, 46

Alyha role, 171–80

American Indians, cross-gender behavior of, 171–80

Anatomy, genital, 13, 74

Andrenogenital syndrome, 23

Androgen insensitivity syndrome, 12–13, 22, 23

Androgens, 12, 13, 18n., 22, 23, 61, 74–75, 181

Animal psychologists, 10

Anxiety, 27, 38–41, 63, 200. See also Castration anxiety; Separation anxiety; Symbiosis anxiety

Apache Indians, cross-gender behavior of, 178

Bak, R. C., 93, 123, 124, 126, 133, 135

Behavior modification treatment, 121, 170

Berdache role, 171–80

Biologic issues in gender identity, 5, 11, 12–13, 22–23, 38n., 61, 65–76, 131, 182. See also specific biologic disorders

Bisexuality, 13, 123, 125, 152; Freud on, 14, 44, 152n.

Blanket, security, 127

Bloodletting rites, Melanesian, 197 and n., 198

Blum, H. P., 44, 129, 194n.

Bocknek, G., 158

Body ego, 14

Bonding, 130

Boyhood gender disorders, 6, 7–8; fetishistic

cross-dressing, 93–136, 138–51. See also Feminine boy(s); Masculinity, development of

Brain function, and gender identity, 12, 22, 23, 61, 74–75, 131, 155, 182

Cancer, 75–76, 168

Cantwell, D., 38

Castration anxiety, 10, 12, 14, 15, 16, 18, 38, 44; and childhood fetishism, 123, 124, 126, 128 and n., 129, 131–35; Freud on, 128n., 132

Casual cross-gender behavior, 24

Central nervous system, 11

Childhood gender development, general discussion on, 10–18

Childhood gender disorders, 6–7. See also Boyhood gender disorders; Father; Feminine boy(s); Fetishism, childhood; Infancy and infantile sexual experience; Male homosexuality; Masculine girls; Mother; Oedipal situations; Preoedipal situations

Cholesterol, 75

Chromosomal disorders, 13, 22 and n., 23, 25, 74

Chromosomes and gender identity, 12

Circumcision, and childhood fetishism, 96–98, 128, 129, 133

Clitoris, 15; surgical creation of, 153

Complemental series (Freud), 73, 182

Complete androgen insensitivity, 23 and n.

Conflict, 8 and n., 9, 27; lack of, in feminine boys, 38–41, 60–61, 63

Congenital endocrine disorder, 50

Congenital hypogonadism, 5

Constitutional male hypogonadism, 23

Coprolalia, 18

215

Core gender identity, 11–14, 161, 181; Freud on, 16–17, 181

Cross-dressing, 5, 21–22, 23, 60; of child fetishist, 93–136, 138–51; of moderately feminine boy, 77–92. *See also* Transvestism

Cross-gender homosexuals, 22

Cryptorchid testes, 23, 67, 76

Data-collecting techniques, 9, 78 and *n.*, 167, 200–01

Death, fear of, 119–20

Depression, 45, 57

Development of gender identity, 10–18; in feminine boy, 25–56, 59–61, 78–92, 138, 172–73, 175–76, 182, 191, 193 and *n.*, 194, 200, 202–03; Freud on, 8, 10, 14–17, 26, 27 and *n.*, 181; in masculine girl, 57–58, 62; and mother-infant symbiosis, 8, 16, 27–28, 30–33, 36, 39 and *n.*, 40, 47, 79, 130–33, 181, 182–83, 190, 191, 194, 200, 202–03; in Sambia society, 126, 183–99. *See also* Core gender identity; Femininity, development of; Masculinity, development of

Devereux, G., 171, 174, 175*n*, 178, 184

Dickes, R., 127*n.*

DSM-III, 162*n.*

Ego, 26

Electrolysis, 153

Embryonal testicular cancer, 75–76

Endocrine disorder, 66–67

Endocrinologists, 10

Enzymes, 75

Erection, infantile, 131 and *n.*

Estrogens, 12, 19*n.*, 61

Exhibitionism, 18

Eye contact, 33

Family dynamics. *See* Childhood gender disorders; Father; Grandparents; Mother

Fantasies, sex-change, 152

Father, 6–7, 11, 33, 130, 132*n.*; of child fetishist, 93, 106, 108, 124–25, 132, 135; on child's sex assignment, 11–12, 13, 23–24, 65, 66–76; Freud on, 14–17; of male transvestite, 137–38, 141, 144, 149, 151; of masculine girl, 44, 57–58, 67, 73; poorly represented to child by mother, 59–60; role in Sambia society, 187–92, 195, 196; in weak father-son relationship, 29, 31 and *n.*, 32, 35, 37, 41, 42, 44–57, 59–61, 78–92, 176, 179, 183, 202–03

Fellatio, homosexual, as Sambia ritual, 188–91

Female gender disorders, 22; transsexualism, 21, 29, 57–58, 67–68, 73. *See also* Femininity, development of; Masculine girls

Feminine boy(s), 25–57, 132, 134, 179, 202–03; lack of conflict in, 38–41, 60–61; of moderate intensity, 77–92; mother of, 25–42, 45–56, 59–61, 78–92, 138, 172–73, 175–76, 182, 187*n.*, 191, 193 and *n.*, 194, 200, 202–03; in weak father-son relationship, 29, 31 and *n.*, 32, 35, 37, 41, 42, 44–57, 59–61, 78–92, 176, 179, 183, 202–03. *See also* Male transsexualism

Femininity, defined, 11

Femininity, development of, 8, 10–18, 181, 182, 183; Freud on, 8, 10, 14–17, 26, 181; in Sambia society, 188, 195, 196

Feminist movement, 79

Ferenczi, S., 132

Fetal androgens, 12, 13, 74

Fetal hyperadrenalism, 23

Fetal life, 11, 39, 61

Fetishism, childhood, 93–136, 138–51; definitions of, 94, 123, 124–27; Freud on, 132; learning theory model of, 126*n.*; organic explanation of, 126*n.*; passage to adult fetishism, 122–23; and physical trauma, 96–98, 123, 124, 128 and *n.*, 129, 131–35, 139–40, 146, 151

Fisk, N., 161 and *n.*, 170

Fleming, M., 158

Freud, A., 93; on childhood perversions, 122, 123, 124, 133, 135

Freud, S., 12, 44, 61, 73, 122, 134*n.*, 193, 196; on bisexuality, 14, 44, 152*n.*; on castration anxiety, 128*n.*, 132; on development of gender identity, 8, 10, 14–17, 26, 27 and *n.*, 181; on fetishism, 132; on homosexuality, 15, 17, 181; on perversion, 93

Frustration, 9; lack of, in feminine boys, 38–41, 60–61, 63

Galenson, E., 127, 128*n.*, 133

Gender, defined, 6 and *n.*

Gender dysphoria syndrome, 161–62, 170, 179

Gender identity, defined, 10–11. *See also* Core gender identity; Development of gender identity; Femininity, development of; Masculinity, development of

Genetic defects, 22

Geneticists, 10

Genital anatomy, 13, 74

Girlhood gender disorders. *See* Masculine girls
Glover, E., 132, 134
Goodwin, W. E., 66n.
Grandparents, 29, 32, 58, 102, 119, 120
Green, R., 41n., 62, 171, 177n.
Greenacre, P., 128, 129, 134 and n.
Gynecomastia, 23, 75

Hallucinations, 24
Hamburger, C., 152
Hamilton, J. W., 128
Hampson, J. L., 5, 157
Herdt, G. H., 126, 181, 184 and n., 194, 198
Hermaphrodism, 4, 5, 11, 23–24, 67–76, 161
Heterosexuality, 33; origins of, parental influence on, 193 and n.; in Sambia society, 190–91, 192, 196 and n.
Homeovestism, 127
Homosexuality, 125, 154; and core gender identity in infancy, 15, 17, 181; cross-gender, 22; Freud on, 15, 17, 181. *See also* Male homosexuality
Hormonal disorders, 22–23, 66–67, 74–76
Hormonal procedures for sex change, 153, 155, 163, 164, 166
Hormones, 12, 13, 19n., 23, 61. *See also* *specific hormones*
Hostility, 41, 59
Humiliation, 22, 138, 176, 177
Hunt, D. D., 157
Hunter, D., 128
H-Y antigen, 161

Iatrogenic prenatal conditions, 22
Identical twins, 175, 176, 177n.
Identification, 181 and n., 193
Identity, defined, 6n.
Imaginary penis, 57, 58 and n.
Imperato-McGinley, J., 66n.
Incest, 125
Incorrect sex assignment at birth, 65, 66–76
Indians, American male, cross-gender behavior of, 171–80
Infancy and infantile sexual experience, 8, 12, 27, 62–64, 122; erection in, 131 and n.; factors resulting in core gender identity, 11–14, 16–18, 181; father-daughter intimacy in, 57; incorrect sex assignment in, 65, 66–76; mother-son symbiosis, 8, 16, 27–28, 30–33, 36, 39 and n., 40, 47, 79, 130–33, 181, 182–83, 190, 191, 194, 200, 202–03; physical trauma in, and childhood fetishism, 96–

98, 123, 124, 126, 128 and n., 129, 131–35, 139–40, 146, 151
Intersexuals, 22–23

Johns Hopkins University sex change study, 157–60
Jucovy, M. E., 198n.

Kernberg, P., 31
Klinefelter's syndrome, 5, 22, 23
Kohut, H., 8n.
Kubie, L. S., 152, 163

Learning theorists, 10
Learning theory model of fetishism, 126n.
Leowald, 60
Levy, R. I., 184
Lidz, R. W., 197 and n.
Lidz, T., 197 and n.
Limentani, A., 40
Loeb, L., 63
Lorand, A. S., 138
Lothstein, L. M., 159, 166

Mackie, J. B., 163
Mahler, M. S., 44
Malcolm, L. A., 188n.
Male childhood disorders. *See* Boyhood gender disorders; Masculinity, development of
Male homosexuality, 22, 37n., 41 and n., 60, 78, 79, 132; American Indian, 171–80; ritualized, in Sambia tribe, 188–91, 198
Male pseudohermaphrodism, 74–75
Male transsexualism, 27–56; American Indian, 171–80; primary, 16, 19, 20 and n., 27–28, 32, 41 and n., 76, 77, 172, 191, 202; secondary, 20–21
Male transvestism, 178; chidhood origins of, 137–51
Mammoplasty, 19n.
Masculine girl(s), 29, 57–58, 62, 67; father of, 44, 57–58, 67, 73; imaginary penis of, 57, 58 and n.; mother of, 57–58, 67. *See also* Female transsexualism
Masculinity, defined, 11
Masculinity, development of, 8, 10–18, 181–99; failure in feminine boy, 25–56, 59–61, 78–92, 138, 172–73, 175–76, 182, 191, 193 and n., 194, 200, 202–03; Freud on, 8, 10, 14–17, 26, 181; hypotheses about, 182–83; and mother-infant symbiosis, 8, 16, 27–28, 30–33, 36, 39 and n., 40, 47, 79, 130–33,

Masculinity, development of (*continued*) 181, 182–83, 190, 191, 194, 200, 202–03; in Sambia society, 183–99

Mastectomy, 4*n.*, 19*n.*, 153

Medawar, P. B., 2

Media, 165

Merging, 39 and *n.*, 40

Metapsychology, 4 and *n.*

Meyer, J. K., 157–59

Mirror experience, in transvestism, 149–50

Mohave Indians, cross-gender behavior of, 171–80

Money, J., 5

Moral issues of sex change, 153–54, 167–68

Mother, 6, 7, 11–12, 130; of child fetishist, 93–120, 124–25, 129–35; on child's sex assignment, 11–12, 13, 23–24, 65, 66–76; father poorly represented to child by, 59–60; of feminine boy, 25–42, 45–56, 59–61, 78–92, 138, 172–73, 175–76, 182, 187*n.*, 191, 193 and *n.*, 194, 200, 202–03; Freud on, 14–17; -infant son symbiosis, 8, 16, 27–28, 30–33, 36, 39 and *n.*, 40, 47, 79, 130–33, 181, 182–83, 190, 191, 194, 200, 202–03; influence on child's heterosexuality, 193 and *n.*; of male transvestite, 137–51; of masculine girl, 57–58, 67; role in Sambia society, 187–96

Necrophilia, 18

Neurophysiologists, 10

Neurosis, 134

New Guinea societies, gender development in, 126, 183–99

Nunberg, H., 190

Observation, naturalistic, use in psycho-analysis, 1–9

Oedipal situations, 18, 44, 58, 59, 93, 123, 124–25, 128*n.*, 133–34, 135–36, 193, 197*n.*; Freud on, 14–17; in Sambia society, 190, 192–97. *See also* Childhood gender disorders; Father; Mother

Opler, M., 178

Ostow, M., 163

Panhysterectomy, 4*n.*, 19*n.*, 153

Paranoid position, 64 and *n.*

Parents. *See* Father; Mother

Parthenogenesis, 130

Payne, S. M., 128

Peabody, G. A., 128

Pedophilia, 18

Penis: envy, 10, 15, 16, 18, 44, 46; imaginary, in women, 57, 58 and *n.*; infantile erection, 131 and *n.*; surgical removal of, 153

Perversions, 8–9; childhood-to-adulthood, discussed, 122–23; Freud on, 93; meanings of the term, 93, 122. *See also specific perversions*

Phallicness, 56–57

Phobia, 133, 134

Physical trauma, and childhood fetishism, 96–98, 123, 124, 126, 128 and *n.*, 129, 131–35, 139–40, 146, 151

Positive and negative reinforcement, 33

Pregenital fetishes, 123

Pregnancy, 130, 144

Prenatal hormone(s), 12, 13, 61, 161; disorders, 74–76

Preoedipal situations, 18, 26, 44, 93–94, 127, 136; in Sambia society, 194–97

Primary transsexualism, 16, 19, 20 and *n.*, 22, 27–28, 32, 41 and *n.*, 76, 77, 161, 169, 172, 191, 202

Primitive societies, gender development in, 126, 183–99

Progesterone, 12, 22, 23

Prostate, 69

Protofemininity, 16–17, 18, 182, 183

Pseudohermaphrodism, male, 74–75

Psychotics, 24

Puberty, 29, 126

Rape, 18

Read, K. E., 197

Reinforcement, positive and negative, 33

Renik, O., 133, 134

Reter, D. J., 157–59

Ritvo, E., 38

Roiphe, H., 127, 128*n.*, 133

Role, defined, 6*n.*

Sambia society (New Guinea), gender development in, 126, 183–99

Satterfield, S., 159

Scopophilia, 124

Secondary transsexualism, 20–21, 22, 161, 169

Security blanket, 127

Semen, significance in Sambia society, 186, 188–91

Separation anxiety, 114–17, 124, 126, 128*n.*, 129, 135

Separation-individuation process, 39, 40, 44, 59, 183, 197*n.*

17β-hydroxysteroid dehydrogenase deficiency, 75

Sex and sexuality, defined, 6 and *n.*, 122

Sex assignment of infant, 11–12, 13, 23–24; incorrect, 65, 66–76

Sex change, 5, 19 and *n.*, 20 and *n.*, 22, 41, 50, 62, 152–70, 172, 174; controversies, 153–70; and core gender identity, 161; definitions of, 19*n.*, 160, 162–63, 170; ethics of, 154–55; hormonal/surgical procedures and issues, 153, 155, 163, 164, 166, 168; Johns Hopkins University study on, 157–60; legal issues of, 156; long-term effects of, 168–70; moral issues of, 153–54, 167–68; theoretic issues of, 156–57; types of treatment, 155–56

Sex reassignment, defined, 162–63

Shane, M., 63

Socarides, C. W., 127, 128, 163

Sperling, M., 127

Steinman, C., 158

Stern, D., 39*n.*

Stevenson, M. C., 178

Suicide, 125, 154; and sex change, 155, 168

Surgical procedures for sex change, 153, 155, 163, 164, 166, 168

Symbiosis anxiety, 183, 192, 195, 197*n.*

Szasz, T., 154

Tarjan, G., 38

Temporal lobe disorder, 23

Testes: disorders, 4, 22, 23, 67, 69, 74–76; surgical removal of, 153

Testicular cancer, 75–76

Testicular feminization syndrome, 4

Testosterone, 12, 13, 19*n.*, 23, 75

Transference, 7 and *n.*, 120, 131, 144–45

Transsexualism, 3, 4 and *n.*, 13, 19–21, 62, 67 and *n.*, 132, 134, 152–70; and core gender identity, 161; definitions of, 19 and *n.*, 154, 161–63, 170; primary, 16, 19, 20 and *n.*, 21, 22, 27–28, 32, 41 and *n.*, 76, 77, 161, 169, 172, 191, 202; secondary, 20–21, 22, 161, 169. *See also* Female transsexualism; Male transsexualism; Sex change

Transvestism, 21–22, 132 and *n.*, 133*n.*, 178, 198*n.*; defined, 21; male, origins of, 137–51; mirror experience in, 149–50

Trauma, 9, 63, 96; lack of, in feminine boys, 38–41, 60–61, 63; physical, and childhood fetishism, 96–98, 123, 124, 126, 128 and *n.*, 129, 131–35, 139–40, 146, 151

Turner's syndrome (XO), 13, 22

Twins, identical, 175, 176, 177*n.*

Uterus, 15

Vagina, 15, 23; surgical creation of, 153

Volkan, V. D., 163

Voyeurism, 18

Whiting, B., 192

Whiting, J. W. M., 192

Winnicott, D. W., 130, 193

Zavitzianos, G., 127

Zuger, B., 62